LOUIS-SÉBASTIEN MERCIER IN GERMANY

NUMBER EIGHT OF THE

COLUMBIA UNIVERSITY GERMANIC STUDIES

EDITED BY ROBERT HERNDON FIFE

NEW SERIES

LOUIS-SÉBASTIEN MERCIER IN GERMANY

His Vogue and Influence
In the Eighteenth Century

By W. W. PUSEY

NEW YORK: MORNINGSIDE HEIGHTS
COLUMBIA UNIVERSITY PRESS
1939

PREFACE

THE PRESENT STUDY was begun in 1933 at the suggestion of Professor F. O. Nolte of Harvard University and completed under the direction of Professor Robert Herndon Fife of Columbia University. Professor Nolte and Professor J. A. Kelly of Haverford College read parts of my work when it was in preparation and made a number of helpful suggestions. I am also grateful to several of my friends and colleagues for the aid they gave me in the onerous task of reading proof. Above all, however, I am indebted to Professor Fife for his valuable and sympathetic guidance in every phase of this investigation.

W.W.P.

CONTENTS

LOUIS-SÉBASTIEN MERCIER IN GERMANY

I

THE POSITION OF MERCIER IN LITERARY HISTORY

IN THE GREAT wave of French cultural expansion in the Eighteenth Century few writers, it seems, achieved wider renown in foreign lands than Louis-Sébastien Mercier, author of numerous bourgeois plays, of a critical essay on the drama, and of a social and political picture of Paris.[1] Although French critics, past and present, have usually held him in great contempt, calling him scornfully the "dramaturge,"[1a] the "ape of Rousseau,"[2] or the "caricature of Diderot,"[3] his works found readers and audiences throughout Europe and also in America. His name appears on lists of translations in almost every European tongue, and one or another of his varied works was known in Austria, Belgium, Czechoslovakia, Denmark, England, Holland, Italy, Poland, Portugal, Russia, Spain, Sweden, and Switzerland.[4] His play *le Déserteur* was per-

---

[1] This has not been recognized by many critics. There is no mention of Mercier, for instance, in the recent book dealing with French influence on foreign cultures by Louis Réau (*l'Europe française.* "l'Évolution de l'humanité," Nr. 70, Paris, 1938).

[1a] Fréron. According to Léon Béclard, *Sébastien Mercier* (Paris, 1903), p. 353, this appellation was not customary at the time.

[2] Cf. J. Lemaître, *Théories et impressions.* "Nouvelle bibliothèque littéraire" (Paris, no date), p. 251.

[3] F. Brunetière, *les Époques du théâtre français*, nouv. éd. (Paris, 1896), p. 305.

[4] Austria: *Der Schubkarn des Essighändlers.* "Neues Wiener Theater," II (Wien, 1776).

Belgium: cf. Henri Liebrecht, *Histoire du théâtre français à Bruxelles au xvii⁰ et au xviii⁰ siècle* (Paris, 1923), pp. 294f.

Czechoslovakia: cf. O. Teuber, *Geschichte des Prager Theaters* (Prag, 1883-1888), I, 374; *British Museum General Catalogue of Books*, under "Mercier."

Denmark: cf. Ch. Brunn, *Biblioteca Danica* (Copenhagen,1877-1914), IV, 403.

England: cf. *British Museum General Catalogue of Books*, under "Mercier."

Holland: cf. J. A. Worp, *Geschiedenis van het drama en van het tooneel in Nederland* (Groningen, 1904-1908), II, 316.

Italy: cf. T. V. Benn, "Notes sur la fortune de *George Barnwell* de Lillo en France," *Revue de littérature comparée*, VI (1926), 685.

Poland: *ibid.*

Portugal: *Carta de Heloiza a Abeillard, traduzida do francez, de Mr. Mercier* (Lisboa, 1820). Harvard University Library.

Russia: cf. M. N. Rosanow, *Lenz*, German translation by C. von Gütschow (Leipzig, 1909), p. 479.

formed on the New York stage at least eight times in the first
thirty-five years of the Nineteenth Century.[5] His vogue was especially great in Germany. His works were translated and discussed and his plays were performed there repeatedly during the
last three decades of the Eighteenth Century. Although his German appeal did not last far into the next century, he is still mentioned by A. W. Schlegel, Büchner, and Tieck,[6] while as late as
1935 a Berlin periodical quotes from his *Tableau de Paris*.[7]

The present treatise will deal with one phase of Mercier's European vogue, his relation to German literature during the last
third of the Eighteenth Century. Following an introductory study
of the character of his work, his popularity in Germany will be
examined, so far as this can be measured by translations, presentations of his plays, and criticism in contemporary journals.
With the extent and nature of his appeal thus established, an attempt will be made to determine his influence on Wieland, Goethe,
Schiller, the *Sturm und Drang,* and the German middle-class
drama. As a supplement to the chapter, "Mercier in German
Translation," a list of German versions of his works has been
appended.

Various phases of the relation of Mercier to German literature
have been treated before. The field of investigation was opened
in 1899 by Zollinger's *Louis-Sébastien Mercier als Dramatiker
und Dramaturg*.[8] In this work and in "Merciers Beziehungen zur
deutschen Literatur" (1902),[9] Zollinger dealt especially with the
translation into German of a number of the Frenchman's plays
and other works. Rosanow's *Lenz* (1909)[10] gave an enthusiastic

---

Spain: *El Desertor ... traducida en verso español* (Madrid, 1793). Bonn University Library.

Sweden: cf. Benn, *op. cit.,* p. 685.

Switzerland: *Portraits des rois de France* (Neuchâtel, 1783).

[5] Cf. G. C. D. Odell, *Annals of the New York Stage* (New York, 1927-1937),
Vols. II, III.

[6] *Vorlesungen über dramatische Kunst und Literatur,* hrsg. von G. V. A. Amoretti
(Bonn und Leipzig, 1923), II, 100, 103; *Dantons Tod,* Act III; *Tieck and Solger,*
ed. Matenko (New York and Berlin, 1933), p. 316.

[7] *Berliner illustrierte Zeitung,* April 17.

[8] Zürich Dissertation.

[9] *Zeitschrift für französische Sprache und Literatur,* xxv (1902), 87ff.

[10] *Op. cit.,* Chaps. v, vi.

appraisal of Mercier and indicated a connection between his dramatic theories and those of Lenz and other *Stürmer und Dränger*. This problem was investigated in a more scholarly fashion and at greater length by San-Giorgiu in his excellent monograph, *Merciers dramaturgische Ideen im "Sturm und Drang"* (1921).[11] Finally, Schiller's debt to Mercier's essay on the drama was treated by Léon Mis in "Sébastien Mercier, Schiller und Otto Ludwig" (1928).[12] However, no comprehensive study exists of Mercier's relationship to German literature as a dramatic theorist, a playright, a social and political critic, and a novelist. It is hoped that the present work, which of course takes cognizance of the findings of previous students of Mercier, will fill this need and in addition throw some light on the similarity and dissimilarity of taste and ideas in France and Germany during the later *Aufklärung*.

The indiscreet ardor, the curiosity, the intemperance, the verbiage, the presumption, the good-heartedness, the facility for tears, and the instinctive optimism which according to the French critic Faguet[13] typify the Eighteenth Century in France, are especially characteristic of Mercier. He was born in Paris in 1740 as the son of a sword merchant and died there in 1814.[14] He paid brief visits to England and Germany in the eighties, and lived as a political exile in Switzerland for five years (1781-1786). Later, as a result of his protest against the execution of Louis XVI, he was confined in various prisons of Paris for over thirteen months (1793-1794). In 1795 he became a member of the newly founded Institut de France, in the division of moral and political science, and in 1797 an auditor of the national lottery. Despite the overthrow of the Directorate and the rise of Napoleon, he remained to the end of his life an advocate of the moderate republican form of government.

The present chapter will give a rapid summary of the most important of Mercier's works as an orientation, not primarily

---

[11] Basel Dissertation.

[12] *Euphorion*, XXIX, 190ff.

[13] *Dix-huitième siècle* (Paris, preface: 1890), xiif.

[14] For Mercier's life, cf. Béclard, *op. cit.*, and L. Louvet in Hoefer, *Nouvelle biographie générale*, XXXV (1865), 19ff.

for an evaluation of his place in French literature, but chiefly in order to furnish a background for the subsequent discussion of his relations to Germany. Our résumé falls into four sections: dramaturgical treatises; plays; social, political, and philosophical essays; and narrative writings. Within these categories the individual works will be treated chronologically.

Mercier's dramatic theories are to be found chiefly in *du Théâtre, ou Nouvel essai sur l'art dramatique* (1773). However, they also appear in the prefaces to his dramas, in chapters of various social and philosophical treatises, and in the essays, *de la Littérature et des littérateurs* and *Nouvel examen de la tragédie française* (both 1778). The *Nouvel essai* is by far the most extensive of these discussions. Its preface and its thirty chapters contain all of our author's dramatic views. It must be said in justice to Mercier that this work is rather a polemic than a reasoned formulation of clearly analyzed ideas. The verdict of the protégée of Mme du Deffand and friend of Marmontel, Mlle de Lespinasse, that it was a "bad book on the theater in which there is a quantity of good things" (1774),[15] is not far wrong. Critical views of the work range between wide extremes, such as the opinion expressed in Bachaumont's *Mémoires secrets* (1774) that nothing could be more ridiculous than the essay,[16] and on the other hand the exaggerated praise accorded two generations later by the literary critic and student of German culture, Michiels, who calls it the "finest critical work published in the Eighteenth Century."[17]

Of the multitude of ideas that the *Nouvel essai* contains, six may be mentioned as particularly interesting and significant. In the first place, Mercier launches an attack on the French classical tradition which, if not precisely vicious, is in any case very vigorous. He inveighs not only against the imitators of the masters, but also against the great playwrights of the Seventeenth Century themselves. With considerable acumen he points out what he considers to be the weaknesses of their tragedy. It is

---

[15] *Lettres de Mlle de Lespinasse,* éd. E. Asse (Paris, notice: 1876), p. 128; in a letter to Guibert, Oct. 14.

[16] (London, 1784-1789), VII, 217.

[17] *Histoire des idées littéraires en France au xix⁰ siècle* (Paris, 1842), I, 110.

only a phantom clothed in purple and gold. It is like the garden of the time, beautiful, symmetrical, uniform, and magnificently sad. Since Corneille, whose greatness Mercier rather stresses than contests, the tragedy has become involuntarily humorous, a serious farce. Racine, a fine poet, is too feminine and not moral enough. Mercier, although an ardent admirer of Restif de la Bretonne, the author of *le Paysan perverti* and *le Pornographe*, brings the charge of immorality against Molière and his successors, Regnard and Dancourt. He discards, then, the tradition of the *grand siècle* to turn to Diderot and Marmontel.[18]

Secondly, our author supports the *genre sérieux* or "drame," as he calls it, which is to replace the degenerate tragedy.[19] The "drame" is to be bourgeois in subject and treatment, "a fine moment of human life that reveals the interior of a family." It combines by its pathos and its depiction of manners the interest of the tragedy and the naïve charm of the comedy.[20]

Thirdly, the critic emphasizes the popular appeal of this new genre. The "drame" should be composed for the people, although not for the vilest public. It must attempt to reconcile, not to increase the "inhuman" differences which the "horrible inequalities of wealth" have placed between the citizens of the realm.[21]

In the fourth place, Mercier stresses the moral purpose of the theater. The dramatic art can give general instruction, spread useful principles, and cultivate public reason. It is the most active and speedy means of enlightening a people, of awakening a slumbering nation.[22]

The dramaturgist assails, in the fifth place, the established form of the French classical drama as well as its subject matter. In the "drame," he thinks, prose is preferable to poetry. A piece may just as well have two, four, or six acts as five. While Mercier believes that the unity of action, or of "interest," as he calls it with Lamotte-Houdar, must be scrupulously kept, he allows

---

[18] *Nouvel essai*, pp. ix, 97n., 48n., 30, 29, 285n., 87, 73, 280.

[19] According to F. Gaiffe, *le Drame en France au xviii° siècle* (Paris, 1910), p. 93, the term "drame" as a designation for the new genre originated with Desfontaines in 1741.

[20] *Nouvel essai*, pp. 140n., 106, 17.

[21] *Ibid.*, pp. 39f., 202n., ixf., 221n.

[22] *Ibid.*, pp. 141, ivf.

the unity of time to be extended to three days. The unity of place merits still less respect. The scene should be enlarged, but the distance must not become too great.[23]

Finally, Mercier is an eloquent, although none too well-informed advocate of Shakespeare. In his opinion, the English dramatist is assured an immortal crown. He appears ridiculous in France since his plays have been disfigured by envy or stupidity. He is dear to his countrymen because he discovered the secret of speaking to the whole nation. His heroes are real men, simple, and at the same time great.[24]

There is little to be added from the other writings of Mercier to this summary of his dramatic theories. In *sur la Lecture* (1764) the author seems to have been carried away by the exuberance of youth, for he makes the sweeping generalization that no rules exist in any art! The preface of *Jenneval* (1769) gives special attention to the moral purpose of the theater, that of *Olinde et Sophronie* (1771) to its sentimental appeal. The chapter of *l'An 2440* (1770) devoted to the stage contains a plea for a more modern and bourgeois theater, while the dramatic treatises of 1778 continue the attack on the unities and call Shakespeare the perfect model for the "drame." The *Tableau de Paris* (1781ff.) scores the "disfigured" French tragedy and praises the great British dramatist. The introduction to *la Destruction de la Ligue* (1782) states the thesis that dramatic poetry should be directed towards dissipating intolerance and error. Finally, the *Satires contre Racine et Boileau* (1808) contains the following parody of a verse of the lawgiver of classicism:

> Qu'en un jour, qu'en lieu, un seul fait accompli,
> Bon! voilà le théâtre à jamais démoli.[25]

It is evident that Mercier's theories correspond in many ways to those of his contemporaries, for instance Beaumarchais, and especially Diderot. This similarity induced the French critic

[23] *Ibid.,* pp. 295, 253, 147, 31n., 146.
[24] *Ibid.,* p. 206.
[25] Cf. Boileau's *Art poétique,* Chant III:
> "Qu'en un lieu, qu'en un jour, un seul fait accompli
> Tienne jusqu'à la fin le théâtre rempli."

Brunetière to conclude that all Mercier's views are merely exaggerations of those of the author of *le Père de famille*.[26] Mercier, however, along with Beaumarchais, went a step further than Diderot. He saw clearly the faults of the great French poets of the Seventeenth Century and was bold enough to attack them. Then too, he stressed the popular and national appeal of the "drame" more than other critics. He was rather a man of politics than a philosopher. He led an early crusade against the unfairness of class distinction. His high conception of the moral purpose of the theater he had, to be sure, in common with the whole age, and strangely enough, also with the very classicists whom he hated. However, his attack on the unities is more radical than that of his predecessors. Finally, he had a greater and more lasting appreciation of Shakespeare than Voltaire or any of his fellow dramaturgists in France. In a certain sense, then, the words of Brunetière are true. However, it is just this conglomeration of ideas that summed up the dramatic treatises of the Eighteenth Century in France, and by its very exaggeration, advanced dramatic theory in the direction of Benjamin Constant, the preface of *Cromwell*, and romanticism. Herein I see the chief importance of the *Nouvel essai* and of Mercier's other comments on the theater.

Mercier wrote a considerable number of plays, most of which are "drames." They carry out his theories in many, although not in all respects. He did write sentimental, bourgeois pieces, moral in tone, but he did not break entirely with the unities nor write in an unrestrained or Shakespearean manner. Few save literary historians read Mercier's thirty-one printed pieces today. They are not, to be sure, devoid of interest to the student of ideas. Considered as works of art, however, they are highly artificial, too much concerned with morality, long-winded, in a word, dull. It will be necessary to give in brief résumé the plots of some of the most important of them in order to show what subjects our dramatist treated and how he treated them.

The subtitle of Mercier's first play, *Jenneval* (1769), indicates its source. *Le Barnevelt français* is an adaptation to French

[26] *Op. cit.*, p. 306.

taste of Lillo's bourgeois tragedy, the *London Merchant* (1731). Like his English model, Jenneval is encouraged by a courtesan, first to rob his foster father, then to murder his rich uncle. At the last moment, however, the French hero experiences a change of heart, rescues the uncle and receives pardon from all. *Jenneval* is not the worst of Mercier's dramas, but the happy conclusion weakens its total effect both artistically and morally.

Le Déserteur (1770), on the other hand, has a tragic ending, and in this respect is unique among Mercier's plays. Even that, however, was altered in later editions. *Le Déserteur* is in spirit the most nearly classical of his dramas. A young Frenchman, Durimel, flees from the army when he is treated unjustly by his superior officer and is then employed in a small German village near the French frontier by a Mme Luzerne. However, he is unmasked as a deserter and is eventually executed by order of his father, a major, despite the protests of the son's bride Clary. The conflict in the mind of Durimel between his military duty and his affection for his father, and his love for Clary, is slightly reminiscent of Corneille's *Cid*. Valcour, the amorous officer who before his change of heart attempts to seduce Clary, and Hoctau the informer, are among Mercier's most successful characters. *Le Déserteur* is almost a good play, but it is marred by an overabundance of virtuous declamations, excessive sentimentalizing, and propaganda against war and against capital punishment for renegades.

Olinde et Sophronie (1771) falls far below the level of excellence of Mercier's first two pieces. It is taken, as the author admits in his preface, from Cronegk's work of the same name (1760), and also owes something to the *Gerusalemme liberata* of Tasso. This "drame héroïque"—the appellation itself is a contradiction—relates the love of Olinde and Sophronie for each other and for Christianity. The evil high priest of Jerusalem, Ismen, has himself committed sacrilege in the temple in order to have a pretext for persecuting the Christians. To save their fellow believers, both lovers take the blame for having desecrated the heathen sanctuary. Olinde is about to die on the burning pile of fagots when the Persian princess, Clorinde, who like Corneille's

Infante secretly loves the hero, stabs Ismen and frees Olinde and Sophronie. *Olinde et Sophronie* is really not a "drame." It is a tragedy in prose, and as Béclard remarks, a poor tragedy.[27]

With *l'Indigent* (1772) Mercier returns to the true "drame." Here for the first time in serious French theater the proletariat plays a large rôle. The action of the piece takes place partly in the miserable chamber of the brother and sister, Joseph and Charlotte, and partly in the sumptuous apartment of the young profligate, de Lys. This reprobate tries to seduce Charlotte and to purchase the friendship of Joseph by putting at his disposal the means of freeing his father from a debtors' prison. He fails in both his attempts, since the brother is virtuous though poor, and the sister has read *Pamela*. *L'Indigent* has a thesis to prove. It is a *Tendenzstück*, like most plays of Mercier and indeed of the second half of the Eighteenth Century, and sets out to be a good one. A melodramatic conclusion, however, that reveals Charlotte as the sister of de Lys and only the cousin of Joseph, smacks too much of the sentimental novel and is out of place in a piece with supposedly social significance. Still there is a certain justification in the dictum of the *Mercure* in 1782 that *l'Indigent* was the most truly moral, the least exaggerated, and the most interesting of Mercier's plays.[28]

Although *le Faux ami* (1772), which is more or less an imitation of *Tartufe*, is free from the romantic surprises that mar *l'Indigent*, it is not much of a play. Merval and his wife are drifting apart, largely as a result of the machinations of the false friend, Juller, but they are finally reconciled and the villain is unmasked. *Le Faux ami* is chiefly interesting as a plea, and a very earnest one, for the sanctity of marriage at a time when adultery was commonplace and the cult of the Marquis de Sade in mode.

A third piece of 1772, *Jean Hennuyer, évêque de Lisieux*, is a mixture of the historical play and the "drame." Here the events of history as they affect a humble family are portrayed. The title hero appears only in the third and last act. By his

[27] *Op. cit.*, p. 294.
[28] Cited by Béclard, *op. cit.*, p. 278n.

brave and spirited intervention he prevents the execution of the
order of the king to slaughter the Protestants of his diocese.
This is again a propaganda play, a condemnation of the policy
of intolerance of Charles IX which brought about the Massacre
of St. Bartholomew's Day, and by implication, a protest against
the misuse of power by any sovereign. Even La Harpe, one of
Mercier's severest critics and an ardent supporter of the classical
tradition, conceded in 1775 that the subject of the piece was
excellent. It contained moments of great interest, he thought,
which deserved a better pen than that of such an author of declamations and platitudes.[29]

Le Juge, which appeared two years later, offers a fine example
of the application of Diderot's theory of the "conditions." The
author of *le Père de famille,* and with him Mercier, maintained
that in the *genre sérieux* representative members of various professions and social ranks should be made the subjects of plays.
In Mercier's piece, a judge, de Leurye, has to decide between the
rights of a peasant and the whims of the village lord. With un-
compromising rectitude and unfaltering courage he pronounces
in favor of the humbler man, although it may cost him the friendship and protection of the aristocrat. However, the seigneur is
reconciled to the verdict, especially since the magistrate turns
out to be his own son. Mercier has attempted to show the methods, duties, and perils of the rural judge, and he has more or less
succeeded, although the large amount of excess baggage in the
form of moral tirades presents an almost insurmountable barrier to the enjoyment of the piece. The reader will want to ex-
claim: "In the name of the devil and his grandmother, *be* virtuous and have done with it." Although La Harpe's one-sided criticism (1774) goes too far when it calls *le Juge* a "ridiculous production,"[30] it is not a good play.

Despite, or perhaps because of its banality, *la Brouette du
vinaigrier* (1775) was Mercier's most popular, and is today his
best known drama. Dominique, the son of a vinegar merchant, is
employed as a clerk by the rich Delomer. He is also in love with

---

[29] *Œuvres diverses* (Paris, 1826), x, 77f.
[30] *Ibid.,* x, 48.

the latter's daughter, but because of his inferior social position does not dare to ask for her hand in marriage. Delomer suffers severe financial reverses and Dominique-père, by means of his vinegar cask filled with money, is able to aid him and to put his son in a position to wed the daughter. The preface of *la Brouette du vinaigrier* states that anything tending to break the excessive inequality of the various social ranks, "the source of all evil," is politically advantageous. That is just what our author has done. He has written a daring piece of democratic propaganda, which is the more significant when it is recalled that *la Brouette du vinaigrier* antedates Beaumarchais' *Mariage de Figaro* by nine, and the outbreak of the Revolution by fourteen years.

Natalie, which appeared in the same year as *la Brouette du vinaigrier,* is one of the most romantic pieces of our author. It contains all sorts of melodramatic complications and improbable recognitions. The heroine lives in sin with a certain Fondmaire for eighteen years. Their only child, a daughter, is taken by a nurse to Natalie's father. Then, after almost two decades, Fondmaire falls in love with a young girl who turns out to be his daughter. Natalie arrives on the scene. However, everything is eventually explained to the satisfaction of all, and the play, typically enough, ends in a "silent and touching" pantomime. *Natalie* is not a dull piece, and has been called by one critic Mercier's best.[31] Along with *Zoé* (1782), an improbable story of an abduction, it points toward the melodrama of Pixérécourt and the romantic drama of the Nineteenth Century.

While *l'Habitant de la Guadeloupe* (1782) relates the fortunes of a man who returns to France after a long sojourn in the colonies, *la Destruction de la Ligue* (1782) shows "how religious ideas, when wrongly understood, cause political errors and destroy national felicity." As in *Jean Hennuyer,* the Massacre of St. Bartholomew, so in *la Destruction de la Ligue,* the occupation of Paris by Henry IV is shown against a bourgeois background. On the one hand, Mercier pictures the middle-class family in the clutches of starvation; on the other, the priests who are the blackest of villains and the most despicable of fanatics. Finally,

---

[31] J. Lemaître, *op. cit.,* p. 262.

Henry IV, always one of Mercier's favorites, is portrayed in highly idealized fashion and as if he were a disciple of Rousseau.[32] Bachaumont's *Mémoires secrets* pointed out in 1782 that *la Destruction de la Ligue* suggested the manner of Shakespeare, although it was more regular in form.[33] The modern reader would find it a far cry from the Englishman's *Richard II*, for instance, to Mercier's play. The justification for the critic's verdict lies in the breadth of the interest and in the national and popular nature of the action of the latter. While in one scene the people of Paris appear on the stage and speak as individuals and in chorus, the entire last act is laid in the "palace of vengeance," the Bastille.

The *Portrait de Philippe II,* preceded by an essay, or *précis historique* (1785), is another historical "drame." It relates the well-known story of the cruelty and tyranny of the Spanish king. Because of jealousy, the hypocritical monarch has both Elizabeth, his wife, and Don Carlos, his son by a former marriage, destroyed. Again Mercier has produced propaganda. While Philip is the incarnation of all that is base and evil, his son and his wife are representatives of the spirit of humanity.

Le Ci-devant noble (1792), a revolutionary version of an earlier play, *le Gentillâtre,* is one of Mercier's few comedies. It was written to poke fun at the sudden disintegration of the "feudal monster," and at the nobles who did not want to become good citizens. The Baron de Tempesack and his henchman who wishes to marry his daughter are members of the insolent nobility. Eraste, a saner gentleman with democratic inclinations, puts both of them to shame, and just as the Revolution breaks out, succeeds in winning the daughter.

We do not need to concern ourselves with Mercier's other comedies, adaptions from the English, or historical pieces. It is already clear what types of subjects he treats and how he deals with them. It was characteristic of the *genre sérieux* to portray contemporary bourgeois life. In this respect Mercier follows in the footsteps of Diderot, Sedaine, and Beaumarchais.

[32] Béclard, *op. cit.,* p. 310.
[33] *Op. cit.,* XXI, 44.

Like them, he lays emphasis on the moral lesson and indulges in lachrymose sentimentalism. His method is, as Fréron rather aptly put it, "to indoctrinate and bore all humanity for its own good."[34] Nevertheless, Mercier brings one new tone into these family tableaux. While the *genre sérieux* of Diderot glorifies the virtues of the middle class, the "drame" of Mercier contrasts the bourgeoisie with the aristocracy, gives its preference to the former, and attacks the privileges of the higher order. Thereby Mercier introduces what is almost a revolutionary note into serious French drama. With him, militant social protest invaded the French stage.

From Mercier's theories, we should expect his plays to make a distinct break with established form. That is not the case. They are, to be sure, in prose and vary in the number of their acts. Nevertheless, there is no evidence that more than twenty-four hours elapse in any of them. Although the unity of place is not always strictly kept, the action is never shifted further than to another room or another spot in the same town. The external realism of his pieces, however, is frequently very marked and can be called almost Zolaesque. In this respect, Mercier advanced a step further in the direction suggested by Diderot. Still, the characters he portrays are not at all real and the action is often marked by romantic coincidences. With Mercier the "drame" doubtless reached its highest, or if one will, its lowest point. Then it passed gradually on the one hand into the melodrama, and on the other into the problem play of the next century.

The motto of *l'An 2440*, "the present is pregnant with the future,"[35] is the basic idea of Mercier's social, political, and philosophical works, to which we now turn. They are practically all polemics against tyranny, intolerance, and abuse of power, and not in the least objective philosophical treatises. In line with his century Mercier was both destructive and constructive. He joined eagerly in the assault on the established authorities of the preceding age, the church and the absolute monarchy, but he was

[34] Cited by Béclard, *op. cit.*, p. 354.
[35] Taken by Mercier from Leibnitz.

likewise very productive in suggestions for a newly organized society.

His incredible optimism is already quite apparent in the *Songes philosophiques* (1768).[35a] This is a collection of often highly allegorical dreams on such subjects as cupidity, optimism, a happy world, royalty, and tyranny. In them he shows an almost limitless belief in the perfectibility of man, his eventual felicity on earth, and in God's love for him. Mercier is never held in check by artistic scruples. Nevertheless, despite their exalted tone, the *Songes philosophiques* ring true. They were composed by a man who was convinced that he was doing his part to disperse the shadows of darkness and pave the way for a new and happier order.

The same enthusiastic optimism characterizes *l'An 2440* (1770). This picture of the future in the utopian tradition relates the experiences of the author when he awakens in a perfected society after a sleep of almost seven centuries. He visits the various public buildings, goes to the theater, sees the library of the king. He learns of the systems of taxation, commerce, government, and religion. The government is a limited monarchy, the religion an enlightened, deistic morality. Everybody is serious, pious, and well-meaning. The ideal world of *l'An 2440* is an abstract creation, a society made over in accord with its author's hopes and wishes rather than with any political experience of mankind. It is, as is remarked in the *Mémoires secrets* of Bachaumont (1771), a kind of "apocalypse."[36] The footnotes with which the book is generously supplied are, as in Bayle's *Dictionnaire historique et critique,* of great importance. While the main body of the text paints the utopian picture of 2440, Mercier's annotations offer a biting criticism of the conditions of the year 1770. *L'An 2440* was considered so revolutionary in Spain that it was condemned to be burned by the king in 1778 and was forbidden by the Inquisition.[37]

[35a] An augmented version, *Songes et visions philosophiques,* appeared in 1788.

[36] *Op. cit.,* v, 297.

[37] Cf. Zollinger, "Eine Utopie des 18. Jahrhunderts vor der spanischen Inquisition," *Zeitschrift für französische Sprache und Literatur,* xix (1897), 305ff. All references to *l'An 2440* are to the edition, Londres, 1772.

A group of Mercier's prize essays, bearing the title *Éloges et discours philosophiques* (1776), contains eulogies of Charles the Wise, Henry IV of France, and Descartes, along with discussions of the man of letters, reading, and the horrors of war. These discourses were written for the most part in the preceding decade, and are thus among the earliest works of our author. They are in general of little interest to the modern reader. Of note, however, are the panegyric on the *littérateurs* who castigate tyranny, speak in an exalted fashion on behalf of their fellow men, and live as freemen in their thoughts; and in another vein, the realistic portrait of the mutilated bodies that litter up the battlefield when the guns have ceased firing.[38]

If Mercier has escaped at all from literary oblivion, it is because of his *Tableau de Paris*. This gigantic work, which between 1781 and 1788 grew to twelve volumes, gives a complete picture of the French capital on the eve of the Revolution. It sums up the spirit of the century: the political currents, the social customs, the literary movements of the time.[39] Mercier wrote in the fourth volume of his work: "Escape, my book, escape from the flames and the barbarians! Tell future generations what Paris really was!" Our author omits nothing from his exhaustive but not exhausting description of the metropolis. Literature, music, architecture, religion, the nobility, women, churches, hospitals, cemeteries, public latrines, police courts, are among the subjects the disconnected chapters treat. They are written with the same naïve faith in progress, with the same emphasis on morality, and in the same democratic tone that characterize Mercier's other literary productions. Mercier knew his Paris. He went every-

---

[38] Mercier, who expressed great appreciation for the Quakers, was an early French pacifist. Cf. the following passage from *les Malheurs de la guerre* (German translation, Leipzig, 1777-1778), I, 178f.: "Wenn meine Hand den königlichen Mantel, welcher dich (Krieg) umgibt, wegreißt, was werde ich gewahr werden? Großer Gott! Wunden, Blut, Würgen, gräuliche Blessuren, verstümmelte Leiber, Rümpfe von Menschen, Werkzeuge des Schmerzens, Verzuckungen, Geschrei, klägliche Seufzer, Wehklagen . . . die Tränen der Gattinnen, der Mütter, der Kinder, der Freunde, die Flüche der Verzweiflung, das Geheul der Wut. . . ."

[39] According to Ch. Aubertin, *l'Esprit public au xviii᷎ siècle*, 2d ed. (Paris, 1873), p. 11, these three elements go to make up the "spirit of a century." All references to the *Tableau de Paris* are to the edition, Amsterdam, 1782ff.

where and saw everything, and his talent for description is not far below that of La Bruyère or Saint-Simon. The *Tableau de Paris* was composed by an Eighteenth Century reporter.

The *Portraits des rois de France* (1783), Mercier's one attempt to write history, relates the story of France under its various monarchs. It is in the main political history, written in a liberal, although not revolutionary tone. It contains chapters of a wider scope on feudalism, the customs of the Tenth Century, literature under Louis XIII, and is not without the merit of seeing now and then the broader perspectives of history. Mercier notes, for instance, the French sense of gaiety which appears even at the most serious moments. This is obviously no scholarly history in the modern sense. Footnotes are rare and there is in general no effort made to give sources.

"I am in the habit," wrote Mercier, "of writing down every evening what has impressed me during the day, what I have seen, felt, thought, or read. In short, I entrust everything to paper."[40] The result of this activity is *mon Bonnet de nuit* (1784), a four-volume collection of disconnected essays on all imaginable subjects entirely unrelated to each other, a kind of Mercier potpourri. The prevailing tone is, as one would expect, optimistic, sentimental, and moral. The observation in Bachaumont's *Mémoires secrets* (1784), how astonishing it was that a gifted man could publish such stuff,[41] is not without justification. However, *mon Bonnet de nuit* does contain a very spirited sketch of the Alps, and shows, too, an increasing interest in foreign literatures. Mercier refers to Dante, Fielding, Milton, Newton, Ossian, Richardson, Shakespeare, and Tacitus.

La Solitude considérée relativement à l'esprit et au cœur (1788) is a translation in condensed form of *Über die Einsamkeit* (1784-1785) of J. G. Zimmermann (1728-1795), the Swiss doctor and popular philosopher. Zimmermann's work treats in twelve long chapters the advantages and disadvantages of the solitary life. It also contains an attack on the mode of life of monks and other "Christian rogues." In general, *Über die Einsamkeit* shows

[40] *Mon Bonnet de nuit* (German translation, Berlin, 1784-1786), I, 5.
[41] *Op. cit.*, XXVI, 65.

that its author had much in common with Rousseau. It is not at all strange, then, that Mercier, in many respects a follower of the Geneva philosopher, devoted himself to making Zimmermann's disquisition available to his countrymen. Although his version reduced the four large tomes of the original to two small volumes, leaving out most of the discussion of the solitude of the hermit, French critics still found it too detailed, filled with misplaced erudition, and not always in good taste.[42]

The colors of le Nouveau Paris (1797-1800) are quite different from those in the original picture of the French city, for as the author states in his preface, "the model and the painter have undergone the most stormy events."[43] This work sketches in Mercier's usual desultory fashion the happenings of the years following 1789. It is really a collection of political essays composed in accord with the author's relatively conservative republicanism. Later historians, Thiers, Mignet, Carlyle, and Louis Blanc made use of le Nouveau Paris as a source book.[44] It lacks, however, the general appeal of the earlier portrait of the great metropolis.

Mercier contributed a final series of sketches of Paris to an English-French-German anthology, translated into German and published by K. F. Cramer, the exile from Kiel. It appeared in 1807-1808 with the title, Ansichten der Hauptstadt des französischen Kaiserreichs vom Jahre 1806 an. The Ansichten, whose purpose was to contribute to the progress of mankind,[45] contains essays by the Scottish antiquary and historian, Pinkerton, by the publisher, Cramer, and by Mercier. None of the twenty-odd sketches by the Frenchman is of any particular interest or importance.

In the later years of his life, Mercier turned more and more to political subjects. Among his most important works in this field are the Notions claires sur les gouvernements (1787), which contains propaganda in favor of a limited monarchy; de l'Associa-

---

[42] E. Eggli, Schiller et le romantisme français (Paris, 1927), I, 10, cites the Année littéraire (1790), I, 34.

[43] I, 33. My references are to an edition published at Brunswick in 1800.

[44] Zollinger, Mercier als Dramatiker, p. 6.

[45] Cf. Cramer's introduction, I, 20.

tion des princes du corps germanique (1789), a translation of
Johannes von Müller's *Darstellung des Fürstenbundes* (1787);
and the *Fragments de politique et d'histoire* (1792), a collection,
as the title indicates, of miscellaneous essays of a general political
character. During the latter part of his life, Mercier also engaged
in journalistic activity, which attests his indefatigable energy, but
does not pertain to the present study.

Mercier's importance in his social, political, and philosophical
works lies in the sociological significance of his opinions and in
the detailed pictures of contemporary life which he painted. He
was not a philosopher or moralist of the calibre of Montesquieu,
Voltaire, Diderot, or Rousseau, though many of his views can
indeed be traced back to this quadrumvirate. Nevertheless, he is,
in the broader sense, one of the earliest French social critics. He
described the life of all classes, not merely that of the aristocracy.
Although he repeatedly called democracy the worst form of government,[46] he was a precursor of the Revolution, and his often
inflammatory writings contributed their small part to the growing fire of popular resentment. He was a philanthropist and like
Plato wished to harness the forces of art to the wagon of social
progress. He employed whatever literary endowment he had, not
to produce works of artistic merit, but to campaign for the betterment of his fellow men. The *Tableau de Paris* and perhaps
l'An 2440, because of their author's enthusiastic love of humanity and the keenness of his observations, come near to being masterpieces. For Mercier was with the pen what Greuze was with
the brush, a genre painter of great merit.[47] He was one of the
most realistic authors of his day.

Active as he was in almost every literary genre imaginable,
from didactic poetry to lexicography, Mercier maintained that
every great poet should at some time write a novel. He himself produced several, and also a number of short stories. All of them
fall far below the high standard set by Prévost, Voltaire, Diderot,
Rousseau, and Marmontel. *L'Homme sauvage* (1767) is a romance in the vein of the Abbé Prévost about the inhabitants of

---

[46] *Notions claires,* I, 337; *Fragments de politique,* III, 164.
[47] Mercier himself noted this similarity. Cf. Béclard, *op. cit.,* p. 205n.

the New World.[48] A young and virtuous savage grows to young manhood alone with his father, sister, and a faithful servant. He marries his sister, and seems to be destined to live virtuously and happily ever after. A European intruder, however, disturbs his bliss and causes him to leave his desert refuge after the death of his father and to undergo all kinds of adventures. The whole novel is shot through with the sentimentalism, deism, and the love of nature characteristic of Rousseau. Still our author is a bit sceptical of the virtuous savage, and cautions his readers that "nature alone is a bad guide."[49] *L'Homme sauvage* is written with some warmth, and despite its lack of local color, its grotesque plot, and its unnatural style, is not dull reading. It offers, too, an interesting contrast to the uncritical glorification of nature which characterizes the *Paul et Virginie* (1788) of Rousseau's follower, Bernardin de Saint-Pierre.

Mercier's longest original novel *Jezennemours* (1776)[50] is a genuine, although not very successful romance of adventure, with all the surprises that are so typical of the genre. Jezennemours, an illegitimate son of a Jesuit priest, becomes "enlightened" by reading Fontenelle and Voltaire, falls in love with a Protestant girl, Suzanne, and runs away with her. They remain together as brother and sister until they are separated by a band of robbers. Jezennemours is adopted by the hedonistic philosopher Monval, falls in love with the philosopher's virtuous mistress, is, however, disenchanted, and flees. Then he is taken in by an old officer, who turns out to be the father not only of the mistress, but also of a son who has just married Suzanne. The mistress retires to a convent, the son goes to America, and Jezennemours follows him to the New World. Here the son dies and the title hero finally returns to wed his first love. The book abounds, then, with improbabilities. The part of the first volume which is imitated from Wieland's *Agathon*[51] is about all that is in any way palatable to the modern reader.

[48] Cf. E. Rovillain, "l'Abbé Prévost et *l'Homme sauvage* de Sébastien Mercier," *PMLA*, XLV (1930), 822ff. For the relationship of *l'Homme sauvage* to Pfeil's *Wilde*, see below, pp. 46f.

[49] P. 10.

[50] Mercier also translated or adapted Meissner's *Alcibiades* in 1789.

[51] See below, pp. 105f.

Mercier also wrote short moral tales, which are more moral and less interesting than those of Marmontel, the acknowledged master of the *conte moral.* A collection of these appeared in 1792 with the title *Fictions morales.*[52] The avowed purpose of the three volumes is to combat vice, which the author considers more dangerous than mere ridiculousness.[53] They contain numerous stories that had appeared before, including *l'Homme sauvage,* and also a tale supposedly taken from an "old German chronicle."[54] In general Mercier's stories are a bit tedious. Unlike Marmontel, he stresses the moral more than the narrative.

The narrative works of Mercier make little if any contribution to the development of the French novel and short story. Full of the melodramatic elements of the romance of adventure, and burdened with a superabundance of the didactic element, they are not alleviated by any charm of style. At best they can be excused in view of the sincerity of their author in his effort to better the world and its people.

There is considerable literature on Mercier's position in the history of the arts in France. While one critic goes to extremes, praising him to the skies and attributing the rebirth of French literature in the Nineteenth Century to his influence, another denies that he contributed anything new or lasting at all.[55] This is not the place to investigate the question of his relationship

[52] Not to be confused with the *Contes moraux,* four stories which appeared in 1769.

[53] I, vii.

[54] I, 58ff.

[55] Michiels, *op. cit.,* I, 124f.; R. Doumic, *Études sur la littérature française* (Paris, 1896-1909), V, 122, 133. For other appraisements of Mercier, cf. G. Desnoiresterres, "Étude sur la vie et les ouvrages de Mercier," in his edition of the *Tableau de Paris* (Paris, 1853), pp. v-xlvi; J. Janin, *Histoire de la littérature dramatique* (Paris, 1855-1858), IV, 223-242; Ch. Monselet, *les Oubliés et les dédaignés* (Alençon, 1857), I, 51-99; Louvet, *op. cit.* (1865); P. Albert, *la Littérature française au xixe siècle* (Paris, 1882), I, 329-347; C. Lenient, *la Comédie en France au xviiie siècle* (Paris, 1888), II, 378-390; du Bled, *le Prince de Ligne et ses contemporains* (Paris, 1890), pp. 227-252; H. Hettner, *Geschichte der französischen Literatur im achtzehnten Jahrhundert,* 5 ed. (Braunschweig, 1894), pp. 410-412; Brunetière, *op. cit.* (1896), pp. 305-310; Zollinger, *Mercier als Dramatiker* (1899); Béclard, *op. cit.* (1903); Lemaître, *op. cit.,* 249-268; Ernest-Charles, *les Samedis littéraires* (Paris, 1903-1904), II, 301-311; Suchier und Birch-Hirschfeld, *Geschichte der französischen Literatur,* neuer Abdruck (Leipzig und Wien, 1905), p. 579; H. Lion in Petit de Julleville's *Histoire de la langue et de la littérature française* (Paris, 1908-1912),

to Hugo and the other romanticists. In the preceding pages, however, an effort has been made to define the general characteristics of his work and to indicate his relation to predecessors and contemporaries in his fields of artistry. Attention has been called to the note of social protest and to the external realism that characterize his philosophical works as well as his dramatic theories and his plays and distinguish them from other writings of an earlier or the same period. That he was not a genius nor a great artist is evident at the first glance into his work. He was rather a man of ideas, ideas that he more often than not borrowed from more original thinkers. All of these are concerned with one point, an implicit belief in human progress. He unites the rationalism of Diderot, the sentimentalism of Rousseau, and the combative liberalism of Voltaire. While at home, where his ideas were already familiar from other sources, his writings could not arouse any enthusiasm, Germans and other foreigners found in his works a cross section and a convenient summary of the most progressive contemporary French thought. That is certainly one of the reasons why he was more popular in other countries than in his native land.

---

vi, 617-619; Gaiffe, *op. cit.* (1910), p. 443; Lanson's classical *Histoire de la littérature française,* 21 ed., mentions Mercier only in a footnote. Later Mercier scholars treated his relation to foreign literatures rather than his position in France.

II

MERCIER IN GERMAN TRANSLATION

THE EXTENT of Mercier's vogue in Germany is attested by the large number of translations, adaptations, and imitations of his works that appeared in the last three decades of the Eighteenth Century. According to a review of a German version of his *Jezennemours* in the *Allgemeine deutsche Bibliothek* in 1787, not one line had flowed from the pen of this prolific writer that had not been seized at once and repeatedly by eager German translators.[1] All kinds of people undertook to adapt the work of the Frenchman for the German public. Prominent figures in German literary history, such as Schiller, Heinrich Leopold Wagner, and Christian Weisse, knew and translated Mercier's works. Men of less importance, nowadays known only to the scholar, K. F. Cramer, A. von Knigge, and H. A. O. Reichard, were also translators of Mercier. Men of the theater, such as Schröder, Iffland, and Dalberg, found his plays worth adapting and imitating. Scholars, such as Heydenreich, and publishers such as C. F. Schwan, translated his literary productions. In a period of thirty years ending with the tern of the century, at least seventy-five editions of Mercier in German were published in German-speaking territory, six appearing in 1778 alone.[2]

In the following pages the character of the translations, and the men who made them will be discussed. Those German versions that were available to me will be treated at some length in respect to any omissions or additions which may have been made.[3] As regards the others, which, if they still exist at all, are

---

[1] LXXVII, 122.

[2] Cf. the appendix: "German Translations of Mercier's Works." French editions were also published in Germany of *l'Homme sauvage, Jenneval, l'An 2440, Tableau de Paris, la Destruction de la Ligue, mon Bonnet de nuit, le Nouveau Paris,* etc.

[3] I have examined the translations of Mercier in the university libraries in Hamburg, Jena, Bonn, at Columbia and Harvard, and in the Bibliothèque nationale and the New York City Public Library. No attempt has been made to examine all the translations of Mercier into German. Such an effort to be exhaustive would

scattered throughout the various libraries in Germany,[4] we must rely on contemporary criticism. First Mercier's plays will be considered, since these enjoyed the earlier vogue, having been translated most extensively between 1770 and 1785. Then his other works, mostly philosophical, social, or political in nature will be taken up. These appeared in German chiefly between 1780 and 1795. In both cases we shall proceed chronologically, beginning with the first translation of the work into German.

Mercier's first appearance before the German public in its native tongue was in 1770, when *Jenneval, oder der französische Barnevelt* was published at Frankfort on the Main. Since the original, Lillo's *London Merchant* (1731), had been translated into German at least twice before 1770 and performed in Germany as early as 1749,[5] it it not strange that this translation of Mercier was received with no great enthusiasm. A critic in the *Almanach der deutschen Musen* in 1771 remarked briefly and to the point that he would like to know why the French *Barnwell* had been translated at all.[6] The author of the German version was J. H. Faber (17..-1791),[7] professor of law and belles-lettres in Mainz and later secretary to Count Neiperg in Frankfort. Faber's interest lay mainly in the operetta. He translated many of Favart's works for Marchand in Frankfort. He also wrote German versions of plays by Dancourt and Sedaine.[8] This

---

contribute little toward the fulfillment of the purpose of the present study. For this it was sufficient to explore the extent of the knowledge of Mercier in Germany and to establish the general character of his appeal to German readers. This implied a firsthand examination of a number of representative and popular translations, together with the listing and description of all other translations so far as bibliographical research has revealed them. The result seems to justify quite fully the conclusion that Mercier was one of the foreign authors most frequently translated into German in the last third of the Eighteenth Century.

[4] Translations not available to me are indicated here and in the appendix by an asterisk.

[5] Cf. C. Flaischlen, *Otto Heinrich von Gemmingen* (Stuttgart, 1890), p. 4n., and *Bibliothek der schönen Wissenschaften*, I (1757), 161.

[6] P. 152.

[7] Attributed wrongly to Johann André, the early friend of Goethe and the music director of the Döbbelin Theater in Berlin, by Reichard, *Theater-Kalender*, 1776, p. 205.

[8] Cf. Meusel, *Lexikon der vom Jahr 1750 bis 1800 verstorbenen deutschen Schriftsteller* (Leipzig, 1802ff.), III, 256ff., and A. Iacuzzi, *The European Vogue of*

seems to be the only direct translation of *Jenneval,* while most of Mercier's other dramas of the seventies enjoyed greater popularity. This is due, of course, to the fact that the English original was well known and repeatedly translated during the next twenty years.[9] However, in a slightly modified form, with the title *Die Gefahren der Verführung,* Mercier's work had at least six further editions. This adaptation was published in 1781 by Friedrich Ludwig Schröder, the theater director in Hamburg and actor in Vienna, and was considered an improvement over Mercier's *Jenneval* by a contemporary critic in the *Allgemeines Verzeichnis neuer Bücher,*[10] and by E. von Bülow, the editor of Schröder's works.[11] It introduced German names for the characters, and had recourse to the English original for the trait that the heroine reveals her love for Jenneval by making up the money he has stolen and not by opening her heart, as in Mercier's play, to an unnecessary confidante.[12] The latter part of the German version was considerably shortened by the omission of lengthy tirades and the last two acts were made into one, although this necessitated a change of scene within the act.[13] Schröder, with the trained eye of a man closely connected with the theater, made his hero leave the seductive woman with the intent to save his uncle, while Mercier's Jenneval sets out to kill him and changes his mind somehow or other before the encounter. Otherwise, however, Schröder's adaptation is practically a word-for-word translation of the French original, and a very excellent and natural one.[14] He attempted to make the French *Jenneval* more German,

Favart (New York, 1932), pp. 175f. I was unable to discover the date of Faber's birth.

[9] Cf. Flaischlen, *op. cit.,* p. 4n.

[10] (1781), p. 761.

[11] *Friedrich Ludwig Schröders dramatische Werke* (Berlin, 1831), I, lxxiv: "Ich ziehe die Merciersche Bearbeitung dem Originale, und . . . die Schrödersche der Mercierschen vor."

[12] Act III, Sc. 1, in the three plays.

[13] Act IV, Sc. 1, "Ein schlechtes Zimmer"; Act IV, Sc. 10, "Woldemars Zimmer."

[14] Cf. for example the following: Act I, Sc. 6, Jenneval, seul: "J'étais prêt de tomber à ses pieds. Qui m'arrêtait? Rosalie, Rosalie, laisse-moi respirer. Tu maîtrises tout mon être. Tout ce qui n'est pas toi n'a plus d'empire sur mon âme . . . Cruelle! tu semblais me promettre le bonheur. Hélas! au lieu de te rendre heureuse, je me perds avec toi . . .." Act I, Sc. 10, Adolph, allein: "Ich war im Begriff,

more artistic, and more fit for the stage, and succeeded to such an extent that fifty years later Tieck could still express the wish that this now long forgotten piece with its "mild scenes" and its "clever solution" might be performed again.[15]

The year after 1770, when Mercier was first introduced to the German public in translation, saw the appearance of two more of his plays in German, le Déserteur and Olinde et Sophronie. Le Déserteur was published in France in 1770 and at once took the country across the Rhine by storm. Translations appeared at Mannheim, Berlin, Hamburg, and Prague in the following year. The author of the Mannheim *Deserteur, Schiller's friend C. F. Schwan (1733-1815), was one of the first in Germany to receive the French play, perhaps having got it from Mercier himself.[16] Schwan was head of the publishing firm that bore his name. His literary activity consisted chiefly of translations from French, for instance of another of Mercier's plays,[17] Sedaine's Philosophe sans le savoir and his operetta le Déserteur, and Beaumarchais' Eugénie. He also published a French and German dictionary (1782ff.). His interest in French literature made him, together with Reichard, one of the chief German intermediaries between France and Germany in the second half of the Eighteenth Century. He was friendly with such men as Götz, Gotter, Lenz, Maler Müller, Schubart, Lessing, Wieland, Herder, Goethe, and Dalberg.[18] It is to be expected, then, that a work that interested Schwan would soon become known to a large number of German men of letters. His translation, which was supplied with the new happy conclusion, does not seem to

mich zu seinen Füßen zu werfen! Wer hielt mich ab? O Lina, Lina! außer dir hat nichts mehr Macht über meine Seele. Von dir versprach ich mir alles Glück and Seligkeit eines fühlenden Menschen und anstatt dich und mich glücklich zu machen, stürze ich mich mit dir ins Verderben . . ."

[15] "Die geschichtliche Entwicklung der neueren Bühne" (1831), Kritische Schriften (Leipzig, 1848-1852), II, 357.

[16] Cf. K. H. von Stockmayer, Das deutsche Soldatenstück des 18. Jahrhunderts. "Literarhistorische Forschungen," hrsg. von J. Schick und M. von Waldberg, Nr. 10 (Weimar, 1898), p. 92.

[17] L'Indigent, 1772. Cf. below, p. 33.

[18] Cf. Meusel, Das gelehrte Deutschland, 5. Ausgabe (Lemgo, 1796ff.), VII, 403f.; J. Minor, Weiße und seine Beziehungen zur deutschen Literatur (Innsbruck, 1880), pp. 197f.; and Allgemeine deutsche Biographie, XXXIII, 176f.

have been a particularly good one, if we can believe a contemporary critic in the *Almanach der deutschen Musen*.[19] It did, however, attempt, at least superficially, to Germanize the French work, giving German names to the characters.[20] This procedure was typical of the time. It has already been noted in Schröder's *Gefahren der Verführung* and will come to our attention repeatedly in later translations of Mercier's plays.

The Berlin *Deserteur*, which was also reprinted three years later, was the work of K. A. von Beulwitz (1735-1799), a Prussian officer who ended his long military career with the rank of lieutenant-colonel. He was doubtless attracted to the play because it presented a problem with which he might come in contact in the course of his service. The first edition followed the original French tragic version, while the second had like Schwan's translation the "new fifth act in which the play comes out happily," this being brought about by a pardon granted Durimel by the commanding officer.[21] Beulwitz' translation is exact and better than the others, although the reviewer in the *Almanach der deutschen Musen* finds that he had difficulty with the touching passages.[22]

The Hamburg **Deserteur*, according to the same periodical a weak reproduction of the original,[23] appeared anonymously and cannot be assigned with certainty to any author. It may be the work of a Madam Zink, or of A. Wittenberg (1728-1807) of Hamburg, who about this time was actively engaged in translating from French and English.[24]

[19] 1772, p. 161.

[20] Cf. Stockmayer, *op. cit.*, p. 92.

[21] Cf. *Almanach der deutschen Musen*, 1775, p. 90, and Zollinger, *Mercier als Dramatiker*, p. 78.

[22] 1772, p. 161. Compare, however, the following: Act IV, Sc. 2, Saint-Franc, seul: "Impénétrable providence! tu veux rendre la fin de ma carrière triste et funeste! Hélas! il devait faire la consolation de ma vieillesse. Ah! quand ma main guidait en paix ses premiers ans, j'étais loin de prévoir que cette même main devait un jour le conduire à la mort!" Saint Franc, allein: "Unergründliche Vorsehung! du willst, daß das Ende meiner Tage in Trauer gehüllt sei! Ach! er sollte der Trost in meinem Alter sein! Ach! da meine Hand seine ersten Schritte ruhig leitete, war ich weit entfernt, zu denken, daß ihn dieselbe Hand einst zum Tode führen sollte!"

[23] 1772, 161.

[24] Cf. the bibliography.

The Prague *Deserteur, a "rührendes Lustspiel,"[25] was prepared by J. J. Nunn (1744-about 1805), and had likewise the
modified conclusion. Nunn, a one time pupil of Sonnenfels, went
to Prague in 1770 and held various positions of a secretarial nature there with the archbishop. Aside from translations from
French and Italian, his chief writings were of a philological and
theological nature.[26]

C. H. Schmid's *Deserteur is an adaptation for Koch's company based on Beulwitz' version. Schmid, professor of rhetoric
and poetry at Giessen and a literary critic of some merit, attempted to improve le Déserteur by cutting down the moral
tirades of the major, by a clearer characterization of Valcour,
and by preparing adequately for the pardon of the deserter in
several additional scenes.[27] It is typical of the translators of Mercier's works, political and social as well as dramatic, that they
usually attempt to shorten or omit his lengthy declamations and
repetitions.

A critic in the Frankfurter gelehrte Anzeigen remarked in
1774 that any one who knew how many translations of le Déserteur had appeared in Germany and how often it had been produced on the stage, would not be surprised to learn of a new
edition of it.[28] Its vogue, however, was not yet over, for besides
*Der Deserteur (1774) of F. F. Westarp (1734-1797), a high
government official in Upper Silesia,[29] it was frequently translated and imitated during the next forty years. Further editions
of Schwan's translation appeared in 1791 and 1814, the latter
being an adaptation for the Vienna stage by the actor Stegmayer,
who was also the author of numerous operettas.[30]

The imitations of Mercier's play are very numerous. Influence
of at least the title is evident in both Stephanie's and Gotter's

[25] The terminology is interesting. The other versions are called "Drama," or
"Schauspiel."
[26] Cf. C. von Wurzbach, Biographisches Lexikon des Kaisertums Österreich (Wien,
1856-1890) xx, 434f.; and Meusel, Das gelehrte Deutschland, v, 465, x, 374.
[27] Stockmayer, op. cit., p. 93.
[28] Sept. 13.
[29] Cf. Meusel, Lexikon, xv, 49.
[30] Cf. Wurzbach, op. cit., xxxvii, 327ff.

Deserteur aus Kindesliebe, and in *Der österreichische Deserteur* (1790-1791) and *Der ungarische Deserteur* (1814). The
Austrian *Deserteur* was written by K. F. Hensler (1761-1825),
the author of numerous plays and later the director of the Leo-
poldstädter Theater in Vienna;[31] the Hungarian *Deserteur* by a
C. W. Schall. An anonymous "collection of tales by German,
French, and English writers," published in 1778, also contained
a "truly touching story," *Der Deserteur*, that was possibly de-
rived from Mercier.

The problem of insubordination for the sake of humanitarian
ideals had a great appeal to the discipline-loving Germans of the
Aufklärung. It was treated by the younger Stephanie, a very
fruitful producer of worthless plays, in *Die Kriegsgefangenen*
(1771);[32] by H. C. H. von Trautzschen, lieutenant-colonel in the
Electorate of Saxony, in *Der Freiherr von Bardenfels* (1773);
and by Grossmann, author of *Nicht mehr als sechs Schüsseln*, in
Henriette, oder sie ist schon verheiratet (1777). Insubordination
was also the subject of one of the most popular plays of the seventies, *Der Graf Walltron* (1776), by the prolific Heinrich Ferdinand Möller (1745-1798). Here the hero has quarrelled with his
superior and has been condemned to die. His wife arrives on the
day when he is to be executed, and like Clary in the French
play, begs in vain for the life of her beloved. This motif also
crops up in Klinger's *Die falschen Spieler* (1781), Iffland's *Albert von Thurneisen* (1781), and Schröder's *Fähndrich* (1782).[33]

Similarity of title or theme does not necessarily signify actual
borrowing. The various German works that have been discussed
as imitations of *le Déserteur* belong to the genre of sentimental
and lachrymose humanitarianism that owed its origin to both
France and England and replaced in the Soldatenstück the more
virile realism of Lessing's *Minna von Barnhelm*. They may owe
their similarity to Mercier's work to the fact that the question
was in the air and the theme available to all[34] as much as to any

[31] Wurzbach, *op. cit.*, VIII, 312ff.
[32] Cf. Stockmayer, *op. cit.*, pp. 31f.
[33] See below, "Mercier, Lessing, and the German Middle-Class Drama."
[34] On the question of similarity and influence, cf. Gaiffe, *op. cit.*, p. 76.

direct knowledge of the Frenchman. However, if he did not exert a direct influence on all the German military plays, his influence on the tradition of the Soldatenstück cannot be denied.

The second of Mercier's plays to be translated into German in 1771 bore the title *Olint und Sophronia, ein heroisches Drama in ungebundener Rede,* and appeared at Frankfort on the Main. Here we encounter the strange phenomenon of the translation of a work into German that Mercier had taken from that language. *Olinde et Sophronie* is an adaption, with alterations, of Cronegk's play of the same name, which came out in 1760 and was reviewed by Lessing in the opening chapters of his *Dramaturgie.* We are not concerned here with the changes Mercier made in adapting the German work.[35] However, a reviewer in the *Almanach der deutschen Musen* in 1772 stated that the French work deserved to be translated all the more because Mercier had used, improved upon, and completed Cronegk's fragment.[36] It seems that German critics still looked up to France and were glad to find the merit of their countrymen recognized and confirmed by their neighbors across the Rhine. A preference for things French still lingered on in spite of Lessing's iconoclasm. This led a later critic to ask sarcastically, who wouldn't read Mercier rather than Wieland, since the former was a foreigner.[37]

Cronegk's play was well known in Germany, and it is not strange that only one more translation of *Olinde et Sophronie* appeared, and that not until 1788. Its author, Bernard Christian d'Arien (1754-1793), made various translations for the Hamburg stage, and wrote a number of original tragedies, comedies, and operettas.[38] The verses of *Olinth und Sophronie* are irregular, often misplace the natural accent, and sometimes do not scan. The play seems to have been written too hurriedly, a criticism that was directed at some of d'Arien's works by a reviewer in the *Allgemeine deutsche Bibliothek* in 1783.[39] The following comparison,

[35] Cf. W. Gensel, *Cronegk, sein Leben und seine Schriften* (Berlin, 1894), pp. 100ff., and Zollinger, *Mercier als Dramatiker,* pp. 33ff.

[36] Pp. 154f.

[37] *Allgemeine Literaturzeitung,* Feb. 5, 1795.

[38] Cf. Meusel, *Das gelehrte Deutschland,* 1, 89, and Reichard, *Theater-Kalender,* 1783, pp. 187f.

[39] LVI, 124.

taken from the opening monologue of the dramas of Cronegk, Mercier, and d'Arien, is interesting in that it contrasts three mediums of dramatic expression, the Alexandrine, prose, and blank verse.

Cronegk: Noch schläft Jerusalem; doch niemals schläft mein Kummer:
Mein Herz kennt keine Ruh, mein Aug kennt keinen Schlummer.
Ist dies Jerusalem, der Völker Königin?
Wo ist nunmehr ihr Stolz, wo Macht und Schimmer hin?
Ein wildes Pferd zerstreut der Könige Gebeine:
Wo sonst der Tempel stand, sind jetzo Schutt und Steine . . .
Der Himmel hört uns nicht, und sieht nicht unsre Tränen.

Mercier: Triste Jérusalem, ô ma patrie! qu'est devenue ta gloire? Mes yeux ont peine à te reconnaître: est-ce-là cette ville, la reine des cités! Tes murs solitaires portent l'empreinte du courroux d'un dieu. . . . Dieu t'a rejetté, il n'entend plus tes prières, il ne reçoit plus tes sacrifices. L'infidèle triomphe; il arbore l'étendard du croissant sur ces mêmes remparts où j'ai vu le signe auguste de la croix.

d'Arien: Bedrängtes Vaterland! Jerusalem!
Wo ist dein Ruhm? Kaum kennt mein Auge dich
Der Städte Königin! Auf einsamem
Gemäur, ruht schwer der Gottheit Zorn. Du bist
Verbannt von Gott! Er hört nicht deine Stimme,
Will deiner Opfer nicht! Der Frevler siegt!
Der halbe Mond hebt nun die stolzen Hörner,
Wo das Panier des heil'gen Kreuzes stand.

While Cronegk's play was written in the accepted verse of his day, Lessing's *Nathan der Weise* had started a new vogue in Germany, and every second-rate author tried his luck with this new style. D'Arien's translation follows the French original scene by scene and almost speech for speech. Only very rarely are a few lines omitted, for instance in the long scene in which Sophronie reveals to her confidante that she intends to sacrifice herself for the Christians and that she loves Olinde.[40]

In 1772, the year following the first translations of *le Déserteur* and *Olinde et Sophronie,* two German versions of *l'Indigent* ap-

---

[40] Act II, Sc. 1 in both versions.

peared. One was published at Mannheim, and was the work of
C. F. Schwan, who, as we have seen, made a mediocre translation
of *le Déserteur*.[41] *Der Dürftige* is a literal and a poor translation.
Schwan did not always choose the best German word to express
the idea of the French. Thus, for instance, "quelle impéritie" would
be better rendered "wie unerfahren" or "wie ungeschickt" than
"wie dumm," and "avide" better by "gierig" than "neidisch."
Clumsy, too, is the expression "möchten doch alle Leiden, die wir
noch erdulden müssen, nur mich allein treffen," for the simple
French phrase, "Oh! si j'étais la seule à souffrir."[42] The Mannheim
Dürftige is careless work done in too great haste.

The other translation appeared at Breslau and was made by
J. Milack (1736-1785), a professor of Hebrew and Greek at Brieg
in Silesia, and an active translator of French works.[43] The Breslau
*Dürftige was reprinted six years later in the first and only volume of **Dramatische Werke des Herrn Mercier,* along with *le
Faux ami,* to which we shall shortly turn. A third translation, **Die
dürftige Familie,* appeared anonymously in Hamburg in 1773,
and may be the work of a certain H. Heinrichs. According to a
contemporary critic in the *Almanach der deutschen Musen,* its
dialogue was better than that of the other two versions, and its
scene had been shifted to Germany.[44] This offers another example,
then, of the superficial efforts made by translators to Germanize
French works. Finally, another translation, also entitled **Die
dürftige Familie,* appeared at Vienna in 1781 and two years later
in a collection of **"Im kaiserl. königl. Nationaltheater aufgeführte
Schauspiele,"* also published in the Austrian capital.

The relationship of C. F. Weisse's *Armut und Tugend* (1772)
to *l'Indigent* was indicated by a contemporary reviewer. He found
that the difference between Mercier's work and the "little play
by Weisse" lay especially in the fact that Mercier pictured the life
and feelings of the rich reprobate at greater length than did the
German author and that his play had a more romantic conclu-

---

[41] See above, pp. 27f.
[42] Schwan's translation, pp. 141, 23, 25.
[43] Cf. Meusel, *Lexikon,* IX, 172f.
[44] 1774, p. 104.

sion.[45] Since *l'Indigent* appeared early in 1772, it seems probable that Weisse knew it, especially since he translated other works by Mercier, one of them, *Das Jahr 2440*, coming out in this same year. Although *Armut und Tugend* may be based on a French dramatic proverb,[46] certain likenesses to Mercier's play are very evident. The stage setting is the same for both pieces, a wretched room with worn-out furniture. Similar is the attempt of the rich nobleman to seduce the poor but virtuous heroine, and in both works virtue triumphs over poverty as she flees from his clutches.[47]

Another of Mercier's plays, *le Faux ami*, was translated into German in 1772. In his preface to *Der falsche Freund*, the translator, J. Milack, who was also, as we have seen, the author of the German version of *l'Indigent*, remarked that one could not fail to recognize the author of *le Déserteur* in this play.[48] Nevertheless, it did not have the popular appeal of the latter piece, and besides reprints in 1778 and 1805, only one other translation of it appeared. This, also entitled *Der falsche Freund*, was published in 1774 and was the work of F. F. Westarp, whom we have already met as a translator of *le Déserteur*. Le Faux ami was greeted by enthusiastic reviews in the *Göttingische Anzeigen* in 1772[49] and the *Almanach der deutschen Musen* in 1775,[50] but otherwise it did not receive much attention in Germany. It is indeed surprising, in view of its extreme mediocrity, that it was translated even twice.

Jean Hennuyer, Mercier's drama of tolerance, was also translated only twice. C. F. Weisse's *Johann Hennüyer* appeared at Leipsic in 1773, while another German version, attributed to J. G.

---

[45] *Almanach der deutschen Musen*, 1773, p. 123.

[46] According to *Almanach der deutschen Musen*, 1773, p. 61, and Minor, *Weiße*, p. 125.

[47] Compare: Mercier, "Le théâtre représente une misérable salle basse sans cheminée. Les tabourets sont dépaillés. Les meubles sont d'un bois usé," and Weisse, "Das Theater stellt ein sehr armseliges Stübchen mit etlichen alten halbzerbrochenen Stühlen, und einem Tische vor." Mercier, "Venez donc, ma belle enfant, venez . . . De quoi avez-vous peur?" He then takes her hands which she withdraws (Act II, Sc. 5), and Weisse, "Ach mein schönes Kind! sehen wir einander hier?" He tries to take her hand, but she draws back (Sc. 4). Zollinger, *Mercier als Dramatiker*, pp. 53f., points to other apparent similarities, which are, however, not very close when taken in their context.

[48] Cited by the *Almanach der deutschen Musen*, 1775, p. 91.

[49] Nov. 16.

[50] P. 91.

P. Thiele (1748-   ), was published at Hamburg in the following year. Thiele's *Hennüyer, according to a critic in the *Almanach
der deutschen Musen* in 1774, did not change or add to the original,
and was almost identical with that of Weisse, although its dialogue
was not as good. It was prepared specifically for the use of the
theater in Hamburg.[51] This would indicate that the translations
of Mercier's plays were made primarily for the stage and only
secondarily to be read, and indeed, as we shall see later, most of
them were performed in Germany. It is interesting to note that
Jean Hennuyer was attributed by this translator and others to
Voltaire, doubtless because one edition of it appeared in a volume
that otherwise contained only works of the Patriarch of Ferney.[52]
That Thiele was rector of a Lutheran school and later a Lutheran
minister did not keep him from being an ardent advocate of tolerance. He had already translated two "heroic" letters of the religious martyr Calas to his wife,[53] and this evidently led him to
the "republican" *Jean Hennuyer*.[54]

No work of Mercier, *le Déserteur* included, and few plays of
any French dramatist of the Eighteenth Century enjoyed such
popularity in Germany as *la Brouette du vinaigrier*. Mercier could
indeed boast that his wheelbarrow had been rolled across all the
stages of Europe.[55] *La Brouette du vinaigrier* was translated at
least eight times into German, one translation coming as late
as the seventh decade of the Nineteenth Century. Heinrich Leopold Wagner, the friend of Goethe and the author of *Die Kindermörderin,* was one of the first to translate *la Brouette du vinaigrier*.
Since Wagner was essentially bourgeois and naturalistic in his literary tastes, Mercier's glorification of the middle-class and his external realism could not but appeal to him. His *Schubkarn des
Essighändlers* first appeared in Frankfort on the Main in 1775
and was reprinted a number of times in the following years. It is a

---

[51] P. 103.
[52] Entitled *l'Évangile du jour*. Cf. Zollinger, *Mercier als Dramatiker*, p. 68, and
G. Bengesco, *Voltaire, Bibliographie de ses œuvres* (Paris, 1882-1890), I, 87.
[53] Cf. Meusel, *Das gelehrte Deutschland*, VIII, 41f.
[54] So called by the *Göttingische Anzeigen*, Nov. 26, 1772. I was unable to discover
the date of Thiele's death.
[55] Cf. Monselet, *op. cit.*, I, 55.

literal translation of the original and is not without merit. It adds nothing and omits nothing. In connection with the translation of Mercier's works, it must be remembered that his prose style was not too difficult to render into German. Since the Frenchman was more interested in ideas than in the form of their expression, and since he was utterly devoid of artistic taste, the translator could put the original into German without devoting much attention to the style.

Der Essigmann mit seinem Schubkarrn, prepared for the use of the Hoftheater in Gotha, was published in the following year, 1776. Its author was Christian Georg von Helmolt (1728-1805) of the court of the Duke of Gotha, a translator of works from English and French.[56] Although we cannot say with the enthusiastic editor of the *Theater-Kalender,* Reichard, that it was so perfect that it did not seem to be a translation,[57] it does reproduce the sense of the original excellently and is every bit as good as Wagner's version.[58] It also called forth a poem of thanks from an enthusiastic playgoer:[59]

> Wer so, wie Du, aus Galliens Sprache
> Die Sprache der Natur entlehnt,
> Der sei hinfort kein Übersetzer,
> Der werfe fremde Pinsel weg.

Other German versions of *la Brouette du vinaigrier* were made by Becker, Marchand, and M. von Brahm. Von Brahm's *Schub-*

---

[56] Cf. Meusel, *Das gelehrte Deutschland,* III, 193f.

[57] 1776, p. 29n.

[58] Compare the following monologue of old Dominique in the versions of Mercier, Wagner, and Helmolt. Mercier (Act III, Sc. 5): "Métal pernicieux! tu as fait assez de mal dans le monde, fais-y du bien une seule fois. Je t'ai exchaîné pour un moment d'éclat; voici le moment tant désiré; sors, va fonder la paix et la sureté d'une maison où habiteront l'amour et la vertu." Wagner: "Schädliches Metall! Du hast Übels genug in der Welt gestiftet, tue auch einmal etwas Gutes. Ich versperrte dich bis zur Zeit, wo du etwas Großes tun könntest; jetzt ist sie da, die gewünschte Zeit; geh heraus, tue deine Wirkung! gründe die Ruhe und Sicherheit eines Hauses, wo Liebe und Tugend wohnen werden." Helmolt: "Schädliches Metall! Du hast Unglück genug in der Welt angerichtet, stifte nun auch einmal etwas Gutes. Du warst mein Gefangener, bis zu dem Augenblick, dich mit Ehren loszulassen. Dieser längst gewünschte Augenblick ist erschienen, heraus mit dir, stifte den Frieden und die Sicherheit eines Hauses, welches Liebe und Tugend bewohnen werden."

[59] *Theater-Kalender,* 1776, p. 29f.

karn was published in Vienna in 1776, and according to a critic in the *Almanach der deutschen Musen* in the following year, was not so well done as those of Wagner and Helmolt.[60] Its author, a knight of the Holy Roman Empire and a police inspector in Innsbruck, was the translator of numerous works, including Sedaine's *Déserteur*. The latest rendering of *la Brouette du vinaigrier* or of any of Mercier's plays into German was the stage version of Karl Grunert (1810-1869), a famous actor and interpreter of Shakespeare, Goethe, and Schiller. His **Essighändler* appeared in Stuttgart in 1868 and, typically enough, was shortened considerably. The rival for the hand of Mlle Delomer became a second Riccaut de la Marlinière. Only the rôle of the old Dominique, the part Grunert loved and played, remained unchanged.[61]

Finally, a continuation, *Das Erbteil des Vaters*, was made by Iffland and performed in Berlin in 1800. It traced the fortunes of young Dominique, his wife, and his father-in-law in Germany, where they took refuge during the Revolution. References to *la Brouette du vinaigrier* are frequent and even the famed wheelbarrow appears on the stage, causing, of course, a general *attendrissement* on the part of the three exiles. Iffland's play has little intrinsic value and is interesting only in showing how he attempted to "cash in" on the successful idea of another.

Although *Natalie* appeared in France in the same year as *la Brouette du vinaigrier*, it was not translated into German until three years later, in 1778, when two versions were published, both by men who had already translated Mercier, Helmolt and Beulwitz. The *Natalie* of the former, which also appeared in a Gotha *Theater der Ausländer* in the same year, was of the same excellent quality as his *Essigmann*. Its style is clear and the dialogue is well handled. Beulwitz' **Natalie* was published in Berlin, also in 1778. That the German public was still eager to receive foreign plays is shown by the comment in the *Allgemeines Verzeichnis*, that this translator deserved the thanks of the entire German public for having made *Natalie* accessible in German.[62]

[60] Pp. 72f.
[61] Cf. Zollinger, *Beziehungen*, p. 97.
[62] 1778, pp. 465f.

Le Juge was translated in 1779 by A. von Knigge (1742-1796), the well-known popular philosopher. Knigge, we recall, corresponded with men of letters such as Lavater, Klopstock, and Bürger, was a friend of Grossmann and Schröder, and wrote reviews for Nicolai's *Allgemeine deutsche Bibliothek*. He was dependent on his pen for his living and filled many volumes with his writings.[63] While one reviewer of his *Richter* in the *Almanach der deutschen Musen* complimented him on the transcription of the legal language,[64] another in the *Frankfurter* wished that he had translated more freely, changed the scenes around a bit, shortened the long monologues, and made the play less French.[65] This last complaint was repeated by a critic in the *Allgemeine Literaturzeitung* in 1785. In his opinion, the fact that the characters bore German names did not make the play any less French, and really only tended to increase the improbability, since German law was so different from French law.[66] Knigge's translation was reprinted in a *Sammlung ausländischer Schauspiele* in 1784, and was adapted by Schröder for the theater in Vienna in 1781. Schröder's *Richter* made two acts of the three of the original. The long account of the duties of the magistrate was shortened and other scenes omitted entirely. No additions were made. The characters have German names, but Schröder, like Knigge, did not attempt to make the play less French by the introduction of German law and custom.

In the decade between 1770 and 1780 Mercier made his greatest contribution to the practice and the theory of the stage. His later plays had little importance either for France or Germany. Only three of them appeared in German, *la Destruction de la Ligue*, the *Portrait de Philippe II*, and *le Ci-devant noble*. The first of these, a historical drama or "pièce nationale" as Mercier called it, was translated by C. A. Wichmann (1735-1807), who wrote mostly about government. His *Zerstörung des heiligen Bundes* was published in Leipsic in 1782. Another version, entitled *Die*

---

[63] *Allgemeine deutsche Biographie*, xvi, 288ff.
[64] 1780, p. 55.
[65] April 13-16, 1779.
[66] May 19.

Zerstörung der Ligue, appeared anonymously in the same year at Geneva, one of the seats of tolerance in Europe.

Another historical drama, again a condemnation of tyranny, the *Portrait de Philippe II,* preceded by a historical account of the reign of the king, was published in France in 1785. The historical essay was translated by Schiller in 1787.[67] Schiller's *Philipp der Zweite, König von Spanien,* was used almost word for word by the anonymous translator of the complete play, which appeared in the following year with the title *Philipp der Zweite, König von Spanien, ein dramatisches Gemälde von Mercier.*[68] A reviewer in the *Allgemeine deutsche Bibliothek* in 1790 pointed out several awkward translations in this rendition and considered it in general to be more French than German.[69]

Le Ci-devant noble was the only comedy of Mercier to be translated into German. *Der Adliche, wie er weiland war* appeared anonymously in Hamburg in 1792. It is difficult to understand what could have caused this worthless piece to have been translated at all. It must have been Mercier's name and the glorification of the Revolution that the translator thought would appeal to the liberal element in Germany.

It was not Mercier's *Montesquieu à Marseille* that was the source of *Montesquieu, oder die unbekannte Wohltat* (1787) by Dalberg (1750-1806), the friend of Schiller and the director of the National Theater in Mannheim, but *le Bienfait anonyme* of J. Pilhes. Only a few insignificant traits seem to have been taken from Mercier's play. While Pilhes calls his hero Saint-Estieu, Dalberg follows Mercier in identifying his with the great French philosopher. Likewise, the German's discussion of the hardships of a poet may owe something to Mercier.[70] Otherwise *Montesquieu, oder die unbekannte Wohltat* follows Pilhes' piece very closely.

A summary of our discussion of the translations of Mercier's plays yields the following results. At least twelve of his dramas were translated and some fifty German versions and editions of

---

[67] See below, pp. 147ff.
[68] Cf. Schiller, ed. Goedeke, IV, 88n.
[69] XCV, 233f.
[70] Act I, Scs. 3, 4.

them appeared in the last three decades of the Eighteenth Century, *la Brouette du vinaigrier, le Déserteur,* and *Jenneval* being the most popular. Imitations of his plays were also very numerous. The translators were men of various professions: actors, scholars, publishers, soldiers, men of letters, courtiers. In general, they prepared their translations for use on the stage. The translations adhered closely to the original, often, however, omitting or condensing Mercier's repetitions and long moral harangues. They were in most cases none too well made, although Schröder, Wagner, and Helmolt seem to have been fairly successful in their efforts. The translators frequently tried to make the plays seem less French by giving the characters German names and transferring the scene to the east of the Rhine, thus falling in line with the increasing national feeling of German critics and men of letters since Lessing and the "Hainbund."

Although Mercier's plays were much more frequently translated than his other works, his philosophical, social, and political treatises and his novels and short-stories were not overlooked by German translators. The revolutionary utopian dream, *l'An 2440,* was translated two years after its appearance in French, in 1770, by C. F. Weisse, who, as we have seen,[71] also translated *Jean Hennuyer* and imitated *l'Indigent. Das Jahr 2440* is exact, leaves out nothing, includes Mercier's footnotes, and contains nothing which is not in the original except one note, which explained to the Germans the geographical divisions of Paris.[72] The style is in general acceptable without being distinguished.

In addition, Mercier's work called forth several imitations.*Das Jahr 1850,* which appeared at Frankfort and Leipsic in 1777, contained "thoughts on the institutions for the poor, public religious service, and the oath of allegiance of a Swiss canton." It gave a utopian picture in the frame of a dream, but was more conservative than *l'An 2440.*[73] *Das Jahr 2440, zum zweitenmal geträumt, ein Traum, deren es wohl träumerischere gegeben hat* was published at Leipsic six years later. It treated many of the

---

[71] See above, pp. 34f., 33f.
[72] P. 43.
[73] Cf. Zollinger, *Beziehungen,* p. 93.

subjects discussed in Mercier's work, such as the stage, laws, women, and antiquity, but was intended as an antidote for the Frenchman's overenthusiastic optimism. According to a critic in the *Allgemeine deutsche Bibliothek*, it was not only well written, but also especially good for those people whose heads were dizzy with the "supposedly highest degree of enlightenment, culture, and refinement."[74] It is generally attributed to K. H. Wachsmuth (1760-   ), a tax-collector in the Electorate of Saxony, and an adapter of Ossian into German. Finally, *Das Jahr 2550, oder der Traum Alradis, aus einer arabischen Handschrift des 16. Jahrhunderts*, which was printed in Berlin in 1794-1795, told of a future age when the human race would be more perfect and wisdom and virtue would replace the present degeneracy.[75] It was the work of D. G. G. Mehring (1759-   ), an army chaplain who also wrote several works on education.[76]

Mercier's *Nouvel essai sur l'art dramatique* was translated into German by Heinrich Leopold Wagner in 1775-1776 at the instigation of Goethe. It will be discussed below in the chapter on Mercier and Goethe.

The first translation of Mercier's *Éloges et discours philosophiques* appeared at Leipsic in 1777-1778. The *Philosophische Abhandlungen und Lobreden* came from the pen of K. A. Caesar (1744-1810), a professor in Leipsic and the author of numerous philosophical works. In the preface Caesar relates how a happy chance made him acquainted with the collection which he then translated in his spare time. Although he is not always in accord with the views of the "lover of humanity," he tells us that he has suppressed his desire to insert his own notes, since the book already had too many. The translation itself was found excellent by a contemporary critic in the *Göttingische Anzeigen*.[77] Another translation of the *Éloges et discours* appeared at Salzburg some ten years later with the title, *Philosophische Abhandlungen über verschiedene wichtige Gegenstände*, but was apparently unsuccess-

---

[74] LVIII (1784), 124ff.
[75] Cf. *Neue deutsche Bibliothek*, XXI (1796), 482.
[76] I was unable to discover the date of Mehring's or Wachsmuth's death.
[77] *Zugabe*, Feb. 7, 1778.

ful. According to a reviewer in the *Allgemeine Literaturzeitung,* it contained many unnatural phrases and overliteral translations. The critic did not understand how any one who used such expressions as "gerechte Geister" and "großmütige Wissenschaften," would dare to translate Mercier's philosophical writings.[78]

Jezennemours, the imitation of *Agathon,* was translated a number of times into German. The earliest version, with the title **Jezennemours, ein dramatischer Roman,* was printed at Leipsic in 1778, two years after the publication of the French original. In reviewing this translation, a critic in the *Allgemeines Verzeichnis* takes the opportunity to condemn the original as a plagiarism of Wieland. He remarks with biting sarcasm that the subtitle, "dramatic novel," is very appropriate, since the French author is nothing more than a supernumerary who can disappear without the work suffering in the slightest degree.[79] A second version, entitled **Geschichte eines jungen lutherischen Frauenzimmers,* came out at Leipsic about a decade later and was evidently very poor. A reviewer in the *Allgemeine deutsche Bibliothek* in 1787 called it the work of a blunderer, and found it timid, stiff, too literal, and not German, being full of gallicisms such as "ausschreien" for "s'écrier," "auspfeifen" for "persifler," and "abseiten" for "de la part."[80] Nor was **Belcour und Antonie,* the translation that appeared at Neustadt on the Aisch in 1791 much better, for, according to a contemporary critic in the *Allgemeine Literaturzeitung,* it too was filled with French expressions.[81] It was made by Leopold von Lehndorf-Bandels (1771-   ), an East Prussian count, at the age of nineteen.[82] The critic in the *Allgemeine Literaturzeitung* complains that Lehndorf undertook to translate *Jezennemours* at all, and is sure that only a few German noblemen would rather read Mercier than Wieland, as the translator maintained. A fourth translation of Mercier's novel, a **Geschichte einer jungen Protestantin,* appeared anonymously in Frankfort on the Main in 1793.

[78] Feb. 18, 1791.
[79] 1778, p. 461.
[80] LXXVII, 122.
[81] Feb. 5, 1795.
[82] Cf. Meusel, *Das gelehrte Deutschland,* IV, 392f. I was unable to discover the date of Leopold's death.

Again we see, as in the case of *Olinde et Sophronie,* an example of almost blind respect for even the most mediocre works of French literature in a Germany that had already produced Lessing and Goethe.

The *Tableau de Paris* was translated into German two years after it began to appear in French. The *Schilderung von Paris,* which was published in Breslau in 1783, was made by Samuel Gottlieb Bürde (1753-1831), a financial secretary in Breslau and the author of several tragedies and comedies. Bürde shortened many chapters and omitted many others entirely, a procedure that the reviewer in the *Allgemeines Verzeichnis* thought excellent.[83] There are, to be sure, a number of French words such as "Population" and "Akteur" in his version, but nevertheless his style is fast-moving and easy to read.

Another translation, entitled *Paris, ein Gemälde von Mercier,* was published at Leipsic in 1783-1784. It was the work of B. G. Walch (1746-1805), the librarian and director of archives at Meiningen, and a reviewer for the *Allgemeine deutsche Bibliothek* and the *Allgemeine Literaturzeitung.*[84] Walch states in his preface that since the value of the *Tableau* is generally recognized, no justification of his translation is needed. The time is past, he continues, when it was necessary to curb the German love of Paris and French customs and it cannot but be valuable for those Germans who do not read French to know an enlightened and clever writer's opinion of the great metropolis. Walch realized the difficulty of putting a book like the *Tableau de Paris* into German and asked pardon for any errors he might have made, since his version was not a result of avarice or the mania for translating. He added a few footnotes and omitted at least one chapter of the original that was mere repetition.[85]

The later volumes of the *Tableau de Paris* were translated into German by H. A. O. Reichard (1751-1828), the publisher of the *Theater-Kalender* and the *Theater-Journal.* Reichard became acquainted with the authors of the French Enlightenment at an early

[83] 1782, p. 531.
[84] Cf. Meusel, *Das gelehrte Deutschland,* VIII, 313f.
[85] Cf. *Paris, ein Gemälde,* VII, 127n.

age, and this knowledge aided him in becoming one of the chief intermediaries for the spread of French literature in Germany. After a gay student life at Göttingen, Leipsic, and Jena, he settled down in his native city, Gotha, and devoted himself chiefly to the theater, eventually becoming the financial manager of the Gotha Court Theater.[86] His *Merciers neustes Gemälde von Paris, für Reisende und Nichtreisende,* which appeared at Leipsic in 1789, not only shortened the original but also arranged the chapters in a more logical sequence. This seems to be one of the rare cases in which Mercier's lack of form was felt to be a fault by Germans. A reviewer in the *Allgemeine Literaturzeitung* in 1790 found Reichard's translation better than the other two, of which Walch's especially must have caused sighs to those who knew the original. In addition, the critic thanked the translator for having kept in check Mercier's "political and moral hobby-horse," which he thought often went beyond the limits of enjoyment and caused the reader to waste considerable time.[87]

The **Historisch-kritische Enzyklopädie* (1787) of H. G. Hoff, the author of various works of a moral and historical nature, included translations of passages on d'Argenson and the lieutenant of police taken from the *Tableau de Paris.* Aside from such a glaring error as the following: "Der Philosoph würde über seine Mitbrüder erstaunen" for "Le Philosophe étonnerait tous ses confrères," those parts that I have seen were adequately translated.[88]

The *Tableau de Paris* also called forth a collection of 96 prints which were supposed to illustrate it. They were the work of an obscure German artist by the name of Dunker, who was living in Bern.[89] One German critic in the *Allgemeine Literaturzeitung* in 1788, the year following their publication, found them very poor

[86] For Reichard, cf. Meusel, *Das gelehrte Deutschland,* VI, 256ff.; Wilhelm Hill, *Die deutschen Theaterzeitschriften des 18. Jahrhunderts.* "Forschungen," hrsg. von Muncker, Nr. 49 (Weimar, 1915), pp. 46ff.; and the *Allgemeine deutsche Bibliothek,* XXVII, 625ff.

[87] Sept. 18.

[88] Cited in Schiller, ed. Boxberger (DNL), VIII, 209ff. Cf. also Ludwig Stettenheim, *Schillers Fragment: "Die Polizei"* (Berlin, 1893), p. 35.

[89] Cf. Béclard, *op. cit.,* pp. 628f.

and thought they would only increase the price, but not the value, of Mercier's "highly esteemed" book.[90]

The *Neustes Gemälde von Berlin,* which appeared anonymously at Kölln in 1798, contained a number of articles on contemporary life in Berlin. It treated such subjects as English styles, Greek costumes, clergymen, Jews, picnics, and marriage, and owed its title and general method of approach to Mercier. It was concerned, however, exclusively with conditions and people in Berlin.

"We are not even spared *mon Bonnet de nuit,*" remarked the critic in the *Allgemeine deutsche Bibliothek* who reviewed the *Geschichte eines jungen lutherischen Frauenzimmers* in 1787.[91] *Merciers Nachtmütze* was published at Berlin in 1784-1786 by Reichard, the translator of the *Tableau de Paris.* Reichard also translated the first part of *mon Bonnet de nuit* himself, while the second volume owes something to several of his friends, and the last two parts were written by another or by others than the Gotha theater manager.[92] In the preface to the first volume, Reichard states that he has tried to translate according to the sense of the original and not word for word. His version is, to be sure, fairly accurate, but it tends to be stiff, and is not free from gallicisms and mistranslations, all of which gives the impression of haste. We certainly cannot share the enthusiasm of the reviewer in the *Frankfurter Gelehrte Anzeiger,* who found the *Nachtmütze* so well translated that he threw away the few chapters he himself had begun to put into German, and wished that the publisher of the *Theater-Kalender* might be pensioned so that he could devote himself exclusively to translation.[93] Reichard added an occasional explanatory footnote and left out numerous poems, since he considered it a thankless task to translate French poetry into German verse. Interesting is his omission of Mercier's discussion of Homer on the grounds that his respect for the great epics would not permit him to include such unfavorable criticism.[94] The tone of the

---

[90] April 23.
[91] LXXVII, 122.
[92] Cf. *Nachtmütze,* I, IV, and III, 3n.
[93] Sept. 17, 1784.
[94] Cf. *Nachtmütze,* I, 206n. Reichard does not seem to have read the original very carefully, for he believes that Mercier had translated some of Homer. The

later volumes becomes somewhat better, although French words and expressions are still in evidence and it is quite impossible to forget that the original was French. Friederika Unger (1751-1813), the wife of the publisher in whose firm the book appeared, and a J. K. Müchler probably had a hand in translating them. Friederika translated a number of French comedies and wrote the novel *Julchen Grünthal,* while Müchler may be the military advisor in Berlin who dabbled in literature and whose *Feierstunden* appeared in 1782.[95]

It is a matter of dispute whether Mercier's *Homme sauvage* (1767) is an original work or an adaptation of a story by the German J. G. Pfeil. The title page contains the words, "Histoire traduite de . . .," and Pfeil himself claimed that *l'Homme sauvage* was nothing more nor less than a plagiarism of his *Der Wilde,* which had appeared ten years earlier in a collection of *Moralische Erzählungen.*[96] Contemporary criticism was silent on Pfeil's original, which according to the *Allgemeine Literaturzeitung* was rare even in 1787.[97] More proof is certainly necessary than the mere statement of the German author to show that Mercier's story owed anything to *Der Wilde.* In the first place, the fiction "translated from . . ." was a common cover in the Eighteenth Century for the expression of radical ideas. In addition, this caption was suppressed when *l'Homme sauvage* was reprinted in 1784[98] and when it appeared in the *Fictions morales* in 1792. Secondly, it would be difficult to explain how Pfeil's work could have been available to Mercier, since he could not read German and there is no record of any French translation of it.[99] Thirdly, *l'Homme sauvage* is quite in the spirit of Rousseau, and, as we have seen,[100] the Abbé Prévost. It did not need, then, to have a German model at all. In

---

Frenchman, however, *discusses* Homer, especially in French translation. Cf. *mon Bonnet de nuit,* I, 266ff.

[95] Karl Friedrich Müchler (1763-1857). Cf. Meusel, *Das gelehrte Deutschland,* v, 304ff.

[96] Zollinger, *Beziehungen,* p. 110, cites Pfeil's accusation from the *Journal von und für Deutschland,* hrsg. von S. von Bibra (1787), I, 92f. The *Allgemeine deutsche Biographie,* xxv, 655ff., lists Pfeil's *Versuche in moralischen Erzählungen.*

[97] Dec. 5, 1787.

[98] Béclard, *op. cit.,* p. 45n.

[99] Cf. Quérard, *la France littéraire* (Paris, 1827-1864), VII, 115.

[100] Cf. above, pp. 20f.

fact, it is much more probable that it was influenced by the two Frenchmen than by an obscure German. Finally, neither Grimm in France,[101] nor the reviewer of the original in the *Göttingische* in 1768,[102] nor the announcement in the *Allgemeine Literaturzeitung* of its translation into German,[103] said anything about its being an adaptation of a foreign work.

In any case, *l'Homme sauvage* was translated into German in 1787, twenty years after its original publication in France. This version, made by a certain C. A. J. Brückmann, and appearing at Hamburg with the title *Der Naturmensch*, was found to be in good taste by a contemporary reviewer in the *Allgemeine Literaturzeitung*. The critic, however, advised his countrymen to read Pfeil's work, which he evidently considered the original, rather than the German translation of *l'Homme sauvage*.[104]

Two translations of Mercier's *Songes et visions philosophiques* appeared in Germany in the same year, 1791. The Leipsic *Erscheinungen und Träume* was the work of G. Schatz (1763-1795), a private scholar, a reviewer for Nicolai and the *Allgemeine Literaturzeitung*, and the author of numerous translations from French, Italian, and American.[105] It also contained a dozen "dreams" by German scholars, of which some were counterparts to Mercier's *Songes* and others independent. While, according to contemporary critics, the German dreams were more profound and freer from contradictions, they lacked the rich fantasy, the freshness, and the elegance of the original.[106] The contributors of these visions were J. G. Dyk (1750-1813), the author of several essays on the French Revolution and the publisher of the *Neue Bibliothek der schönen Wissenschaften*, J. G. E. Maass (1766-1823), a defender of the old Leibnitz-Wolff philosophy against Kant and later a professor of philosophy at Halle, and J. K. F. Manso (1760-1826), the noted historian.[107] Dyk contributed the counterparts to two of Mercier's

[101] *Correspondance littéraire*, éd. Tourneux (Paris, 1877-1882), VII, 299f.

[102] Sept. 15.

[103] Oct. 25, 1786.

[104] March 11, 1790.

[105] Cf. Meusel, *Lexikon*, XII, 92f.

[106] *Allgemeine Literaturzeitung*, Sept. 24, 1792; *Neue Bibliothek der schönen Wissenschaften*, XLV (1792), 141ff.

[107] For Dyk, cf. Meusel, *Das gelehrte Deutschland*, II, 119f.; for Maass, *Allgemeine deutsche Biographie*, XX, 1f.; for Manso, *ibid.*, XX, 246ff.

dreams, "Das Mißbündnis," and "Der Soldat," and an independent essay on Franklin. The chief contribution of Maass was a serious allegory on literary styles, while according to contemporary critics Manso's "Traum des Empedokles" was particularly noteworthy. The three essays by the publisher, Schatz, on Lessing, immortality, and German poetry, seemed to the reviewer in the *Allgemeine Literaturzeitung* not only to have Mercier's elegance but also to be better thought out.[108] The translation itself omitted various passages of the original and added an occasional footnote. It was considered excellent by reviewers.

A more literal version appeared anonymously at Dresden with the title *Merciers philosophische Träume und Visionen*. It seems to have lacked the power of expression that was to be found in the Leipsic translation. In fact, it was alleged by the *Neue Bibliothek der schönen Wissenschaften* in 1792 that it compared with Schatz's as "lead with silver."[109]

---

[108] Sept. 24, 1792; the *Erscheinungen und Träume* is discussed there, in the *Neue Bibliothek der schönen Wissenschaften*, XLV (1792), 141ff., and in the *Göttingische Anzeigen*, Oct. 29, 1791.

[109] XLV, 152. The critic is quoting a "Berlin reviewer." Compare the original, the Leipsic and the Dresden translation, and Reichard's version included in the *Nachtmütze*:

Mercier, "de l'Amour": Le triste mois du sagittaire annonçait déjà l'hiver aux cheveux blancs; le flambeau des cieux ne jetait plus qu'un éclat pâle, et la nuit plus longue succédait rapidement au jour. Adieu les plaines riantes, les bois ombragés, les ruisseaux tranquilles. Le froid vieillard qui s'assied sur les orages, tout hérissé de glaces et de frimas, chassait l'automne expirante. Il fallait retourner á la ville, á cette ville tumultueuse, où toutes les passions fermentent, et semblent de leur souffle impur corrompre l'air qu'on y respire. J'abandonnais à regret ces belles campagnes, où six mois s'étaient écoulés comme un seul beau jour.

Leipsic translation (cited by the *Allgemeine Literaturzeitung*, Dec. 23, 1793): Schon verkündigte der traurige Dezember die Annäherung des Winters mit dem Tannenkranz. Die Fackel des Himmels verbreitete nur matten Schimmer, und die längste Nacht folgte schnell dem Tage. Dahin war der Reiz der lachenden Ebenen, der schattigen Wäldchen, der stillen Bäche. Der frostige Alte, der, bedeckt von Eis und Reif, auf den Stürmen daherfährt, verjagte den sterbenden Herbst. Es war Zeit, nach der Stadt, der geräuschvollen Stadt, zurückzukehren, wo alle Leidenschaften gähren, und mit ihrem unreinen Hauch die Luft, die man da atmet, zu verpesten scheinen. Mit Widerwillen verließ ich die reizenden Fluren, wo sechs Monden wie Ein schöner Tag verflossen waren.

Dresden translation (cited by the *Allgemeine Literaturzeitung*, Dec. 23, 1793): Der traurige Monat des Schützen verkündigte bereits die nahe Ankunft des eisgrauen Winters; die Fackel des Himmels verbreitete nur noch einen schwachen blassen Schein, und der kurze Tag floh schnell vor der lange daurenden schwarzen Nacht. Verschwunden waren die blumigen Wiesen, das schattige Gehölz, und der sanft

The dream "de l'Amour," contained in Mercier's collection, also served as the basis for a play, *le Cri de la nature, by a certain Armand. This was in turn translated into German in 1775 with the title, *Die Stimme der Natur, by M. von Brahm, whose rendering of la Brouette du vinaigrier was noted above.[110] In this form it was played in Vienna and on several German stages.[111]

A year after the translations of the Songes et visions in 1791, the German version of the Portraits des rois de France began to appear. It was the work of Friedrich Samuel Mursinna (1754-1805), a school inspector and a prolific writer of popular history in the form of readers.[112] His *Gemälde der Könige von Frankreich was so poor that a critic in the Allgemeine Literaturzeitung, after pointing out many blunders, concludes ironically with the hope that a second or third translation[113] would be better. For, he says, due to the prevailing mania for translation, German literature is not safe from repeated translations of productions that it can well get along without.[114] A reviewer in the Neue deutsche Bibliothek is not so severe. He finds it strange that although practically everything Mercier had written had appeared in German, the Portraits had not yet been translated. He recognizes some value in Mursinna's

---

murmelnde Bach; der kalte phlegmatische Greis, der auf Stürmen thront, und seine Scheitel mit Eis und Schneepflocken bekränzt, jagte den hinsterbenden Herbst eiligst vor sich her. Alles eilte nach der Stadt, nach diesem Schauplatz des Taumels, wo alle Leidenschaften in ewigem Kampf begriffen sind, und mit ihrem unreinen Hauch die Luft, die man atmet, zu vergiften scheinen. Ungerne, reuevoll, verließ ich die schöne, ländliche Gegend, wo mir sechs Monate wie ein einziger schöner Tag verschwunden waren.

Reichard (I, 104): Der traurige Monat des Schützen verkündigte schon den Winter mit den weißen Haaren. Die Fackel des Himmels gab nur einen bleichen Schimmer, und längere Nächte folgten den kürzeren Tagen. Lebt wohl lachende Ebenen, schattige Gehölze, ruhige Bäche, denn der kalte Greis, der auf Stürmen sitzt, und von Frost und Eise starrt, vertreibt den falben Herbst, und zwingt uns die Stadt, die lärmende Stadt aufzusuchen, wo alle Leidenschaften gähren, und mit ihrem unreinen Hauch die Luft vergiften, die man dort atmet. Ungern schied ich von den schönen Gefilden, wo sechs Monate verflossen waren, wie ein einziger schöner Tag.

[110] See above, pp. 36f.

[111] Cf. Göttingische Anzeigen, April 24, 1777; Nachtmütze, I, 144n.; P. Legband, Münchener Bühne und Literatur im 18. Jahrhundert. "Oberbayerisches Archiv für vaterländische Geschichte," Nr. 51 (München, 1904), p. 423.

[112] Meusel, Das gelehrte Deutschland, v, 367.

[113] Mursinna's title read "zum erstenmal übersetzt."

[114] July 10, 1794.

version, but nevertheless feels obliged to call attention to errors made by the translator and to the useless footnotes he had added.[115]

The first volume of *Moralische Dichtungen* appeared anonymously at Hamburg in 1792 and seems in all probability to be a translation of Mercier's *Fictions morales*, which had been published earlier in the same year. German criticism was silent as to the merit of the German translation and a copy was not available to me.[116] The *Moralische Erzählungen* which appeared in Leipsic in 1771, however, were translated from an anonymous collection of tales, *Contes moraux, ou les hommes comme il y en a peu*, and have nothing to do with either Mercier's *Fictions morales*, or his *Contes moraux*.[117]

With the appearance in 1797 of Karl Heinrich Heydenreich's translation of Mercier's adaptation of Zimmermann's *Über die Einsamkeit*, we meet again the phenomenon of a German translation of a work that was originally German, as was the case with *Olinde et Sophronie*. *Mercier über die Einsamkeit . . . nach Zimmermann . . . übersetzt von Heydenreich*, subtitled "a book for the mature youth of both sexes," also contained a few psychological reflections by the German translator. The present version, according to a reviewer in the *Allgemeine Literaturzeitung* in 1798, follows Mercier in reducing the number of exaggerations and in modifying the polemical character of Zimmermann's original, and has thus become a more useful work.[118] The translator, Heydenreich (1764-1801), was a professor of philosophy at Leipsic and the author of various odes and other poems and of essays on aesthetic and philosophical subjects.[119]

Le Nouveau Paris, the continuation of the *Tableau de Paris*, appeared in German at Braunschweig in 1800. The author of *Das neue Paris* was K. F. Cramer (1752-1807), the son of J. A. Cramer, the friend of Klopstock and Gellert. Until 1794 the younger Cramer was a professor of Greek and oriental languages at Kiel. Due

---

[115] VI (1793), 338f.; XXI (1796), 156; XXVII (1796), 181f.

[116] Criticism of the original can be found in the *Allgemeine Literaturzeitung*, Jan. 19, 1793.

[117] For the *Contes moraux*, cf. Béclard, *op. cit.*, p. 63n.

[118] March 10.

[119] Cf. Meusel, *Das gelehrte Deutschland*, III, 295ff.

to his sympathy with the Revolution, however, he was forced to re-
tire from his position, and took up his residence in Paris. He was
a fervent admirer of Klopstock and the translator of works by
Rousseau and Diderot.[120] *Le Nouveau Paris* contained a quotation
from Cramer's *Menschliches Leben* in which the *Tableau de Paris*
is extravagantly lauded,[121] and this praise evidently led to Mercier's friendship with the German exile, his "councilor" and
staunch ally "amidst the injustices of his contemporaries."[122] In
any case, Mercier suggested early in 1796 that Cramer translate
le Nouveau Paris, and promised him his own manuscript.[123] In
1798 the translation was partly finished,[124] but it did not appear
until two years later. A contemporary critic writing for the *Neue
deutsche Bibliothek* found *Das neue Paris in general quite satisfactory, but one barbarous rendering, "Denn es gibt keine, noch
so kleine Anstrengung, deren Kraft nicht *unberechbar* wäre,"
called forth the exclamation: "Bürger Cramer-Krämer und Wort-
krämer! wie übersetzen Sie oft! wie notzüchtigen und verstüm-
meln Sie die deutsche Sprache!"[125]

The *Ansichten der Haupstadt des französischen Kaiserreichs
vom Jahr 1806 an,* which appeared in 1807-1808 at Amsterdam,
contained, as we have seen, a number of essays by Mercier, Pinkerton, and Cramer. Cramer, the editor of the collection, hoped by the
combination of French, English, and German elements to produce
a "not unpiquant mixture."[126] About his method of translating he
stated that he had elsewhere justified his custom of including the
French expression in parentheses to show the inadequacy of his
own word, whenever the translation was particularly difficult.[127]
Mercier's essays were insignificant and Cramer's German style
was not especially good. The footnotes show that the German ex-

---

[120] Cf. *Allgemeine deutsche Biographie,* IV, 557f.
[121] *Nouveau Paris,* I, 24ff.
[122] *Ibid.,* I, 23.
[123] Cf. *Briefe von und an Klopstock,* hrsg. von J. M. Lappenberg (Braunschweig, 1867), p. 368; Cramer to Klopstock, March 14, 1796.
[124] Cf. Leyser, *Joachim Heinrich Campe* (Braunschweig, 1877), II, 217f.; Cramer to Campe, Nov. 28, 1798.
[125] LXV (1801), 140ff.
[126] Introduction, pp. 11f.
[127] I, 459nf.

ile had discussed many of the matters with Mercier. They served either to explain the content or often to praise the Frenchman, "notre maître à nous tous," as Cramer calls him.[128]

At least thirteen of Mercier's philosophical and narrative works were translated into German, some twenty-three editions appearing in all. *Jezennemours* and the *Tableau de Paris* were translated several times, while *l'An 2440* called forth a number of German imitations. As in the case of the plays, the translators tended to shorten the original. In general their work is none too good, and one feels as if it had been done too hastily. The translations of the *Tableau de Paris* made by Bürde and Reichard, however, are not without merit.

The interest of Germans in Mercier during the last three decades of the Eighteenth Century is clearly indicated by the numerous translations and imitations of his plays and other works. Despite the flowering of their own literature, Germans still looked to France for patterns and for stimulation, and led by such men as Schwan and Reichard,[129] who might be called Mercier's intermediaries, eagerly devoured in translation the literary productions of this mediocre Frenchman. In fact, they even went so far as to retranslate into German, works that Mercier had translated from that language. Our discussion of the extent of Mercier's German appeal, however, would not be complete without a consideration of the performance of his plays in Germany, a subject to which we now turn.

---

[128] Introduction, p. 12.

[129] The *Theater-Kalender* contained a list of plays which had appeared in Paris, "for the use of translators." Mercier's *Juge* and his historical portrait, *Childéric I*ᵉʳ, *roi de France,* are listed in 1775, pp. 164f.

III

MERCIER ON THE GERMAN STAGE

The German translations of Mercier's dramas were, we have noted, intended chiefly for use on the stage. In the last thirty years of the Eighteenth Century at least nine of these in translation and some three in the original language were performed in Germany. One, *Der Essigmann,* was played during a period of almost a hundred years, and attracted many famous actors. The histories of the various German stages and the biographies of the actors consulted are deficient as regards plays and parts, and offer but little descriptive material. Due to the nature of the sources, then, no pretense to completeness can be made. However, it is hoped that this study will suffice to measure the extent of Mercier's vogue on the German stage and to indicate the nature and the duration of his appeal.

Mercier's plays were not performed in Paris until the ninth decade of the century, long after they had been given in the French provinces and in Germany. *Jenneval,* the first one of them to appear on the Paris stage, met with a mixed reception when it was first presented in 1781, although it had been sensationally popular in Bordeaux.[1] According to the report of Bachaumont, one part of the metropolitan audience greeted the end of the first performance with cries that it was terrible, while another shouted that it was perfect.[2] In Germany *Jenneval* had already been given a number of times in the translation of Faber, and was later to be presented more frequently in Schröder's adaption. Faber's version, *Jenneval, oder der französiche Barnevelt,* was acted by Seyler and his players in Weimar and Gotha seven times between 1772 and 1775,[3] and was also included in the repertory of Marchand, whose

[1] Gaiffe, *op. cit.,* p. 202.
[2] *Op. cit.,* XVII, 61.
[3] Cf. R. Hodermann, *Geschichte des Gothaischen Hoftheaters, 1775-1779.* "Theatergeschichtliche Forschungen," hrsg. von Litzmann, Nr. 9 (Hamburg und Leipzig, 1894), pp. 130ff.

troupe was giving performances in the Rhenish cities of Frankfort, Mainz, and Cologne, about the year 1775.[4]

Schröder's adaptation, *Die Gefahren der Verführung*, enjoyed a greater and more extended popularity. It had its première under the direction of its adapter in Hamburg in 1778 or early in the following year.[5] When it was given again in the same city in 1787, the rôle of the garrulous old uncle was played by Schröder himself, and that of the seductive woman by his wife.[6] *Die Gefahren* was also produced in Berlin, in 1783, where Johann F. F. Fleck (1757-1801), genial interpreter of Franz Moor and Wallenstein, took the part of the uncle.[7] Mercier's plays seem to have been well liked by the actors because of the character parts they offered. This factor will doubtless help to account for whatever popularity the present play achieved, and was also instrumental in the greater success of *la Brouette du vinaigrier*. *Die Gefahren* was given five times in Mannheim between 1780 and 1783,[8] and once in Bonn in 1783 under the direction of Grossmann,[9] the author of *Nicht mehr als sechs Schüsseln*. It was likewise presented in the Austrian capital in the early eighties.[10] It had its greatest success in Munich, however, where it came on the stage thirteen times in a period of fifteen years, enjoying three presentations in 1782, the year of its Bavarian première.[11]

Le Déserteur, the first drama of Mercier to be given in Germany, enjoyed a tremendous success there, according to C. Schmid's contemporary account, appearing in all possible German theaters.[12] In the original tongue it was presented in 1771 in celebration of the visit of Prince Henry, the brother of Frederick the Great,

---

[4] Cf. *Deutscher Merkur* (1775), 3. Vierteljahr, p. 271.

[5] Cf. Bülow, *op. cit.*, I, lxxiii. According to B. Litzmann, *Schröder* (Hamburg und Leipzig, 1890-1894), II, 268, the date of the first performance was Oct. 2, 1778.

[6] Bülow, *op. cit.*, I, lxxiii.

[7] Cf. E. Groß, *Fleck*. "Schriften der Gesellschaft für Theatergeschichte," Nr. 22 (Berlin, 1914), p. 157.

[8] Cf. F. Walter, *Archiv und Bibliothek des großh. Hof- und Nationaltheaters in Mannheim* (Leipzig, 1899), II, 396.

[9] Cf. Jos. Wolter, *Großmann* (Köln, 1901), p. xviii.

[10] Walter, *Archiv*, II, 103f.

[11] Cf. Legband, *Münchener Bühne und Literatur im 18. Jahrhundert*, p. 508.

[12] Cf. *Chronologie des deutschen Theaters*, hrsg. von Legband. "Schriften der Gesellschaft für Theatergeschichte," Nr. 1 (Berlin, 1902), p. 202.

to the court of the Reichsgraf von Kayserling in Königsberg. The Count himself wrote a prologue to the play and members of the upper nobility acted in it.[13] Some years later, during the French occupation of the Rhine, le Déserteur was performed by a French troupe, the Comédiens de Liège, in Cologne.[14]

The German version, Der Deserteur, was given by Seyler in Hanover in March, 1771, in Hildesheim two months later, and twice more in Northwest Germany.[15] When the Seyler troupe moved to Weimar it kept Der Deserteur in its repertory, presenting it twice, in 1772 and 1773. When the company was established in Gotha after the destruction by fire of the ducal chateau in Weimar, it also performed Mercier's play at the Hoftheater there in 1775 and 1776.[16] The impression that the presentations in Gotha made on one spectator is indicated in the following poem in Reichard's Theater-Kalender of 1776. It is addressed to a certain actor Schmelz, who played the part of the father of the deserter:[17]

> Wenn weinen wieder alle Väter
> In deinem Schmerz, weil du das Urteil hörst,
> Und den geliebten Übertreter
> Die große Kunst zu sterben lehrst?
>
> O komm uns doch bald wiederum zu täuschen,
> Daß wir mit tausend Seufzern deinen Sohn
> Vom Richter losgesprochen heischen:
> Komm in der nächsten Woche schon!

While the poetry is bad, the appreciation is sincere and shows clearly the desire so typical of the period, to be moved to tears, to be moved by tears to noble actions. Another rôle was also a favorite of German players, that of Clary, the fiancée of the deserter. In Seyler's troupe it was taken by Charlotte Brandes, the wife of the actor playwright Johann C. Brandes, who also interpreted Rodogune, Zaïre, Minna, and Weisse's Julie.[18]

---

[13] Cf. E. A. Hagen, Geschichte des Theaters in Preußen (Königsberg, 1854), 347f.

[14] In 1796-1797. Cf. O. Kasten, Das Theater in Köln während der Franzosenzeit. "Die Schaubühne," Nr. 2 (Bonn, 1928), p. 186.

[15] Cf. R. Schlösser, Vom Hamburger Nationaltheater zur Gothaer Hofbühne. "Theatergeschichtliche Forschungen," Nr. 13 (Hamburg und Leipzig, 1895), p. 69.

[16] Ibid., pp. 72, 75.

[17] Pp. 19f. The poem is signed "Mad. Karschin."

[18] Cf. Johann Ch. Brandes, Meine Lebensgeschichte, hrsg. von W. Franke (München, 1923), p. 437.

The popularity of *Der Deserteur* was so great in Königsberg
that the playgoers could not see it often enough. The bravery of
the major and the courage with which his son prepared to die
made a deep impression that could not be lessened by constant
repetitions. Madame Schuch, who played Clary's mother, was herself often overcome by tears.[19] *Der Deserteur* was also performed
in the seventies by Koch in Berlin,[20] by Bondini in Dresden,[21]
by Wäser in Stralsund,[22] and by Döbbelin in northeastern Germany.[23] It was given four times in Munich between 1775 and
1785,[24] and quite frequently in Mannheim in the early eighties.[25]
In the latter city, to be sure, the performances were not always
successful. In September, 1783, the director Dalberg complained
of the poor acting in this drama and the consequent lack of applause. Even the masterful Iffland, who could play the rôle of the
major so "warmly, clearly, and naturally," appeared artificial,
while Beck's interpretation of the gallant reprobate Valcour was
too heavy, and a Mlle Baumann did not achieve the grace which
she usually bestowed on the character of the heroine.[26]

Mercier's play and Sedaine's operetta of the same name called
forth a large number of plays somewhat similar in title which were
also popular on the German stage. Besides those dramas discussed
above in the chapter on Mercier in German translation, we learn
of *Der französische Deserteur, Der vermeintliche Deserteur, Der
weibliche Deserteur, Der adliche Deserteur,* and even of *Der Esel
als Deserteur.*[27] It is little wonder a contemporary observer remarked: "What, another Deserter already? Every cause seems
to have its period. . . . The fair sex cries with the deserter and then
finally rejoices with him."[28]

[19] Cf. Hagen, *op. cit.*, pp. 400, 367.
[20] Cf. A. E. Brachvogel, *Geschichte des königlichen Theaters zu Berlin* (Berlin,
1877-1878), I, 230.
[21] Cf. R. Prölss, *Geschichte des Hoftheaters zu Dresden* (Dresden, 1878), p. 306.
[22] Cf. O. Altenburg, "Aus der Geschichte des Theaters in Pommern," *Baltische
Studien*, N. F., XXXIII[1] (1931), 208.
[23] Cf. *Deutsche Bibliothek der schönen Wissenschaften*, hrsg. von Klotz, XXIV
(1771), 655.
[24] Cf. Legband, *op. cit.*, pp. 421ff.
[25] Cf. Walter, *Archiv*, II, 385; nine times.
[26] Cf. W. Koffka, *Iffland und Dalberg* (Leipzig, 1865), pp. 347f.
[27] Cf. Legband, *op. cit.*, pp. 504, 507.
[28] Cf. Wenzel Dennerlein, *Geschichte des Würzburger Theaters* (Würzburg, 1853),
p. 428.

In this sentimental age when tears came easily to all eyes, *le Déserteur* achieved a popularity in Germany entirely disproportionate to its intrinsic worth. The audience wanted to be moved, but not too deeply. Mercier's plays were calculated to do just that. Sentimentality only thrives in a sentimental period, however, and hence the appeal of *le Déserteur* could not last. It was, to be sure, given on the Vienna stage in 1814 in an adaptation made by the actor Stegmayer,[29] but this is the only indication I have found that it was performed in Germany or Austria in the Nineteenth Century.

L'Indigent, which Grimm found to be not without effect on the stage and Bachaumont considered interesting and full of new and picturesque tableaux,[30] was performed in Paris in 1782 with considerable success.[31] Like *Jenneval* and *le Déserteur*, it had already been acted in German a number of times before its première in the French capital. According to the *Journal helvétique*, it was played successfully on a number of German stages in 1772.[32] Eight years later *Der Dürftige* was presented by the "Evangelical Agents" at Kaufbeuren,[33] and by Grossmann in Bonn.[34] Translations bearing the title *Die dürftige Familie* came on the stage in Dresden in 1778,[35] in Vienna in 1781, where Schröder's wife performed the part of the poor but virtuous heroine,[36] and in Mannheim in 1781-1782.[37] In the latter city a presentation of it "carelessly played and poorly memorized" called forth director Dalberg's ire. He was unwilling to admit the actors' excuse that the piece itself was imperfect as a justification for their unfamiliarity with the parts.[38] *Die dürftige Familie* was popular at Munich, being given there

---

[29] Cf. *Joseph Schreyvogels Tagebücher*, hrsg. von Karl Glossy. "Schriften der Gesellschaft für Theatergeschichte," Nrs. 2, 3 (Berlin, 1903), II, 403.

[30] Grimm, *op. cit.*, XIII, 235. Bachaumont, *op. cit.*, XXI, 202.

[31] Cf. Béclard, *op. cit.*, p. 699.

[32] April, 1772, p. 62. Cited by Béclard, *op. cit.*, p. 358n.

[33] Cf. H. Vasterling, *Das Theater in der freien Reichsstadt Kaufbeuren* (Braunschweig, 1934), p. 112.

[34] Cf. Reichard's *Theater-Journal*, 1782, 20. Stück.

[35] Cf. Prölss, *op. cit.*, 306.

[36] Walter, *Archiv*, II, 104; Schink, *Zusätze und Berichtigungen zu der Gallerie von deutschen Schauspielern und Schauspielerinnen*, hrsg. von R. M. Werner. "Schriften der Gesellschaft für Theatergeschichte," Nr. 13 (Berlin, 1910), pp. 231f.

[37] Cf. Walter, *Archiv*, II, 386.

[38] Cf. Koffka, *op. cit.*, pp. 319f.

six times. Like its imitation, Weisse's *Armut und Tugend,* it was
a play with social implications and hence appropriate for charity
performances. Its first presentation in the Bavarian city, in 1784,
was for the benefit of the poor.[39]

Although *le Juge* is not one of Mercier's best plays, it was given
in translation surprisingly often in Germany. It was played in
Hamburg in 1779,[40] in Vienna two year later,[41] and in Dresden in
1784.[42] In Mannheim, where *Die Gefahren der Verführung, Der
Deserteur,* and *Die dürftige Familie* were also given, it was the
most popular of all Mercier's pieces, being performed seven times
in 1783 and 1784 alone and sixteen times in all before 1795.[43]
Iffland appeared in it there in 1790.[44] When it was presented in
Berlin in 1783, the character rôle of the wronged peasant was taken
by Fleck who, as we have seen, appeared in *Die Gefahren* in the
same year.[45]

Before turning to *la Brouette du vinaigrier,* which would occupy
the next position in a strictly chronological treatment, the other
plays of the Frenchman that were less popular on the German
stage will be discussed. *Olinde et Sophronie* was performed in
German at Hamburg in 1771,[46] while *Jean Hennuyer* was translated in 1774 for use on the stage in the same city.[47] *Die Stimme
der Natur,* the adaptation of Armand's play based on a "dream" in
Mercier's *Songes et visiones,* was given, as was noted above, at
Vienna and on several German stages in the middle seventies.[48] A
critic in the *Allgemeines Verzeichnis* expressed the wish in 1779
that *Natalie,* which the Comédie-française had refused to produce
in 1775, might soon be presented in his native land.[49] Besides a
solitary performance that had already been given in Gotha in

[39] Cf. Legband, *op. cit.,* pp. 507, 446.
[40] Cf. *Almanach der deutschen Musen* (1780), p. 55.
[41] Walter, *Archiv,* II, 104.
[42] Prölss, *op. cit.,* p. 309.
[43] Walter, *Archiv,* II, 406.
[44] Cf. *Ifflands Briefe, meist an seine Schwester nebst andern Aktenstücken,*
hrsg. von L. Geiger. "Schriften der Gesellschaft für Theatergeschichte," Nr. 6
(Berlin, 1905), p. 28.
[45] Groß, *op. cit.,* p. 157.
[46] Schmid, *op. cit.,* pp. 202f.
[47] Cf. *Almanach der deutschen Musen* (1774), p. 103.
[48] Cf. above, p. 49.
[49] P. 127.

1777,[50] the German version of *Natalie* was seen four times in Mannheim in 1782 and 1783, despite Iffland's criticism of it as a "shallow drama."[51] *Le Ci-devant noble*, according to its title page, was given in the original language at Coblenz in 1791, a year before it was published in France.[52] When *l'Habitant de la Guadeloupe*, which so far as I could ascertain was not translated into German, was performed in Lyon in 1786, it was greeted with enthusiastic applause. A Swiss visitor to that city relates that the whole audience was enkindled with the feeling of brotherhood and humanity, while one old man cried and sobbed like a child and praised the hero and cursed the villain.[53] *L'Habitant* was played at the French theater in Cologne once in 1795-1796 and twice in the following season.[54]

La Brouette du vinaigrier was the most popular of Mercier's plays on either side of the Rhine. It was given at the Comédie-Italienne for the first time in 1784, having the same success in the French metropolis that it had earlier in the provinces.[55] It appeared on almost every German stage and was played well past the middle of the Nineteenth Century. Its continued success was doubtless due more to the opportunity that the old vinegar merchant, a true "philosophe de la rue,"[56] offered to character actors than to any other factor.[57] Otherwise it would most probably have been popular only for a few years, and then like Mercier's other plays, would have vanished completely from German repertories.

Reichard gives a list of the performances on fourteen different German stages in 1776. According to his count, *Der Essigmann* is in second place with forty-eight presentations, only two less than Sedaine's operetta, *le Déserteur*, and twenty more than, for instance, Lessing's *Minna von Barnhelm*.[58] If these figures of

[50] Cf. Hodermann, *op. cit.*, p. 175.
[51] Walter, *Archiv*, II, 402; Koffka, *op. cit.*, p. 370.
[52] "Représenté à Coblenz le 2 Novembre 1791."
[53] Cited by Zollinger, *Beziehungen*, p. 101.
[54] Cf. Kasten, *op. cit.*, pp. 185f.
[55] Cf. Béclard, *op. cit.*, p. 701.
[56] Lemaître, *Théories et impressions*, p. 260.
[57] Zollinger, *Beziehungen*, p. 97, cites on this point the introduction of Grunert's *Essighändler*.
[58] Cf. F. Rupp, *Reichard* (Marburg, 1908), pp. 106ff. Reichard's figures are for the stages of Hamburg, Amsterdam, Berlin, Gotha, Innsbruck, Munich, Münster, St.

Reichard are anywhere near correct, then the German translations of *la Brouette du vinaigrier* were given more frequently in Germany in this year than any other legitimate play.[59]

The fragmentary source material at my disposal reveals that this play was given in German or French on at least twenty-five stages in Germany and Austria. Iffland gave a guest performance of *Der Essigmann* in 1796 at Berlin where it had already been staged twenty years before.[60] According to a contemporary letter from Marianne von Eybenberg to Goethe, the German actor let the part of the vinegar merchant drag a bit and played the rôle of an old German rather than of a Frenchman. Still, she believed, he was consistent in his interpretation, and one was always aware of his great ability.[61] *Der Essigmann* was presented sixty-five times in the Prussian capital in the next fifty-odd years.[62] We have record of performances of it by Grossmann in Bonn in 1780,[63] by Seyler and Bondini in Dresden in 1775-1776 and 1781,[64] and by Marchand in Frankfort on the Main in 1776-1777.[65] Dominique was a favorite rôle of the latter actor and troupe-leader.[66] Ekhof's company gave it ten times in Gotha between 1775 and 1779.[67] The first performance with Ekhof himself in the part of the vinegar merchant received much applause, Prince August of Gotha praising the translation and the acting very highly. He noted that Ekhof had given his rôle such simplicity and naturalness that every one must have been touched and deeply moved, and expressed his appreciation in a poem:[68]

Petersburg, Prague, Königsberg, Dresden, Brandenburg, the Rhine region, and Esterhazy.

[59] Rupp, p. 106, warns against exaggerating the accuracy of these figures.

[60] Cf. Brachvogel, *op. cit.*, I, 272.

[61] "Einundzwanzig Briefe von Marianne von Eybenberg," hrsg. von L. Geiger, *Goethe-Jahrbuch*, XIV, (1893), p. 32.

[62] Cf. C. Heine, "Die ausländischen Dramen im Spielplane des Weimarischen Theaters unter Goethes Leitung," *Zeitschrift für vergleichende Literaturgeschichte*, N. F., IV (1891), 318.

[63] Reichard's *Theater-Journal*, 1782, 20. Stück.

[64] Prölss, *op. cit.*, pp. 288n., 308.

[65] Cf. E. Mentzel, *Geschichte der Schauspielkunst in Frankfurt am Main* (Frankfurt, 1882), pp. 517ff.

[66] Cf. *Allgemeine deutsche Biographie*, XX, 296ff.

[67] Hodermann, *op. cit.*, p. 174. Reichard's *Theater-Journal* (1780), 13. Stück, records only nine performances.

[68] Cf. Reichard, *Selbstbiographie*, hrsg. von H. Uhde (Stuttgart, 1877), p. 119, and *Theater-Kalender*, 1776, 29f.

Empfange den verdienten Dank
Für jede süßvergossne Zähre,
Die gestern meinem Aug' entwich,
Als ich den alten Dominique
Durch Dich auf uns'rer Bühne sah!

As in the case of *Der Deserteur,* the appeal of this play on the stage was also an emotional one. The sentimental German playgoer wanted to be gently moved, to shed a few painless and "sweet" tears in vicarious enjoyment of the experiences of others. Mercier, who hoped to better mankind by appealing to emotion, fulfilled this wish completely.

The Gotha repertory in the middle and late seventies gives a good picture of the shifting vogue of several of Mercier's dramas. While *Jenneval* had disappeared entirely from the boards, *Der Deserteur* was still being given, and *Der Essigmann* was at the height of its popularity.[69] Even twenty-five years later Iffland was rolling Dominique's wheelbarrow across the Gotha stage, and receiving a handsome sum from the Duke of Gotha for doing it.[70]

The stage presentations of *Der Essigmann* were not limited to any part of Germany. In Göttingen, Karl Friedrich Abbt, who took such parts as Odoardo in *Emilia,* Werner in *Minna,* and Walltron in Möller's piece of that name, also acted the rôle of Dominique.[71] The democratic appeal of the play to Germans is clear from the announcement of a performance in Königsberg. The spectator, it was maintained, would feel with the author that the coarsest garment could be as important on the stage as the robe of majesty.[72] In Hamburg the drama was given for the first time in November, 1775.[73] Two years later it was revived there at the request of the minister to France.[74] When Iffland played Dominique in the Hansa city in 1805, the actor Costenoble remarked that the vinegar merchant of the great actor was very personal,

[69] Schlösser, *op. cit.,* p. 52.

[70] Cf. J. Wahle, *Das Weimarer Hoftheater unter Goethes Leitung.* "Schriften der Goethe-Gesellschaft," Nr. 6 (Weimar, 1892), p. 113.

[71] Cf. O. Deneke, *Göttinger Theater im 18. Jahrhundert.* "Göttingische Nebenstunden," Nr. 8 (Göttingen, 1930), pp. 39, 46.

[72] Hagen, *op. cit.,* p. 400.

[73] Cf. L. Wollrabe, *Chronologie sämtlicher Hamburger Bühnen* (Hamburg, 1847), p. 66.

[74] Cf. Zollinger, *Beziehungen,* p. 95.

and also both bourgeois and gallant at the same time.[75] Costenoble
evidently held the play in great esteem, for he complained of the
poor performance of the difficult main rôle by a certain Schwarz,
and elsewhere condemned ranting in this part.[76] Dominique was
also one of the favorite rôles of Karl Seydelmann (1793-1843).
According to his biographer, Rötscher, his vinegar merchant was
a combination of goodness, honesty, and straightforwardness, and
showed clearly the marks of the Frenchman of the old régime who
was faithful, satisfied with the world, himself, and his son.[77]

Continuing the review of the presentations of *Der Essigmann* in
Germany, we find that it was given at Kaufbeuren in 1786,[78] and
by Marchand in Mainz in 1776.[79] It was still being given in the
latter city as late as 1829-1833.[80] It appeared at least a dozen times
on the Mannheim stage during the directorship of Dalberg, having
four performances there in 1788 alone.[81] The actor Johann David
Beil (1754-1794), who specialized in just such bourgeois parts,
received as Dominique the greatest of applause from his audience.[82] The lengthy report of Dalberg on a performance of *Der
Essigmann* late in 1787 indicates the importance he attached to
this piece. He gives a detailed criticism of the acting of the various
rôles. While in general he concurs with the public's enthusiastic
praise of Beil, he nevertheless would have preferred a greater
calmness in the opening scenes and a more gradual development
toward the "fiery climax" than the actor had given to Dominique.
The director, always a severe critic of his actors, is even less
charitable to other members of the cast. A certain Boek, for instance, is scored for having played the wealthy merchant so carelessly that even his own friends accused him of spoiling a "popular

[75] *Costenobles Tagebücher*, hrsg. von Weilen. "Schriften der Gesellschaft für
Theatergeschichte," Nrs. 18, 19 (Berlin, 1912), I, 222.
[76] *Ibid.*, I, 152, 63f.
[77] *Seydelmanns Leben und Wirken* (Berlin, 1845), p. 205.
[78] Vasterling, *op. cit.*, p. 113.
[79] Cf. J. Peth, *Geschichte des Theaters und der Musik zu Mainz* (Mainz,
1879), p. 46.
[80] Cf. H. Maas, *Das Mainzer Theater vom Beginn der zweiten Franzosenherr-
chaft bis zur Einweihung des Neuen Schauspielhauses* (Gießen, 1928), p. 159.
[81] Walter, *Archiv*, II, 389.
[82] Cf. E. Witzig, *Beil.* "Germanische Studien," Nr. 47 (Berlin, 1927), p. 52.

and good piece." While admitting that the title rôle is better, Dalberg none the less maintains that the "most tender paternal feelings of the merchant" toward his daughter can be successfully portrayed by a good actor. Real art was especially necessary to interpret correctly the scenes of his bankruptcy and of the bestowal of his daughter on young Dominique. Finally, another actor, Beck, is criticised for having played the latter part with too much reflection and not enough ardor.[83] In Munich *Der Essigmann* was apparently well received, being produced there fifteen times in the last quarter of the century.[84] It was also given at Nürnberg between 1775 and 1780 under the direction of Franz Joseph Moser.[85] It had its Vienna première in July, 1775, and was performed in that city over seventy times in the next seventy-five years.[86] Finally, it was played twice at Weimar under Goethe's direction, in 1798 with Iffland in the main rôle, and in 1802.[87]

La Brouette du vinaigrier was also produced in the original language at the court of Frederick II of Hesse-Cassel by a troupe of French actors in 1788.[88] Deep into the Nineteenth Century the vinegar merchant continued to appear with his wheelbarrow on the German stage. Iffland's masterful Dominique was enthusiastically received in Pressburg in 1807.[89] *Der Essigmann* also came on the boards at Darmstadt, Düsseldorf, Leipsic, and Stuttgart in the following years.[90] Between 1779 and 1870 it was performed at

---

[83] Koffka, *op. cit.*, pp. 403ff.

[84] Legband, *op. cit.*, p. 519.

[85] Cf. Th. Hampe, *Die Entwicklung des Theaterwesens in Nürnberg* (Nürnberg, 1900), p. 211. Hampe speaks of plays by Frenchmen including Mercier. In all probability this refers to *Der Essigmann*.

[86] *Deutscher Merkur*, 1775, 4. Teil, p. 274, and E. Wlassack, *Chronik des kaiserl. königl. Hof-Burgtheaters* (Wien, 1876), p. 302.

[87] Cf. Burkhardt, *Das Repertoire des Weimarischen Theaters unter Goethes Leitung.* "Theatergeschichtliche Forschungen," Nr. 1 (Hamburg und Leipzig, 1891), pp. 28, 113.

[88] Cf. Jean-Jacques Olivier, *les Comédiens français dans les cours d'Allemagne au XVIII° siècle* (Paris, 1901-1905), IV, 29.

[89] Cf. J. Pukánszky-Kádár, *Geschichte des deutschen Theaters in Ungarn.* "Schriften der deutschen Akademie in München," Nr. 14 (München, 1933), p. 142.

[90] For Darmstadt, cf. D. Fuchs, *Chronologisches Tagebuch des Großherzoglich Hessischen Hoftheaters* (Darmstadt, 1832), p. 30; for Düsseldorf, cf. Fr. Vogl, *Das Bergische Nationaltheater* (Düsseldorf, 1930), p. 29: "Kotzebue nach Mercier"; for Leipsic, cf. K. T. Küstner, *Rückblick auf das Leipziger Stadttheater* (Leipzig, 1830), p. 48; for Stuttgart, cf. R. Krauß, *Das Stuttgarter Hoftheater* (Stuttgart, 1908), p. 173.

Mannheim as often as *Faust* and more frequently than *Minna von Barnhelm*. During these years Mercier was played there more often than Kleist or Molière.[91] Grunert, the author of the latest German version of the play, tells us in 1868 that *Der Essigmann* was given in Augsburg, Breslau, Brünn, Hanover, Magdeburg, Pest, Regensburg, and elsewhere with great success.[92] Even Iffland's mediocre sequel, *Das Erbteil des Vaters,* enjoyed some popularity. It was given in Berlin in 1800 where it was more popular than Voltaire's *Alzire,* and in Hamburg in the following year.[93]

Mercier's plays, then, were performed repeatedly in translation on almost every stage in Germany in the Eighteenth Century. The première usually followed shortly after the appearance of the piece in German. Famous actors of the day, Ekhof, Schröder, Marchand, Beil, Iffland, and later Seydelmann, played in them. Their popularity on the stage was chiefly due to their middle-class sentimental appeal and was consequently short-lived, ceasing to exist when excessive sentimentalism passed out of mode. Only one, *Der Essigmann,* could maintain itself on the German boards. This was due partly to its democratic appeal, and partly to the character part of the vinegar merchant. A series of six prints by Wilhelm Henschel (1781-1865) and his brothers, drawn in the first twenty years of the Nineteenth Century, represents Iffland as Dominique. He is short, corpulent to the point of bulging, and has long hair. The implements of his trade stick out of his pockets. After he and his cask of money have made possible the marriage of his son, he puts his left hand on his side and his right to his head and exclaims, "the dear children."[94] German actors enjoyed

---

[91] Cf. A. S. Fühler, *Das Schauspielrepertoire des Mannheimer Hof- und Nationaltheaters im Geschmackswandel des 18. und 19. Jahrhunderts* (Heidelberg, 1935), pp. 157ff.

[92] Cf. Zollinger, *Beziehungen,* p. 96.

[93] Cf. R. Weil, *Das Berliner Theaterpublikum unter A. W. Ifflands Direktion.* "Schriften der Gesellschaft für Theatergeschichte," Nr. 44 (Berlin, 1932), p. 161, and Costenoble, *Tagebücher,* i, 158.

[94] Cf. H. Härle, *Ifflands Schauspielkunst.* "Schriften der Gesellschaft für Theatergeschichte," Nr. 34 (Berlin, 1925), xxx. For a picture of a porcelain figure of the vinegar merchant constructed in the 1770's, cf. *Mannheimer Geschichtsblätter,* hrsg. vom Mannheimer Altertumsverein, xxxviii (1937), 97. My attention was called to this by Dr. Hans Knudsen of the Gesellschaft für Theatergeschichte.

playing a part so full of "Gemüt." German theatergoers found in it just that sentimentality and feeling of the equality of man that marked their own thinking and that made all of Mercier's works so appealing in Europe in the last quarter of the Eighteenth Century.

IV

THE RECEPTION OF MERCIER BY GERMAN CRITICS

THE SECOND and third chapters have shown how popular Mercier's plays and other work were in Germany in the last three decades of the Eighteenth Century and have indicated incidentally several of the reasons for this popularity. The present study will be concerned with a more systematic investigation of the nature of Mercier's appeal and will refer constantly to criticism in German literary journals and to other pertinent contemporary comments. The specific relationship of the Frenchman to outstanding German writers and to the *Sturm und Drang* will be treated in later chapters.

Extensive and numerous criticisms of Mercier and his works are to be found in the influential *Göttingische Anzeigen von gelehrten Sachen*. This conservative, middle-class periodical, the journal of various Göttingen professors, in the last quarter of the century under the direction of the philologist Heyne, was not friendly to the Bardic enthusiasm or to the *Sturm und Drang*, but was later affected greatly by the French Revolution.[1]

Some of the lengthiest criticism of the Frenchman's social and political writings occurs in the *Allgemeine Literaturzeitung*. Coming into the world some fifteen years after Mercier had become known in Germany, this publication was freer from the sentimentalism of the earlier decades. Its editors, the Jena professor Christian Schütz and the lawyer Hufeland, prided themselves on the impartiality of their journal which, according to its preface, was not designed to attack or defend any particular class, party, or individual.[2]

Evaluations of Mercier's works can also be found in the *Neue Bibliothek der schönen Wissenschaften*. Founded by the rational-

---

[1] Cf. H. A. Oppermann, *Die Göttinger gelehrten Anzeigen* (Hannover, 1844), pp. 31f.

[2] Cf. R. F. Arnold, *Allgemeine Bücherkunde*, 3d ed. (Berlin und Leipzig, 1931), p. 22, and the *Vorbericht* to the first issue, 1785.

ists Nicolai and Mendelssohn, this periodical remained, under the direction of Christian Weisse and after 1788 of the bookdealer Dyk, true to the obsolete principles of Batteux and hostile to the emotional movement of the seventies.[3] Criticisms appear also in Nicolai's *Allgemeine deutsche Bibliothek*,[4] which like the *Neue Bibliothek der schönen Wissenschaften* stoutly upheld the tenets of the *Aufklärung* throughout the whole period, and in the *Frankfurter gelehrte Anzeigen,* a very mediocre journal that through the contributions in 1772 of Goethe, Herder, Merck, and Schlosser became famous as the organ of the *Sturm und Drang* and then gradually returned to its original rationalistic point of view. Brief comments are likewise contained in the *Almanach der deutschen Musen* of the "Giessener Schmid" and in the *Allgemeines Verzeichnis neuer Bücher,* a bibliographical journal published by the grammarian Johann Christoph Adelung and continued by the Göttingen classical scholar and historian Christian Beck.

Now these journals represented practically every angle of contemporary German criticism. It is to be expected, therefore, that their reaction to Mercier will vary in accordance with their particular editorial policy. Again, the Frenchman was constantly before the German reading public from 1766 to about 1805. That there will be a change of attitude or at least a shift of interest within this period of forty years is evident; for it is clear that a reviewer in the early seventies will differ materially in his outlook on life in general and hence on Mercier in particular from a critic of, say, the Revolutionary period.

In these four decades Mercier rose to a prominent position in the German world of letters, enjoying the crest of his popularity about 1785, and then sank gradually into oblivion. As early as 1773 a translator of *l'Indigent* expects that no one will doubt that the original is an excellent play when he learns that Mercier wrote it.[5] Four years later the *Allgemeines Verzeichnis* lists a collection of the Frenchman's dramas of which each is individually already well known,[6] while in the middle of the eighties the

[3] Arnold, *op. cit.,* p. 21.
[4] Continued under the title, *Neue (allgemeine) deutsche Bibliothek.*
[5] Preface to the Hamburg translation, cited by Zollinger, *Beziehungen,* p. 94.
[6] (1777), p. 297.

Göttingische speaks patronizingly of an Italian journal that devoted much space to the *Portraits des rois de France,* a work that had long been familiar to Germans.[7] The *Allgemeine Literaturzeitung* names him the "famous" Mercier in 1793, and two years later calls him the author of splendid works.[8] By 1803, however, Mercier's German star is on the wane. The *Göttingische,* once his stanch ally, is now in agreement with Palissot's assignment of him to a low position in the history of literature.[9]

While keeping in mind the factors of source and chronology, without which a study of this kind would lack perspective, we will proceed to treat the reactions of German critics to Mercier in five categories. In connection with this ideological grouping, those traits will also be discussed that seem peculiar to the specific genres in which the Frenchman was known in Germany: drama, social and political treatise, novel and short story. Germans noted, as we shall see, Mercier's philosophic views, his love of virtue, his appeal to tender sentiment, his naturalistic conception of art, and his poetic style.

The interest in Mercier as a personality reflects the nature, extent, and duration of his German popularity, and hence a summary of the personal reactions of certain Germans to him will not be out of place here. When the Frenchman visited Lavater in Zürich in the eighties, the Swiss physiognomist, the story goes, looked him over with great care and then informed him that he was a writer, a philosopher, a man of originality and of courage, in short, the author of the *Tableau de Paris.*[10] Iffland, the Mannheim actor-playwright, considered him important enough to entertain when he visited that city in 1787, introduced him in Dürkheim, where a private theater was active, and three years later wrote a letter of introduction to him for a friend.[11] The

[7] April 15, 1786. The *Portraits* had appeared in 1783.

[8] Nov. 28, 1793; Feb. 5, 1795.

[9] (1803), June 11. In 1789 the *Neue Bibliothek der schönen Wissenschaften,* XXXVIII, 326ff., called Palissot's judgment biased.

[10] Cf. Zollinger, *Beziehungen,* p. 119, and C. d'Avalon, *Merciériana* (Paris, 1834), p. ix. Mercier's own interest in physiognomy is evinced by his frequent references to it. Cf. *l'Homme sauvage,* p. 78; *l'An 2440,* p. 254n.; and the *Nouvel essai,* p. 179; etc.

[11] Cf. *Ifflands Briefe an seine Schwester Louise und andere Verwandte,* hrsg. von

Allgemeine Literaturzeitung quotes in 1796 a eulogy of the Frenchman's character. A "well-known German professor" writes from Paris that Mercier is fatherly and affectionate, a man of noble heart and real virtue whose nature is marred by no false politeness or insincerity. An enthusiastic patriot and an ardent striver for the common good, he accepts no bribes and lives in greatest simplicity with his wife and children.[12] This account is certainly more representative of the German conception of him than that of the aristocrat Wilhelm von Humboldt, who meeting him in Paris in 1798, called him lazy and worthless.[13] However, the fact that Kotzebue in 1804 refused to attend a fraternal banquet in the French capital with Mercier and other authors of "drames" for fear of appearing ridiculous,[14] indicates that by that time Germans no longer held him in great respect.

When we turn to the first point, the reaction to Mercier as a philosopher, it becomes evident that German critics appreciated in him just those qualities that characterized their own thinking at the time. He appealed to them as a representative of enlightenment, a friend of mankind, a patriotic partisan of democracy, and an exponent of natural religion. His works, according to the German translator of *la Destruction de la Ligue* in 1782, are known to all social classes and are praised by philosophers and by students of political science as well as by friends of literature.[15] Walch, the author of a German version of the *Tableau de Paris,* calls Mercier in his introduction a most intelligent and enlightened author. A year or so later, in 1785, the literary historian Flögel in his well-documented and pioneer *Geschichte der komischen Literatur* speaks of him in similar terms and considers

---

Geiger. "Schriften der Gesellschaft für Theatergeschichte," Nr. 5 (Berlin, 1904), pp. 194, 307, and *Ifflands Briefe, meist an seine Schwester,* p. 202. For Mercier in Dürkheim and his possible influence on its theater, cf. C. Valentin, *Theater und Musik am Fürstlich Leiningischen Hofe.* "Neujarsblätter," hrsg. von der Gesellschaft für fränkische Geschichte, Nr. 15 (Würzburg, 1921), p. 37.

[12] April 30. That Mercier did not marry his wife until he had lived with her for a number of years is a fact that cannot have been known to Germans who extolled his middle-class virtues. Cf. Zollinger, *Mercier als Dramatiker,* p. 6.

[13] *Wilhelm von Humboldts Tagebücher,* hrsg. von A. Leitzmann (Berlin, 1916-1918), I, 431, 633.

[14] *Merciériana,* pp. 1ff.

[15] Cf. Zollinger, *Beziehungen,* p. 114.

his works so generally known and esteemed that a summary of
their contents would be superfluous. Flögel also expresses his
regret that the ideal conditions portrayed in *l'An 2440* are merely
visions that probably will never be realized.[16]

This utopian dream founded Mercier's German reputation as
a philosopher, a reputation that was to continue throughout the
last third of the century. The Swabian *Stürmer und Dränger*
Schubart in his *Deutsche Chronik* of 1774 calls the author of
this "golden book" his favorite philosopher.[17] Its title, *Das Jahr
2440,* came to be a favorite expression in Germany for the millennium. It is thus used for example by Wieland in 1775, 1788,
and 1792,[18] appears in the description of a fantastic postal bal-
loon of 1784,[19] and is so employed as late as 1807 in Salzmann's
Ameisenbüchlein.[20] Gruber states in his Wieland biography of
1816 that the author of *Der goldene Spiegel* shared the hope of
a better world which the "friend of humanity" promised for
2440.[21] A Zürich professor prefaces his *Beiträge zur Geschichte
der deutschen Sprache und National-Literatur* (1777) with the
statement that he will entrust the task of writing the history of
German literature of 2440 to a prophetic historian like Mercier.[22]
Here and there we find dissidents, to be sure. While we are not
surprised at Tieck's comparison in 1816 of Goethe's flight into
the unreality of antique art to that of Mercier and other "bun-
glers" from the present to the year 2440,[23] the adverse criticism
in the rationalistic *Allgemeine deutsche Bibliothek* three decades
before, at the height of the Mercier vogue, comes somewhat un-
expectedly. The reviewer praises an imitation of *l'An 2440* which
questions the efficacy of the reforms suggested in the original.

[16] (Liegnitz und Leipzig, 1784-1787), II, 638.
[17] *Beilage,* p. 50; cited by Rosanow, *Lenz,* p. 128.
[18] Cf. below, "Mercier and Wieland," p. 98.
[19] "Große Postluftkugel, welche den 10. März 2440 nach China und Japan fliegen
wird." Cf. W. Neuse, *Wege zur deutschen Kultur* (Chicago and Philadelphia, 1937),
p. 137.
[20] Cf. Zollinger, *Beziehungen,* p. 93.
[21] *Wieland* (Leipzig und Altenburg), II, 193.
[22] I, xxiv. According to Adelung, *Umständliches Lehrgebäude der deutschen
Sprache,* I, 15 these "unripe, confused, and verbose" contributions were written
by a certain Leonhard Meister.
[23] Matenko, *op. cit.,* p. 316.

He recommends, as we have seen, that *Das Jahr 2440, zum zweitenmale geträumt* should be read and taken to heart by all those who are dizzy from the "supposedly highest degree of enlightenment, culture, and refinement."[24]

Other works of Mercier come in for their share of praise and blame. Soon after the publication of the collection *Éloges et discours philosophiques* in 1776, Heinrich Leopold Wagner, the translator of *la Brouette du vinaigrier* and of the *Nouvel essai*, called its author a "dreamer and philosopher,"[25] while some fifteen years later the *Allgemeine Literaturzeitung* still found the essays philosophic.[26] Indeed, interest in the middle-class philosopher was not limited to any one group in Germany. Hamann liked the *Tableau de Paris* and also examined the first two volumes of *mon Bonnet de nuit* when they appeared in 1784.[27] A translation of the latter work is hailed by a critic in the *Frankfurter gelehrte Anzeigen* in 1784 as a splendid book designed for intelligent readers.[28] Old Klopstock himself, we learn from a letter written to him in 1796 by the Mercier enthusiast Cramer, was waiting impatiently for the continuation of the *Tableau de Paris*.[29] Even a translation of the romance *l'Homme sauvage* is found by a critic in the *Allgemeine Literaturzeitung* in 1787 entertaining and often really philosophic.[30]

To be sure, a contrary opinion of the philosophical value of certain of Mercier's works is not entirely lacking. In his *Dramatische Fragmente* (1781-1782) Schink, the dramaturgist and playwright of Hanover and Hamburg, finds the Frenchman's plays not only too full of surprises and exaggerated sentiment but also wanting in philosophy.[31] The judgment of the *Allgemeine Literaturzeitung* in 1794 of the *Fragments de politique et*

---

[24] LVIII (1784), 124ff.
[25] Cited from the *Frankfurter gelehrte Anzeigen* (no date) by San-Giorgiu, *op. cit.*, p. 58. Wagner died in 1779.
[26] Feb. 18, 1791.
[27] Cf. Gildemeister, *Hamanns Leben und Schriften*, Zweite Ausgabe (Gotha, 1875), II, 378, III, 96.
[28] Sept. 17.
[29] *Briefe von und an Klopstock*, p. 368; March 14.
[30] Dec. 5.
[31] Cf. R. Bitterling, *Schink*. "Theatergeschichtliche Forschungen," Nr. 23 (Leipzig und Hamburg, 1911), p. 108.

d'histoire is even more severe. The Jena periodical considers the political and philosophical worth of the work as well as its value as a study of mankind to be practically negligible.[32] However, these unfavorable criticisms are not numerous. Generally speaking, Mercier was regarded as a real philosopher, and although the Germans did not always agree with his views, few challenged him in that capacity.

Mercier, the philosopher and the *Aufklärer,* appealed then to Germans because he was a spokesman of their own feelings. As a representative of enlightenment, he was necessarily a benevolent man and a friend of humanity, and this did not pass unnoticed in Germany. At the beginning of his vogue a Zürich clergyman defended *l'An 2440* against those who held that it was merely a confused mixture of disconnected reveries. He considered the author's ardent patriotism, love of truth, good heart, and humanitarianism worthy of great respect.[33] Herder wrote in the same year, 1772, that the funeral oration at the grave of the virtuous and industrious peasant of 2440 honors mankind.[34] Five years later the Leipsic translator of the *Éloges et discours philosophiques* calls the author of *l'An 2440* a philanthropist as well as a pleasant and emphatic writer. On the other hand, however, the *Göttingische* speaks condescendingly in 1791 of the "misanthropic zeal" of his love of mankind.[35] In the following year a reviewer of the translation of the *Songes et visions* in the *Neue Bibliothek der schönen Wissenschaften* extols the Frenchman's writings as contributory to the efforts of the nations of Europe to make the world a better place to live in. Although all of Mercier's suggestions might not be acceptable, he still finds them valuable, since they tend to draw the attention of the public to the basic problems confronting society. Nonetheless, the critic also extends his praise to the dreams appended by the German scholars, finding in them a sound protest against the attempts of so many writers of the time to arouse

[32] Sept. 29.
[33] J. Tobler, *Onyramynt fürs Christentum.* Cf. Zollinger, *Beziehungen,* pp. 91f.
[34] *Frankfurter gelehrte Anzeigen,* Jan. 10. Herder is referring to *l'An 2440,* chap. XLIII. Cf. M. Morris, *Goethes und Herders Anteil an dem Jahrgang 1772 der Frankfurter gelehrten Anzeigen* (Stuttgart und Berlin, 1909), pp. 431f.
[35] April 2: "misanthropischer Eifer der Menschenliebe."

discontent by condemning the classics, the church, and the state.[36]

Mercier's enlightenment and benevolence are supplemented by his democratic views. Contemporary German criticism was acutely aware of his sympathy for the common man, and while its reaction was mixed, to be sure, approval seems to outweigh condemnation. In 1771, it is true, the conservative and orthodox *Göttingische* finds in Mercier the same contradictions that characterize his leader Rousseau and all such "representatives of evil,"[37] and refuses to give serious consideration to his claim that there can be republican plays, taking issue with his suggestion of the "gentle liberator of his country, Cromwell," as a hero.[38] However, in the next year the same journal emphasizes the humanitarian speeches in *Jean Hennuyer* and notes that they are so democratic that the play could not be printed in France.[39] This piece was so much in the spirit of the liberal Voltaire that it was attributed by A. Wittenberg of Hamburg and others to the Patriarch of Ferney himself.[40] It received, however, little sympathy from the *Almanach der deutschen Musen* in 1774. According to its cynical critic the French had written enough such pieces to have atoned for all the despotic deeds of the past, if that were possible.[41] As for *la Brouette du vinaigrier*, there can be no doubt but that its thesis of the equality of man contributed greatly to its immense popularity throughout Europe. The French literary critic Jules Lemaître lists along with its external realism and the character rôle of the vinegar merchant, its democratic appeal as a reason for its enormous success.[42]

Consideration of Mercier's democratic tendencies is not limited to his plays. In reviewing *l'An 2440* for the *Frankfurter gelehrte Anzeigen* in 1772, Herder extols the Frenchman's patriotism and republicanism. In this connection he expresses his

---

[36] XLV, 141ff.
[37] Mercier's dependence on Rousseau is noted by other critics. Cf. *Neue Bibliothek der schönen Wissenschaften*, XXXVI (1788), 355, XLV (1792), 144f.
[38] Dec. 7.
[39] Nov. 26.
[40] Cf. R. M. Werner, *Ludwig Philipp Hahn*. "Quellen und Forschungen," Nr. 22 (Straßburg, 1877), p. 131. Cf. also above, p. 35.
[41] Pp. 102f.
[42] *Op. cit.*, p. 260.

approval of the method of burying the dead in 2440. Mercier
has the corpses of princes, dukes, and ordinary citizens carried
all together in a cart to the crematory.[43] The conservative Weisse
is torn between his appreciation of Mercier's enlightenment and
his fear of his radicalism. Calling *l'An 2440* in the introduction
to his translation of 1772 one of the best recent French books,
he still takes issue with some of the suggested reforms. In his
opinion they would often be impossible, while some of the abuses
they sought to alleviate had compensatory advantages. Weisse
praises Mercier's knowledge of statemanship, but does not fail
to see that his protests against the existing order are often exaggerated and that his condemnation of the powerful and the rich
seems to come occasionally from personal rancor rather than
from hatred of injustice. He notes further that Mercier often
holds the upper class as a whole responsible for the evil deeds
that certain members of it commit, and denies the validity of
his contention that all kings are tyrants and that all those who
rise against them are friends of virtue, freedom, and humanity.
Heinse, in accord with his "immoralistic" attitude, views the
work with greater scepticism. He writes to Gleim in 1772 that
the condition of the world, in which one animal kills another and
lives from it for a few days, far from being improved by all the
golden mirrors of Plato, Helvétius, Wieland, or the "fanciful
author of *l'An 2440*," might even be made worse by some of
them.[44]

Mon Bonnet de nuit and the Tableau de Paris are also considered by German critics as democratic works. A chapter in
the former in which Mercier shows how even tyrants surrounded
by fortifications fear the printed word, and in which he calls attention to the Revolution in America, was greatly to the taste
of a reviewer in the *Frankfurter* in 1784.[45] A critic of the *Tableau de Paris* in the *Allgemeine Literaturzeitung* in 1790 notes

---

[43] Jan. 10. The reference is to Chap. XXVII.
[44] *Sämtliche Werke*, hrsg. von Schüddenkopf (Leipzig, 1903-1925), IX, 72. In
this connection it may be pointed out that there is little similarity between the
utopia in *Ardinghello* and *l'An 2440* other than the general utopian idea. Cf. W.
Brecht, *Heinse und der ästhetische Immoralismus* (Berlin, 1911), p. 43.
[45] Sept. 17. The reference is to *Merciers Nachtmütze*, I, 99ff.

that the work had a cold reception in the elegant circles of Paris, but was welcomed more warmly for that reason among the common people.[46] The French Girondist, Brissot de Warville, who was guillotined in 1793, writes in his *Mémoires* that the *Tableau de Paris* of which more than a hundred thousand copies were spread over Europe, had contributed noticeably to prepare the Revolution.[47] German critics also recognized Mercier as a precursor of the great upheaval. A critic in the *Allgemeine Literaturzeitung* in 1795 of *Ist est wahr, daß gewaltsame Revolutionen durch Schriftsteller befördert werden* differs with the conclusion of its author, the Mercier translator C. A. Wichmann, that Rousseau, Montesquieu, Helvétius, and Mercier were in no way responsible for the Revolution.[48]

The complaint of Weisse, that Mercier confused the aristocrats as a class with the crimes some of them committed, was heard again after the excesses of the early nineties. The *Allgemeine Literaturzeitung* protests that the revolutionary *Annales patriotiques et littéraires de la France* to which Mercier lent his name defends every act of violence of the lower classes as an expression of freedom and decries every measure necessary to keep order as tyranny. The French paper, the critic continues, also insults every decent man who stands above the crowd by virtue of rank, birth, or character.[49] Mercier himself, before the Reign of Terror a stanch apologist of the new order, was only too eager to interpret the changing conditions in France to curious Germans.[50] While indeed many of them later thought he judged the great cataclysm too favorably, nevertheless the fact that he was against the execution of the king was noted with approval in 1798 even by Wilhelm von Humboldt, who was in general a severe critic of the Frenchman.[51]

[46] Sept. 18.

[47] Cited by Lichtenberger, *le Socialisme au xviiiᵉ siècle* (Paris, 1895), p. 194n.

[48] Jan. 12. Wichmann's book appeared at Leipsic in 1793.

[49] March 7, 1791.

[50] Cf. Leyser, *op. cit.*, II, 80; a letter from Mercier to Campe, Dec. 3, 1791.

[51] Cf. *Intelligenzblatt der Allgemeinen Literaturzeitung*, March 1, 1800, and Humboldt, *Tagebücher*, I, 420f. Earlier, in 1789, Humboldt noted with scorn that Mercier was supposed to live in a café and know only the lower classes; cf. *Tagebücher*, I, 132.

Mercier was often called a prophet and also claimed that title for himself.[52] Iffland recalls in his autobiography that as early as his visit to Germany in 1787 Mercier foretold everything that had happened up to the beginning of the second year of the Revolution.[53] Late in 1789 Reichard writes in the preface to the second volume of his translation of the *Tableau de Paris* that this work will be all the more interesting because it contains so many prognostications that have already been fulfilled, at least in part. In the following year a reviewer of Reichard's translation in the *Allgemeine Literaturzeitung* not only emphasizes Mercier's feeling for freedom and his gift of prophecy but also points out that many of the expected events have actually come to pass.[54] A few years later when the storm in France had run its course the same journal remarked that it is a hobby of Mercier to believe that he foresaw the Revolution and helped to prepare for it.[55]

Mercier once described himself as the "most independent of the children of Adam,"[56] and indeed this independence of thought coupled with a rather extravagant fantasy often led him to express radical and highly controversial opinions. He was not left unchallenged as a biased democratic philosopher by German critics. Again and again we encounter the complaint that he is one-sided and partisan in his views, unsystematic and unscholarly in his method. Early in the seventies the *Göttingische* points out that *l'An 2440* is filled with contradictions. The critic scoffs at Mercier's ideal world where one apologizes to the only criminal executed in thirty years while, on the other hand, the author seems in perfect sincerity to suggest the extinction of all Europeans in America, including the French.[57] Weisse prefaces his translation of the book in the next year, 1772, with the re-

---

[52] Leyser, *op. cit.*, II, 80.
[53] *Über meine theatralische Laufbahn.* "Deutsche Literaturdenkmale des 18. und 19. Jahrhunderts," Nr. 24 (Stuttgart, 1886), pp. 76f.
[54] Sept. 18.
[55] Sept. 29, 1794.
[56] Leyser, *op. cit.*, II, 80f.; in a letter to Campe, Dec. 3, 1791.
[57] Dec. 7, 1771.

mark that since Mercier treats almost every branch of human knowledge, he is bound to deal with material with which he is none too familiar. A few years later the Leipsic translator of the *Éloges et discours* warns against believing every word that Mercier wrote, since he does not have the gift of infallibility and his pronouncements cannot always be accepted as true without reservation.[58] A reviewer of this translation in the *Göttingische Anzeigen* in 1778 attributes the Frenchman's exaggerated praise of Descartes to ignorance. He also exposes a contradiction in the statement that men of letters should both live free and indipendent of the common herd and also work for the happiness of others.[59] Another critic in the *Göttingische* in the same year concedes that there are many good ideas in the *Éloges et discours* but also points out that there is some tinsel in it, as is typical of the philosophy of the time.[60]

Similarly criticism of a mixed nature greets the rest of Mercier's philosophical and political works as they come to the attention of the Germans. While critics pay tribute to the engaging manner in which he presents his theories, they are not blind to the superficiality and inconsistency of his ideas. Thus a scribe in Nicolai's *Allgemeine deutsche Bibliothek* in 1788 notes that while the last two volumes of *mon Bonnet de nuit* are entertaining and pleasantly varied in subject matter, much in them cannot survive exact philosophical investigation, however true it may seem at first glance.[61] In the same year the *Göttingische* analyzes at some length the main ideas of the *Notions claires sur les gouvernements*. Realizing that Mercier is carried away by enthusiasm for the party to which he owes allegiance, the reviewer does not give unqualified approval to his thesis that the views of the intelligentsia have a primary influence upon the government of a nation. He is likewise aware of the inconsistencies and lack of system in the work, which he knows will les-

---

[58] Cf. the preface.
[59] *Zugabe,* Feb. 7.
[60] April 25.
[61] LXXXII, 300.

sen its appeal to anyone accustomed to a more exact scientific method.[62] Two years later, in 1791, in connection with the *Annales patriotiques et littéraires*, the influential *Allgemeine Literaturzeitung* even goes so far as to say that Mercier's patriotic and philosophical writings have never been anything but superficial and insipid declamations.[63] In the same year the *Göttingische* calls the *Songes et visions* just as one-sided as all of Mercier's works. On the other hand, it praises the visions added by German scholars, since these dreams enable one to see the evils and injustices of mankind from several angles.[64] In reviewing this book in 1792 the *Neue Bibliothek der schönen Wissenschaften* holds that Mercier's judgment on the same matter often varies. Thus, according to the circumstances, he is either republican or royalist, Stoic or Epicurean, mystic or freethinker.[65] While the *Portraits des rois de France* is lauded by the *Neue deutsche Bibliothek* in 1793 for the ease and charm of tone which is typical of Mercier, it is nonetheless scored for its lack of critical thoroughness. The reviewer admits that it contains many attractive reflections, but even these he often finds useless and not free from historical error.[66] A critic in the *Allgemeine Literaturzeitung* in the next year expresses a keen disappointment in the *Fragments de politique et d'histoire*. Although the name of the author may have led many readers to have great expectations, the work is superficial, biased, and so general that no valid conclusions can be deduced from it.[67] Finally, some years later, a reviewer in the same periodical, while conceding that *le Nouveau Paris* would be read by all with satisfaction and interest, nevertheless feels himself in duty bound to warn future historians that the book must be used with the utmost caution. In the days of the monarchy Mercier had prepared for the overthrow of the existing government by his bold attack on abuses and by his pro-

[62] June 23.
[63] March 7.
[64] Oct. 29, 1791.
[65] XLV, 141ff.
[66] VI, 334ff.
[67] Sept. 29.

clamation of democratic ideas, and hence, concludes the critic, he cannot be entirely objective in his views.[68]

We have seen that Mercier's German appeal was essentially that of the enlightened philosopher. Besides humanitarian tendencies and democratic proclivities, however, an enlightened man of the Eighteenth Century generally also had more or less sympathy for religious tolerance. As an advocate of natural religion Mercier would of course be more appreciated in a France which was traditionally inclined to scepticism than in the deeply religious Germany. In this rôle he probably received more censure than commendation from German critics. Even so, there was a disposition to recognize the sincerity of his religious opinions. Already in 1772 Tobler concedes in his *Onyramynt fürs Christentum* that the views of the author of *l'An 2440* are couched in the language of a genuine worshiper of God. At the same time, however, he believes that the betterment of mankind must be effected on the more orthodox religious basis of the Scriptures.[69] A similar view is entertained by Herder. In reviewing Tobler's book in the now famous issues of the *Frankfurter gelehrte Anzeigen,* the German critic remarks that the otherwise worthy author of *l'An 2440* offends in wishing to banish revelation and clergymen from his utopia.[70] In another review in the *Frankfurter* in the same year, 1772, he scoffs at Mercier's suggestion that youth should be introduced to religion by means of a telescope on a starry night and adds that he would regret it if such instruments were necessary in order to love and admire God and nature.[71] Here the essential dissimilarity of the purely scientific and intellectual conception of religion of the *Aufklärung* and the more intuitive and emotional approach of the *Sturm und Drang* is thrown into clear relief. The conservative and orthodox *Göttingische,* resenting any attack on established religion, is not so charitable to Mercier. In 1772 it condemns Tobler's polite request that the French "dreamer" accept the aid

---

[68] Nov. 28, 1800.
[69] Cf. Zollinger, *Beziehungen,* pp. 91f.
[70] July 17. Cf. M. Morris, *op. cit.,* p. 448.
[71] Jan. 10.

of religion in fashioning his better world. The review also expresses doubts whether Mercier's tree of progress can bring forth the promised fruit if it does not spring from the seed of religion and is not cared for by religion.[72] In the following decade the novelist Pfeil, in alleging that *l'Homme sauvage* is a plagiarism, does not find that Mercier with his few French additions has been any more successful in tackling the problem of natural religion than he had been himself.[73] *Mon Bonnet de nuit,* in which the religious idea is presented in a more eloquent and mystical form, had a more sympathetic reception in Germany. An otherwise none too enthusiastic evaluation of the first volumes of this work in the *Göttingische* in 1784 compliments Mercier on his warm friendship for religion and virtue,[74] while the *Allgemeine Literaturzeitung* in the next year discovers in the work the "well-known" sentiments of the author about religion and humanity.[75] One chapter in the last part of *mon Bonnet de nuit,* which contained rhapsodical musings on God, half mystic, half in the tone of natural religion, is called "most exalted" by another critic in the Göttingen journal in 1786. He can scarcely recall ever having read anything so inspiring about the highest object which the human mind can conceive.[76]

Two of Mercier's plays were examined by German critics in respect to their presentation of religious problems, while still another was praised for its religious sentiments. As early as 1770 a reviewer of *Olinde et Sophronie* in the *Göttingische* lauds the author's efforts to make religious persecution odious,[77] while two years later another critic in the same periodical extols the tolerance of *Jean Hennuyer.* Then, quite characteristically for this period, this latter scribe takes the opportunity to denounce St. Bartholomew's, the "most terrible of all nights," and the more recent persecutions by the Catholic church in Poland.[78] Still another reviewer writing for the same magazine in 1771 expresses

[72] *Zugabe,* Sept. 12.
[73] Cf. Zollinger, *Beziehungen,* p. 110.
[74] June 19.
[75] Jan. 4.
[76] March 30. Cf. *Merciers Nachtmütze,* IV, 67ff.
[77] Nov. 22.
[78] Nov. 26, 1772.

the belief that *le Déserteur* would never be played because it has too much religion. The Protestant major, he adds, is an especially excellent representative of the man of religion and truly noble sentiments.[79]

In general, then, Mercier appealed to the German reading public as a popular philosopher who was imbued with the humanitarian and democratic ideals of the *Aufklärung*. While the critics appreciate his sincere desire to further the welfare of mankind, they are not always in accord with the means he suggests to effect it. In the Revolutionary years less favorable opinions of his political and social views begin to supplant the earlier more enthusiastic estimates. The Germans who in the seventies and eighties welcomed his creed of humanity and freedom, grew more cautious when they saw the theory put into practice across the Rhine. Becoming more and more aware of the Frenchman's inexactness and partisanship, they commenced to regard his work with a very discriminating eye and often to contest the validity of his arguments. They also gave him a hearty welcome for his espousal of the cause of religious tolerance. Nevertheless, they were not so willing as their French contemporaries to replace the traditional church doctrines with a code of morality and natural religion, and hence, under the leadership of the conservative *Göttingische Anzeigen* attacked him bitterly when he attempted to undermine the fundamentals of orthodox Christianity.

Mercier's love of virtue, an integral part of his philosophical code, is a second point with which German criticism was concerned. The sentimentally virtuous age with its utilitarian attitude toward art, approached literature from the angle of usefulness: what good cause it serves, what contribution it makes to the appreciation of virtue and morality. It is characteristic, then, of the German conception of Mercier during the whole period of his vogue that a critic in the *Neue Bibliothek der schönen Wissenschaften* in 1793 can praise his writings for their definite moral purpose, their virtuous atmosphere, their gentle and good characters, and for their attack on vice rather than on folly.[80]

[79] Feb. 11.
[80] XLIX, 137ff.

Earlier comment is similar. In 1772 Herder calls attention in the *Frankfurter* to the ideal of morality that *l'An 2440* recommends,[81] while Weisse also notes that its author is a friend of freedom and virtue.[82] In 1778 the *Göttingische* praises the Frenchman for having stressed in his *Éloges et discours* the high moral character of Descartes.[83] Flögel, the historian of comic literature, recalls in 1785 that Mercier has painted the moral human being in the *Tableau de Paris*,[84] and a critic of the later volumes of this work in the *Allgemeine Literaturzeitung* discovers in them the same gift of philosophy and the same love of freedom and morality that characterize the earlier parts.[85]

However, certain critics do not overlook what seems to them the lack of a moral purpose, or a wrong one. A reviewer in the *Göttingische* at the very beginning of the Mercier vogue pillories *l'Homme sauvage,* a novel in which, in his opinion, the author allowed his hero to commit incest and cannibalism, murder his child, leave his wife to another man, doubt the truth of religion, and still retain a virtuous heart.[86] Later, in 1784, the same periodical notes critically that *mon Bonnet de nuit* has a greater "entertainment" than didactic value.[87] While admitting that the *Fictions morales* is actually very moral in a certain negative sense, the critic in the *Allgemeine Literaturzeitung* in 1793 is offended by its "deathly cold and scholastic portraits of virtue and vice" which have little to do with real morality.[88] More philosophical writers find Mercier's method superficial and outmoded. Thus Wilhelm von Humboldt, who had little sympathy for the Frenchman, expressed in 1798 his dislike for the so-called "philosophical point of view" of *le Nouveau Paris* which he thought sponsored an eternal crusade against folly and vice but lacked real

---

[81] Jan. 10.
[82] In the introduction of his translation of *l'An 2440*.
[83] *Zugabe,* Feb. 7. The same review, however, condemns the exaggerated character of Mercier's praise of the French philosopher. Cf. above, p. 77.
[84] *Op. cit.,* II, 638.
[85] Sept. 18, 1790.
[86] Sept. 15, 1768.
[87] June 19. The final volumes are rated more "instructive" than the first two by the same journal, March 30, 1786.
[88] Jan. 19.

philosophical depth and a true comprehension of the whole of human life.[89]

The critics of Mercier's plays, however, were more nearly unanimous in their approval of his approach to morality. To be sure, the reviewer of *Jenneval* in the *Göttingische* in 1770 is convinced that since the hero, unlike his English prototype, escapes the gallows, the piece has not only lost its moral value but is "harmful and immoral" and may even teach youth that it can commit crimes and still remain virtuous.[90] But this is an exception, and most critics would have been willing to subscribe to J. J. Eschenburg's contention in his *Beispielsammlung zur Theorie und Literatur der schönen Wissenschaften* (1788-1795) that Mercier's dramas, *le Déserteur, l'Indigent, le Faux ami, la Brouette du vinaigrier,* and *Natalie* all have a moral tendency and are filled with noble traits.[91] The major in *le Déserteur,* we remember, was characterized by the *Göttingische* in 1771 as religious and truly noble-minded.[92] A year later the same journal extols the portrayal of virtue in *l'Indigent.* While the critic does not entirely approve of the length and the dogmatic nature of the heroine's tirades on goodness, he nevertheless has nothing but praise for the character of the upright lawyer.[93] A German translator of this play in 1773 calls attention in his introduction to the "torch of virtue" that "shines forth from the impoverished circumstances of the needy family."[94] On similar grounds *le Faux ami* is greeted with enthusiasm by a reviewer in the *Göttingische* in 1772. He is delighted to discover that even in times of corruption a writer who teaches virtue can be successful. In his opinion the noble course that the author follows leads to commendation with greater certainty than do sly innuendoes and a code of morals tending to voluptuousness and degeneracy.[95] The appreciation of a moral purpose induces a later critic in the same

---

[89] *Tagebücher,* I, 430.
[90] Oct. 25.
[91] (Berlin und Stettin), VII, 217.
[92] Feb. 11. Cf. above, p. 81.
[93] May 14, 1772.
[94] Cf. Zollinger, *Mercier als Dramatiker,* p. 53.
[95] Nov. 16.

periodical to prefer Mercier's *Juge* to high tragedy and to the "farces" of Molière and the "witticisms" of Marivaux. While the virtues of a prince do not concern the average man, he thinks, the actions of a brave, upright peasant and of a worthy magistrate, who does not depart from the straight and narrow path of justice even for the sake of a friend to whom he is indebted, are of universal interest.[96] Finally, a critic of the play *Molière* in the *Göttingische* in the same year, 1777, notes with approval Mercier's opinion that it is wrong to crusade against simplicity and the lack of *savoir-faire* rather than against vice.[97]

To German critics of the last decades of the Eighteenth Century, practically unanimous in their demands that a piece of literature be instructive, Mercier's works, novels and plays as well as his social and political treatises, were bound to appeal. Their moral quality was accorded special praise by the *Göttingische*, but the other journals also note it with commendation. In fact it is one of the characteristics that contributed most to his sustained popularity east of the Rhine.

Iffland relates an incident of Mercier's visit to Germany in 1787 that is enlightening. When the two climbed up to the Hardenburg, the seat of the Princes of Leinigen in the Palatinate, the Frenchman looked down into the peaceful valley below and exclaimed with tears in his eyes that he would like to die in just such a spot.[98] Such was the sentimental nature of the man, and it was just this quality, reflected in his works, that appealed to the sentimental German public. No better illustration of this, a third reason for his popularity, can be found than a passage in Bürde's introduction to his translation of the *Tableau de Paris*. He quotes Mercier's belief that his book will have been successful if its readers are induced to give to the poor, and adds his own comment that just these lines will certainly gain for the French author the hearts of most of his readers.[99]

Mercier's works were praised by German critics, as this cita-

---

[96] June 12, 1777.
[97] June 30.
[98] *Briefe an seine Schwester Louise und andere Verwandte*, p. 307.
[99] In the introduction to the second volume of the translation. The passage cited is from the epilogue of the fourth volume of the *Tableau de Paris*.

tion of Bürde indicates, because they were touching. An early reviewer in the *Göttingische,* attributing a short novel concerning a virtuous old man to Mercier, notes that its author has tried to write in a touching fashion and has more or less succeeded.[100] According to an evaluation in the *Neue Bibliothek der schönen Wissenschaften,* written just when the bourgeois tragedy was at the height of its vogue in Germany, there are many terrifying and touching situations in *le Déserteur,* despite its exaggeration of the point of honor.[101] Even the staid *Göttingische Anzeigen* admits in 1771 that notwithstanding certain improbabilities the piece is really moving.[102] A critic in the *Almanach der deutschen Musen* in the following year notes its "lachrymose declamations,"[103] while Herder adds to his *Volkslied,* "Dusle und Bäbele" (1774) a footnote to the effect that the crying girl in the poem reminds him of *le Déserteur.*[104] Still another critic, writing some years later for the *Frankfurter,* calls a story that may have been adapted from this piece a "truly touching narrative."[105]

Other plays of Mercier also impressed German critics by their appeal to tender sentiment. A reviewer of *Olinde et Sophronie* in the *Almanach der deutschen Musen* in 1772 commends the touching scene between Olinde and his father, and the pathetic recognition of Sophronie and Ismen.[106] Most of Mercier's plays struck a similar chord. A critic in the *Göttingische* in 1772 notes the touching prose of *Jean Hennuyer.*[107] In the following year the *Neue Bibliothek der schönen Wissenschaften* assigns *le Faux ami* to the category of touching dramas,[108] while in 1775 the *Göttingische* enthusiastically recognizes *Natalie* as a bourgeois tragedy or a lachrymose comedy. According to the scribe this genre is distinguished by pathetic and touching scenes and by the fact

---

[100] March 12, 1768. I was unable to identify this.
[101] XI (1770), p. 367.
[102] Feb. 11.
[103] Pp. 160f.
[104] *Herders sämtliche Werke,* hrsg. von Suphan (Berlin, 1877-1913), XXV, 23, 659. Herder may, however, have been thinking of Sedaine's operetta.
[105] Jan. 19, 1779.
[106] Pp. 154ff. The references are to Act I, Sc. 2, Act IV, Sc. 3.
[107] Nov. 26.
[108] XIV, 343.

that it evokes pity and noble sentiments rather than laughter. Especial praise is then accorded to the touching interviews between Fondmaire and Natalie and between Natalie and her child.[109] In 1777 the Göttingen journal finds *la Brouette* a moving play and a year later calls attention to the touching language in which the peasant in *le Juge* presents his children to the upright magistrate.[110] In the middle eighties the sentimental, rationalistic *Allgemeine deutsche Bibliothek* singles out the pathetic scenes of *Montesquieu à Marseille* as characteristic of Mercier.[111] A work belonging to another genre, *mon Bonnet de nuit,* is also praised for its touching nature. According to the *Göttingische* in 1786, the essays describing a wretched Parisian writer and a French officer will be read by foreigners and later generations with great sympathy and profound pity.[112] As late as 1793 the reactionary *Neue Bibliothek der schönen Wissenschaften* calls attention to the improvements that Mercier has made to *King Lear* in his adaptation, *le Vieillard et ses trois filles.* According to this critic, the horrors and excesses of the Briton have been replaced by true sentiment and gentle pity. The new happy ending also seems natural and agreeable to the reviewer.[113]

Occasionally, however, it is just this trait of sentimentalism that is condemned in Mercier. A critic in the *Frankfurter* in 1773 notes with disapproval that the situations in *l'Indigent* are touching rather than tragic, and that even the really moving is limited to the scene in which Joseph and Charlotte learn their true identity.[114] Twenty years later the *Allgemeine Literaturzeitung,* unlike the rationalistic *Neue Bibliothek der schönen Wissenschaften,* expresses a preference for the English *King Lear.* Although appreciating Mercier's attempt to adapt a royal tragedy to bourgeois circumstances and granting that in its appeal to tender sentiment his "miniature" surpasses a "whole library" of French tragedies, the Jena periodical has already too

[109] Nov. 9. The references are to Act II, Sc. 5, Act III, Scs. 1, 5.
[110] *Zugabe,* Jan. 27, 1776, and June 12, 1777. The reference is to Act III, Sc. 6.
[111] *Anhang* zu LIII-LXXXVI (1782-1787), Vol. III, pp. 1815f.
[112] March 30. The references are to the *Nachtmütze,* IV, 22ff, 28f.
[113] L, 153.
[114] Dec. 24. The reference is to Act III, Sc. 3.

deep an understanding of Shakespeare to be in sympathy with the change Mercier makes of Lear's "fondness" and passion into "profonde sensibilité." The reviewer points out with considerable perspicacity that since Mercier enthusiastically acknowledges the Briton's greatness, his inability to comprehend him must be due to his French mentality.[115]

The works of Mercier, then, were written in a spirit of sentimental pathos intended to touch the reader or spectator. Those Germans who contemporaneous with *Sturm und Drang* and in the following decades still remained in the "moonlight" of *Empfindsamkeit* and wished to be gently moved, found their desire more than adequately fulfilled by the Frenchman. There is, however, a difference observable between the periodicals of flat rationalism like the *Neue Bibliothek der schönen Wissenschaften* and the more progressive magazines. While the journal of Weisse and Dyk, as we have seen, prefers Mercier's touching *Vieillard* to the English original, the *Frankfurter*, still in 1773 somewhat under the influence of the *Sturm und Drang*, and the *Allgemeine Literaturzeitung*, a periodical not adverse to the irrational in literature, protest against the sacrifice of the tragic to the touching and the sentimental.

One of the reasons Lemaître assigns for the popularity of *la Brouette du vinaigrier*, we remember, is its external realism.[116] This realism was characteristic of Mercier's works in general, and is another angle from which he was viewed by contemporary German critics. Even Wilhelm von Humboldt, writing in 1798, notes with approval a description of a dog at an inn that the Frenchman contributed to the *Journal de Paris*. In his opinion Mercier is really great as a naturalistic painter. His instinctive discernment of things as they are, coupled with his total lack of artistic feeling, enables him to put the characteristic elements into clear relief, especially if they are "ugly and immoral."[117] An appreciation of Mercier as a realist, then, can be traced in German criticism throughout the last thirty-five years of the century. Not infre-

---

[115] Jan. 19, 1793.
[116] *Op. cit.*, p. 260.
[117] *Tagebücher*, I, 523.

quently, however, we find dissenters who complain that he has not paid enough attention to the factor of probability.

The earliest mention of Mercier I have found in any German journal deals with the problem of realism in *l'Histoire d'Izerben, poète arabe*. The *Göttingische* concedes in 1766 that while this novel does not give the proper local color, and the action cannot have taken place anywhere except at Paris, still the fate of the poet portrayed in it is treated realistically.[118] Mercier's descriptive *Tableau de Paris* called forth greater enthusiasm than this early *conte* in the manner of Voltaire. The *Allgemeines Verzeichnis* notes in 1782 that its candid and exact portrayal of the modes and morals of the French capital will be valuable for foreigner and native alike.[119] Somewhat later Reichard writes in the preface to his translation of the work that his own visit to Paris has convinced him that Mercier gives the best and most correct idea of the manners of that city.[120] Toward the end of the century in his *Leben Justus Mösers* Nicolai quotes a description of the French finance minister Turgot from the *Tableau de Paris*, which he terms excellent.[121] Critics also express admiration for the nature pictures in *mon Bonnet de nuit*. In one of its first numbers the *Allgemeine Literaturzeitung* dwells with especial commendation on the chapters "ma Fenêtre" (the view from the author's window in Switzerland), "de la Campagne" (the charms of country life), and the "Lac de Nantua" (a very romantic region).[122] In the following year, 1786, the *Göttingische* singles out for praise from among the many "excellent" pictures of Swiss landscape in the last two volumes of this work the description of a view of the mountains from Neuchâtel.[123] A critic of the *Songes et visions* in the *Allgemeine Literaturzeitung* in 1792 attributes the excellence of Mercier's descriptions to a lively imagination and a happy faculty for realistic portraiture.[124] The

---

[118] Nov. 27.

[119] P. 531.

[120] In 1789.

[121] (Berlin und Stettin, 1797), pp. 48nf. Nicolai writes "Il débuta par *des* réforms absolument inutiles" for "*deux* réformes."

[122] Jan. 4, 1785. Cf. *Merciers Nachtmütze*, II, 303ff, 12ff., 123ff.

[123] March 30. Cf. *ibid.*, IV, 32ff.

[124] Sept. 24.

announcement of the publication of *le Nouveau Paris* in the same journal in 1800 absolves the Frenchman of having deviated from truth and actuality in any way.[125] The review of the work in this periodical notes the "painter's" ability to show an object from a completely new angle and at the same time with consummate realism, and adds that circumstances have forced him to dip his brush into colors more vivid than those used for the original *Tableau de Paris.*[126]

Mercier's realism, an integral part of his effort to break with high tragedy, is also very evident in his plays. The definition of the "drame" that he propounded in the *Nouvel essai* in 1773: "a fine moment of human life that reveals the interior of a family and which, without neglecting the important features, carefully considers the details,"[127] was still well enough known in Germany twenty years later to find a place in the 1792 edition of Sulzer's *Allgemeine Theorie der schönen Künste.*[128] Other Germans do not fail to notice this trait of realism in his "drames." Thus a critic in the *Almanach der deutschen Musen* in 1772 points to the realistic setting of the last act of *Olinde et Sophronie,* in which the fagots prepared for the protagonists appear on the stage.[129] Contemporaneously the *Göttingische,* which extols *l'Indigent* as a production in the serious manner, calls especial attention to the characteristic realism of the scene in which the needy family of the hero awaits ejection from its miserable room in order that a couple of greyhounds may be quartered there.[130] While the *Almanach der deutschen Musen* in 1777 finds *la Brouette du vinaigrier* mediocre, it nonetheless calls attention to its "strange" title and to the wheelbarrow itself which is rolled across the stage.[131] The popular philosopher Knigge refers in the preface of his translation of *le Juge* in 1779 to his own dislike for plays in which the action is melodramatic and the characters are unnatural. Instead, he favors

---

[125] *Intelligenzblatt,* March 1.
[126] Nov. 28, 1800. Wilhelm von Humboldt also refers to Mercier as "le peintre." Cf. *Tagebücher,* I, 430.
[127] P. 106.
[128] Neue vermehrte zweite Auflage (Leipzig, 1792-1799), I, 560b-561a.
[129] Pp. 154ff.
[130] May 14. The reference is to Act I, Sc. 3.
[131] 1777, pp. 134f.

small, realistic scenes from everyday life, a preference that doubtless led him to undertake his translation.[132]

German critics also call attention to Mercier's ability to portray character in a natural and realistic fashion. As late as 1793 Eschenburg notes in his *Beispielsammlung* the excellent characterizations in his dramas,[133] while earlier commendation was garnered from the *Göttingische Anzeigen* by the well-drawn characters of *le Déserteur*.[134] Milack in the introduction to his translation of *l'Indigent* in 1773 finds that the persons of this play are true to life.[135] On the other hand, the *Frankfurter*, in the same year, while conceding that they are in general well depicted, still does not consider them completed or entirely alive.[136] A critic of *le Faux ami* in the *Almanach der deutschen Musen* in 1775 discovers more truth and naturalness in the character of the hypocrite than in any of the personages of *le Déserteur*, with the exception of the informer.[137] Two years later the *Göttingische* praises the characterizations of the magistrate and the child in *le Juge*.[138] However, a dissenting voice is raised by the *Allgemeine deutsche Bibliothek*. In the middle eighties one of its critics, in connection with *Montesquieu à Marseille*, questions the Frenchman's ability to portray character and to individualize his dramatic creations,[139] while another about the same time writes that the novel *Jezennemours* lacks outstanding characters.[140]

The disagreement over Mercier as a realist is not limited to his ability in characterization. Indeed, one of the commonest objections raised by German critics to his dramas and other works is that they contain much that is improbable, or in case of the plays, theatrical. Thus an early reviewer in the *Göttingische* of *l'Homme sauvage* remarks that he is unable to discover either the customs or the way of thinking of an Inca in this "strange, highly praised

[132] Cf. the *Frankfurter gelehrte Anzeigen*, April 13-16, 1779.
[133] VII, 217.
[134] Feb. 11, 1771.
[135] Cf. Zollinger, *Mercier als Dramatiker*, p. 53.
[136] Dec. 24, 1773.
[137] P. 91.
[138] June 12, 1777.
[139] *Anhang* zu LIII-LXXXV (1782-1787), Vol. III, pp. 1815f.
[140] LXXVII (1787), 122.

tale."[141] Some two decades later, in 1790, the *Allgemeine Literatur-zeitung* expresses its doubts whether this "unnatural natural man," who embodies the views of a writer living in the most unnatural of all metropolises, can become popular in Germany.[142] The conversion of the hero in Mercier's first play, *Jenneval,* is called improbable and theatrical by the *Göttingische* in 1770.[143] Soon after, this periodical applies the same epithets to the attempted martyrdom of the Christians in *Olinde et Sophronie,*[144] and in the following year, 1771, condemns the piece for not having observed Eastern customs.[145] While the *Neue Bibliothek der schönen Wissenschaften* in 1770 and the *Göttingische Anzeigen* in 1771 laud *le Déserteur,* both point out that the plot is exaggerated and improbable.[146] The scene in *l'Indigent* in which Charlotte fires a shotgun in order to defend her virtue is called "ridiculous" and melodramatic by the *Göttingische* in 1772 and the *Frankfurter* in 1773.[147] The former journal also attacks *le Faux ami* because of its improbability. Although its reviewer realizes that vanity can blind even a reprobate, he still finds it strange that the villain reveals his evil intentions without need.[148] Three years later, in 1775, the Göttingen journal indicates Mercier's failure in *Childéric 1er, roi de France* to portray the morals and manners of the Merovingian Franks.[149] Finally, the critic in the *Allgemeine deutsche Bibliothek* in 1787 who, as we have seen, condemned the characters in *Jezennemours,* also finds that the few "extraordinary and unexpected" events of the novel are neither interesting nor probable.[150]

The criterion of external realism plays a large part in the judgments that German critics of the last thirty years of the century passed on Mercier's writings. A wide diversity of opinion can be noted without any indication that one journal or one period was

[141] Sept. 15, 1768.
[142] March 11.
[143] Oct. 25.
[144] Nov. 22, 1770.
[145] *Zugabe,* Nov. 30.
[146] XI, 367; Feb. 11.
[147] May 14; Dec. 24. The reference is to Act II, Sc. 5 of *l'Indigent.*
[148] Nov. 16, 1772.
[149] March 2.
[150] LXXVII, 122, Cf. above, p. 90.

more or less appreciative of this quality in him than any other. It is clear, however, that while the critics were divided in their attitude toward the realism of his plays, the vivid accuracy of his social treatises received general approbation, and the romantic improbabilities of his novels and tales met with thorough condemnation.

Germans considered Mercier from still another, and fifth angle: as a stylist. He had the reputation in Germany of writing in a vigorous, colorful language which, however, was marred by declamations, tirades, and paradoxes. The German attitude is summed up well in the leading reviews of the *Allgemeine Literaturzeitung* of November 28 and 29, 1800, which deal with *le Nouveau Paris*. The critic speaks of the Frenchman's clever and witty ideas and of his vivid pictures, but also notes the useless tirades and the exaggerated and incoherent reflections. While conceding the vigor of his expression, the reviewer is disappointed that a man of Mercier's ability, whose *Tableau de Paris* was characterized by such a free and powerful style, has not put the freedom resulting from the lack of supervision by the Académie française to better use. In addition, it is interesting for us to note that German critics seldom call attention to that deficiency in Mercier that was particularly evident to his countrymen, his lack of taste. In fact, if we can believe an ironic French anecdote, they were entirely unaware of it.[151]

The German attitude toward Mercier's style, then, is one of praise mingled with censure. As early as 1768 the *Göttingische* calls the style of the short novel it attributes to him "exalted, epic, and metaphysical,"[152] and in the same year praises the "vivid" description of the hero's struggle between nature and religion in *la Lettre de Dulis à son ami*.[153] The same journal notes in 1770

---

[151] Cf. *Merciériana*, pp. 19f. A Frenchman traveling in Germany met a professor who was translating a "masterpiece" of French literature into his native tongue. The traveler asked the name of the author of the chef-d'œuvre. He received negative replies to his suggestions of Montesquieu, Voltaire, and Racine. The German was translating Mercier, whom he considered the greatest genius of France, with the single fault, so typical of the French, that he attached too much importance to good taste and to the graces!

[152] March 12.

[153] Sept. 5.

that *Jenneval*, although in prose, is written with much fire.[154] Weisse lauds the exceptional power and candor of the style in *l'An 2440*. To him, the pictures in this work are excellently drawn, are full of warmth, and seem almost too vivid. Weisse attributes any appearance of a stilted manner to the Frenchman's exaggerated imagination rather than to frigidity or affectation.[155]

Less favorable criticism greets many of his plays. In 1772 the *Almanach der deutschen Musen* speaks disparagingly of the "lachrymose declamations" of *le Déserteur*,[156] and in the following year the *Frankfurter* continues the attack on the weakness of the Frenchman's style. It scores *l'Indigent, le Déserteur,* and *Olinde et Sophronie* for their long scenes filled with dull dialogue, frequent monologues, and rhetorical declamations. In addition, the *Frankfurter* reviewer finds *l'Indigent* quite uninteresting, its whole technique commonplace, its fourth act dragging, and its conclusion evident almost from the beginning.[157] *Jean Hennuyer* is to the reviewer in the *Almanach der deutschen Musen* in 1774 merely a series of speeches which often lack the necessary fire.[158] While in the following year the *Göttingische* hails *Childéric 1ᵉʳ, roi de France* for its exalted prose interspersed with hexameters, it nonetheless does not overlook the "unbearable" length of the tirades.[159] Later, however, the *Allgemeines Verzeichnis* assails even this "exalted" prose and finds the language of the whole piece "very mediocre."[160]

Critics of other works of Mercier strike a similar mixed note. A reviewer in the *Göttingische* in 1784 of *mon Bonnet de nuit* extols the Frenchman's exalted imagination, but condemns the exaggerated declamations.[161] Another critic in the following year in the *Allgemeine Literaturzeitung* not only fails to find in this work the fire and manly eloquence that characterized *l'An 2440,* the *Tableau de Paris,* and the plays, but also scores its careless and dragging style.[162] In 1787 *Jezennemours* commends itself to a

---

[154] Oct. 25.
[155] In the preface to his translation.
[156] Pp. 160f.
[157] Dec. 24, 1773.
[158] Pp. 102f.
[159] March 2, 1775.
[160] 1777, p. 126.
[161] June 19.
[162] Jan. 4.

rather condescending reviewer in the *Allgemeine deutsche Biblio-thek* solely for its Seneca-like eloquence and its fiery declama-tions.[163] In 1788 the *Göttingische* points to the repetition of ideas in the *Notions claires sur les gouvernements*,[164] while in the next year Reichard expresses his preference for the later and briefer volumes of the *Tableau de Paris*, and omits in his translation many long-winded passages that seemed superfluous to him.[165] Contempo-raneously the *Neue Bibliothek der schönen Wissenschaften* dis-parages Mercier's introduction to his edition of Rousseau because it is couched in too general terms.[166] The same journal in reviewing the *Songes et visions* in 1792 is not altogether unappreciative of his style. But while it praises his ardor, eloquence, and fantasy, and concedes that the complementary German dreams lack the richness of his imagination and his impassioned expression, it nevertheless calls Mercier a rhetorician, a sophist, and a declaimer.[167] Simi-larly, a critic of this work in the *Allgemeine Literaturzeitung* in the same year greets the Frenchman's charming and fertile imagi-nation with commendation and adds that the German dreams often lack the ease and grace of the French. Nonetheless, he also points out the Frenchman's too luxuriant fantasy, his tiresome repetitions, his empty declamations, and his affected style.[168] On the other hand, the *Neue deutsche Bibliothek* in 1793 has nothing but praise for the charming style of the *Portraits des rois de France*.[169]

The *Allgemeine Literaturzeitung* becomes a severe critic of the exaggerated style of Mercier's later works. In 1793 it scores the *Fictions morales* as "declamatory" and "bombastic" and wonders how a French man of letters of some distinction can write with such "carelessness, awkwardness, and lack of taste."[170] In the following year it pillories the *Fragments de politique et d'histoire* for its valueless content and for its "very common, declamatory,

---

[163] LXXVII, 122.
[164] June 23.
[165] Cf. his introduction.
[166] XXXIX (1789), 305ff.
[167] XLV, 141ff.
[168] Sept. 24.
[169] VI, 334ff.
[170] Jan. 19.

long-winded, repetitious style."[171] The aphoristic, rhapsodic, ec-
static manner, and the frequency of antitheses and declamations
in *le Nouveau Paris* are condemned in an otherwise friendly review in 1800 as offensive to good taste,[172] a verdict which is sec-
onded three years later by the *Göttingische*.[173]

While the Germans appreciated Mercier's rare enthusiasm and
his vivid style, they were none the less very critical of his leaning
to bombast and declamation. The *Göttingische,* concerned chiefly
with the Frenchman's earlier and simpler productions, is in general
favorably impressed by his diction. On the other hand, the *Allgemeine Literaturzeitung,* confronted with the exaggerations of his
later works, has a tendency to expatiate upon his stylistic weaknesses. This critical approach becomes more general as the Mercier vogue progressed, and eventually contributed its share to the
termination of his German popularity.

Any survey of Mercier's popularity in Germany must take into
account both the character of the periodical or individual criticiz-
ing him, and the shift in the nature of his appeal within the forty
years of his vogue. The *Göttingische Anzeigen,* which along with
the *Allgemeine Literaturzeitung* devotes the most space to Mercier, judges him from a conservative, middle-class, often somewhat
pedantic point of view. While it commends his love of virtue and
his ability to portray the touching, it attacks him almost savagely
when his liberal opinions do not coincide with the canons of orthodox Protestant religion. It is also very exacting as far as minor
details are concerned and continually points out errors in local
color and contradictions of one kind or other. When the younger
Allgemeine Literaturzeitung began to be published in 1785 it
found Mercier at the peak of his popularity and already established
in Germany as a "famous" writer. Its reviewers, confronted with
his later and more mediocre works, are often at a loss to explain
this popularity. In accord with the objective editorial policy of the
paper they try hard to be fair to him, and do speak with special
commendation of his humanitarianism and of his vivid imagination

---

[171] Sept. 29.
[172] Nov. 28.
[173] Oct. 22, 1803.

and colorful style. Still it is far too intelligent a journal ever to
become an unconditional Mercier enthusiast, and thus never fails
to single out his faults, seemingly with great satisfaction. Due to
the paucity of material it is more difficult to define the attitude of
the other journals. The *Neue Bibliothek der schönen Wissenschaften* usually lauds the Frenchman for his tender sentiment and
his love of humanity, and Nicolai's *Allgemeine deutsche Bibliothek*
also judges him almost entirely from a sentimental, rationalistic
point of view. Similarly, the appreciation of the *Frankfurter gelehrte Anzeigen* is, after its emotional outburst in 1772 and 1773,
that of the typical *Aufklärer*.

In general, there is noticeable a shift of attention of the German
critics from one genre to another, from the dramatic to the social,
and then to the political, rather than a definite change in their attitude toward Mercier. In the seventies the interest of the German
public was directed to his plays. By 1790 most of these had vanished from the German stage, and Mercier himself had long since
turned to other fields of literary endeavor. After 1780 his social
and descriptive works commanded the interest of the readers
east of the Rhine. The year 1785 marks approximately the high
point of his German vogue. Finally, in the Revolutionary period,
his political writings attracted attention. Then, around the turn
of the century, he passed gradually into literary oblivion.

The nature and extent of Mercier's German vogue becomes
clear, then, only when we consider the numerous opinions expressed by German critics over a period of about forty years, as
well as the numerous translations of his works and the frequent
performances of his plays. His German appeal as a dramatist,
novelist, and social and political writer, although subject to the
factors of variety of source and of chronology, can for practical
purposes be reduced to a single formula. Germans saw in Mercier
an exponent of the sentimental, democratic, enlightened, middle-
class, humanitarian philosophy prevalent in western Europe at the
time. In addition, they appreciated the external realism of his
works and praised the colorfulness of his style, although they protested, especially in later years, against its pomposity and its exaggerations.

V

MERCIER AND WIELAND

WITH THE GENERAL nature and extent of Mercier's German appeal defined, we can now turn to his relationship with outstanding German men of letters of his period, few of whom indeed escaped his influence. Wieland, the apostle of enlightenment, was among the first foreign Mercier enthusiasts. The present chapter will give a brief account of his knowledge of the Frenchman and then discuss in detail the relation between *l'An 2440* and *Der goldene Spiegel*. While similarities in these two books have already been pointed out by Zollinger[1] and by Kurrelmeyer, the editor of *Der Spiegel* for the Preussische Akademie der Wissenschaften,[2] the following attempts to give a more complete and unified account of these likenesses. Finally, for the sake of completeness, a brief consideration of the influence of Agathon on Mercier's *Jezennemours* has been added.

Wieland's acquaintance with Mercier's works dates from 1771. Early in January of the following year he wrote to Sophie von Laroche that *l'An 2440* was an "excellent book that deserved statues." His own *Histoire de Scheschian (Der goldene Spiegel)*, he continued, was not so caustic, its style not so emphatic, its satire more benign. However, he was willing to pardon the Frenchman's severity, since he had "genius and a good heart."[3] A few days later his friend Sophie was informed by F. H. Jacobi that Wieland had been urging him constantly to read this "very strange phenomenon," this "prophecy of the Judgment Day of the French constitution."[4] Wieland was likewise the author of the review in the *Erfurtische gelehrte Zeitung* in March of the same year,

---

[1] *Beziehungen*, 88ff.

[2] *Wielands gesammelte Schriften* (Berlin, 1909ff.), 1 Abt. xi¹. All references to Wieland are to this edition, unless otherwise noted.

[3] *Wielands Briefe an Sophie von Laroche*, hrsg. von Franz Horn (Berlin, 1820), p. 153; Jan. 6.

[4] *Jacobis auserlesener Briefwechsel*, hrsg. von Friedrich Roth (Leipzig, 1825-1827), I, 62ff.; Jan. 18.

1772, which lauded the French work.[5] It is clear that he did not know yet who had written *l'An 2440*,[6] which had appeared anonymously at Amsterdam in 1770. A note in the first edition of *Der Spiegel* in 1772 which read, "if the well-known patriotic dream of an unnamed author should be fulfilled," was later amended, "if Mercier's patriotic dream. . . ."[7] In 1776 Wieland sent "Sébastien Mercier's revelation" to Lenz.[8] The phrase, "the year 2440," as an expression for the millennium, became part and parcel of Wieland's vocabulary. It is so used in 1775 in the *Versuch über das deutsche Singspiel*, in 1792 in the *Sendschreiben an Ehlers*, and in 1788 in *Über den freien Gebrauch der Vernunft*.[9] In the last mentioned essay Wieland asks us to recall the venerable and lovable Pope Pius XXVI, "or whatever his name in *l'An* may have been," who by his enlightenment, wisdom, virtue, modesty, and unselfishness was an honor to Christianity.[10]

Wieland also knew others of Mercier's works. He printed in the *Deutscher Merkur* of 1784 a letter from the "famous author of *l'An 2440* and the *Tableau de Paris*." In it the Frenchman protests against an attack on his writings in another German journal by a countryman of his. Wieland reveals that although he is none too eager to devote the pages of his periodical to Mercier's private quarrels, he can scarcely refuse the request of a man of letters whom he so highly esteems. Finally, while he is unwilling to take any responsibility for the content of the letter, he feels sure that his readers will not find it entirely void of interest.[11] The fact that this is the only French correspondence which he published in his journal between 1773 and 1789[12] is a clear indication of the respect he had for Mercier.

---

[5] *Wielands Schriften*, 1 Abt., xiv, a51.

[6] *Wielands Briefe an Sophie von Laroche*, Jan. 6, p. 153: "*L'An 2440* . . . méritera à son auteur une place à Bicêtre, s'il est découvert."

[7] *Schriften*, 1 Abt., ix, 266n.; 1, xi[1], 41.

[8] *Briefe von und an Lenz*, hrsg. von Freye und Stammler (Leipzig, 1918), ii, 43; October.

[9] *Schriften*, 1 Abt., xiv, 75n.; 1, xv, 452; 1, xv, 136.

[10] *Ibid.*, 1 Abt., xv, 145. This is a rather vague allusion to chap. xvii of *l'An 2440*, where, however, no name at all is mentioned.

[11] 3. Teil, pp. 277ff.

[12] Cf. A. Fuchs, *les Apports français dans l'œuvre de Wieland* (Paris, 1934), p. 617.

If we assume that Wieland was familiar with all the material in *Der Merkur,* he must have known several of the Frenchman's dramas. It mentions in 1775 both the performance of *Jenneval* by Marchand in western Germany[13] and the première of *Der Essigmann* in Vienna. The writer of the "Theatralische Neuigkeiten" finds the ideas of the latter play commonplace and the situations of little interest. He attributes the popularity of the piece in France to the appearance on the stage of the cask filled with money.[14]

Wieland was not unfamiliar with Mercier's later political writings. In 1792 he calls the *Chronique du mois,* which contained articles by "Condorcet, Brissot, Mercier" and others, one of the most important journals of the new France,[15] and in the next year refers ironically to "citizen" Mercier's "graceful" proof in this journal that the land of liberty and equality should rightfully extend to the Rhine.[16] Wieland's allusions to Mercier's works, then, are fairly numerous. *L'An 2440,* however, was the only one which had a tangible influence on him.[17]

A study of the genesis of *Der goldene Spiegel,* also called *Die Könige von Scheschian,* indicates that it was written partly before and partly after the summer of 1771 and that it was published in 1772.[18] Wieland informed Gleim in July 1771 that he was busy polishing the style of *Musarion* and *Don Silvio,* and writing a third and fourth part of *Die Könige von Scheschian.*[19] If chronological factors make any influence of Haller's *Usong,* which did not appear until the end of 1771, very doubtful,[20] *Der goldene*

---

[13] 3. Teil, p. 271.

[14] 4. Teil, p. 274.

[15] *Schriften,* I Abt., xv, 742n.

[16] *Ibid.,* I Abt., xv, 583, a141.

[17] There is no evidence that Wieland knew the *Nouvel essai.* The only similarity between the *Briefe an einen jungen Dichter* and it is an admiration for Shakespeare. Compare also, "enflammer toutes les âmes par une *commotion électrique*" (p. vi), and "dummer Blick eines Zuhörers bei einer Stelle, die ihm einen *elektrischen Schlag* hätte geben sollen." (*Schriften,* I Abt., xiv, 387.)

[18] It was revised in 1794. The final version differs little from the original of 1772. Cf. O. Vogt, *Der goldene Spiegel.* "Forschungen zur neueren Literaturgeschichte," Nr. 26 (Berlin, 1904), p. 29.

[19] *Ausgewählte Briefe von Wieland* (Zürich, 1815-1816), III, 63; July 6. According to K. Buchner, *Wieland und die Weidmannsche Buchhandlung,* pp. 44ff., two volumes were ready in manuscript form by March, 1771; cf. *Schriften,* I Abt., xi, 5.

[20] Cf. Seuffert, "Wielands Berufung nach Weimar," *Vierteljahrschrift für Literatur-*

Spiegel does show that its author was familiar with works by Plato, Aristotle, Xenophon, Montesquieu, Crébillon-fils, Rousseau, the elder Mirabeau, Abbt, and Zimmermann, and that he knew the reform plans of Joseph II of Austria.[21] However, one of its chief sources is Mercier's *l'An 2440*. Although Wieland first mentions the French utopia in 1772, he may, of course, have read it in 1770 when it first appeared. In any case, as we have shown above, he was familiar with it when he was engaged in writing the latter half of his novel.

Der goldene Spiegel is a political novel in the tradition of Plato and Fénelon. It is perhaps the best German Staatsroman and is likewise the classical Fürstenspiegel of German literature. In it the history of the rulers of a mythical kingdom is told to one of its princes, who is a descendant of the sultan in the *Arabian Nights*. The crux of the tale is the account of the education, development, and rule of Tifan, an especially philanthropic and well-meaning sovereign. *Der Spiegel* contains much theorizing on questions of government in the tone of virtue and enlightenment so typical of the later Eighteenth Century. It lacks, however, the revolutionary fire and the ardent enthusiasm that characterize *l'An 2440* and in that offers justification for Gervinus' contention that Wieland, "not wishing either to caress or chastise his century, tickled it."[22] While the German sets the stage of *Der Spiegel* in a faraway land, Mercier places his utopia in the distant, and safe, future. The French work is not a novel but an idealized picture of the eventual earthly felicity of mankind. Life in Paris under ideal political and social conditions is revealed to a dreamer who awakens after a sleep of more than six centuries. *L'An 2440* has a fascination that is due to the boldness, and at the same time, the naïveté of its prophecies. One can well understand that it enjoyed countless French editions, was translated, as we have seen, into German, and appealed to the politically and socially minded Wieland.

Having established that Wieland knew *l'An 2440* at a time

---

geschichte, I (1888), 355n. Wieland wrote to Sophie von Laroche early in 1772 that he fell asleep at the seventh page when he tried to read *Usong;* cf. *Briefe an Sophie von Laroche,* p. 153.

[21] Cf. Seuffert, *op. cit.,* p. 359; Vogt, *op. cit.,* pp. 30, 2.

[22] *Geschichte der deutschen Dichtung,* 5 ed. (Leipzig, 1871-1874), IV, 308.

when he was writing the second part of *Der Spiegel,* and having examined the general nature of both works, we shall now proceed to a detailed account of their similarities. Both books contain a great deal of information about the education and the duties of the monarch. The Frenchman devotes a special chapter of his utopia to the instruction given the crown prince.[23] He is not brought up at court where flatterers can persuade him that he is more important than other men and that the rest of mankind are less than insects. He is confided to faithful subjects who vow never to reveal to him that one day he will become king.[24] The physical education of the young prince is especially stressed. He is dressed like the peasants and associates with them and with the ordinary laborers. Thus he learns to respect the common man.[25] He does not seek a foreign princess for a wife, but marries a girl of his own people, who has neither scepter nor crown.[26] He travels through the provinces of his realm and discovers the condition of the poor, whose sufferings he might otherwise never suspect.[27] He listens with tears in his eyes to the speech of his father, who before the assembled multitude exposes his identity and outlines his future duties.[28]

Once he has become king, he has full authority to do right, but is so restricted that he cannot do wrong.[29] There is a tablet on each side of his throne. On one of them the laws of the country and the limits of royal power are inscribed, while on the other the obligations of the monarch and of his subjects are noted.[30] The sovereign realizes the importance of the provinces of his kingdom. Just as in the human body, where each part has its own circulation as well as enjoying the general circulation, so each province, while obeying the laws of the domain, modifies them according to its own particular situation and need.[31] Taxation is levied in 2440 by

[23] *L'An 2440,* chap. xxxvii, pp. 345ff.
[24] *Ibid.,* p. 346.
[25] *Ibid.,* p. 347.
[26] *Ibid.,* p. 358.
[27] *Ibid.,* pp. 347f.
[28] *Ibid.,* pp. 349ff.
[29] *Ibid.,* p. 341.
[30] *Ibid.,* p. 320.
[31] *Ibid.,* p. 332.

means of strongboxes (coffres-forts) in which signed contributions are placed. The amount depends on the wealth of the person
who pays. There are even containers for voluntary gifts, which
often turn out to be greater than the obligatory payments.[32] In
Mercier's utopia the clergy, those "automatons as bored as they
are boring," who have taken the "imbecile oath" never to be men,
have been abolished. Its members are, however, allowed to return
to the world and become good citizens and fathers.[33] Finally, education is so arranged that each child receives the appropriate training for the position which it will eventually occupy in society.[34]

Wieland's ideal prince, Tifan, enjoys an education quite similar
to that of the heir to the throne in Mercier's utopia. He passes his
youth far from the court of his voluptuous cousin. His mentor does
not disclose his parentage to him.[35] He grows up as a shepherd
and hence does not consider himself superior to his fellow men.
Indeed, he respects the man whose work is better and more useful
than his own. His training gives him a strong body, red lips, and
fresh blood. He is incapable of ever believing that the millions
were created just for him.[36] Tifan weds a young shepherdess, for
the kings of Scheschian have always married their subjects.[37] He
visits the various regions of Asia and thus comes into contact with
the woes of mankind and the evils of tyranny.[38] He is almost over-
whelmed with emotion as his guardian publicly reveals his rank
to him and admonishes him to be a benevolent ruler.[39]

King Tifan states that necessary measures must be taken that
his and his successors' freedom to do wrong be curtailed.[40] His code
of laws has two principal divisions, one the duties and rights of
the sovereign, the other the duties and rights of the nation. He
considers it ridiculous that the conduct of the citizen should be
minutely prescribed, while the crowned head is left unrestricted.[41]

[32] *Ibid.*, pp. 380ff.
[33] *Ibid.*, pp. 107ff.
[34] *Ibid.*, p. 372.
[35] *Der Spiegel, Schriften,* 1 Abt., IX, 200ff.
[36] *Ibid.*, pp. 202f.
[37] *Ibid.*, pp. 207f.
[38] *Ibid.*, pp. 212ff.
[39] *Ibid.*, pp. 234f.
[40] *Ibid.*, p. 237.
[41] *Ibid.*, 250.

Tifan stresses the value of the provinces for his realm. They are like the members of a healthy and flourishing body. Each partakes of the common lifeblood, each aids the other and receives nourishment from the whole.[42] This same comparison of the state and its parts to the human organism, as we have seen, is used by Mercier, but it is also a common figure in political thought from the *Republic* to Rivarol.[43] A graduated income tax is paid in Scheschian. Strongboxes (wohl verwahrte Kasten) receive the contributions, each signed by the payer.[44] Here Wieland acknowledges his source and alludes in a footnote to a similar method of taxation in *l'An 2440*. In the later edition of *Der Spiegel* he adds that the Revolution, which Mercier did not dream was so near, has considerably shortened his 645 years.[45] Wieland, more realistic and conservative than his French contemporary, does not, however, suggest the containers for voluntary payments which are described in the French utopia. The clergy, the "Ya-faou,"[46] is considered useless in Tifan's moral and enlightened kingdom. Its members do not render any service to the state, merely taking advantage of the work of others. In addition, they hinder national prosperity through their stupidity and their encouragement of superstition and prejudice. They must therefore disband and may either leave the country or learn a trade and become valuable citizens.[47] Finally, Wieland's enlightened monarch sponsors an educational system in which each class of society receives its own training.[48]

Besides these likenesses in the education and the conception of the duties of the ideal prince, there are numerous other points of similarity in the two works. In both the French utopia[49] and in Wieland's ideal kingdom,[50] the children are acquainted with the laws and manners of the land when they become fourteen years

---

[42] *Ibid.*, p. 260.
[43] Zollinger, *Beziehungen*, p. 89f., cites this passage from *Der Spiegel* as a direct borrowing from *l'An 2440*.
[44] *Der Spiegel, Schriften*, 1 Abt., IX, 266.
[45] *Ibid.*, p. 266n. Cf. also *Schriften*, 1 Abt., XI¹, 41.
[46] The name was doubtless suggested by Swift's "Yahoos," which Wieland mentions elsewhere; cf. *Schriften*, 1 Abt., XV, 115.
[47] *Der Spiegel, Schriften*, 1 Abt., IX, 272ff.
[48] *Ibid.*, p. 293.
[49] *L'An 2440*, p. 92.
[50] *Der Spiegel*, p. 57.

old. In Mercier's dream, the reins of government are confided to wise and strong hands. Thus the laws are supreme and general happiness is brought about.[51] Similarly, Danischmend, the philosopher of Scheschian, tells his master that there have always been kings who believed they fulfilled their duties and insured general prosperity only with the assistance of the most sagacious members of their nation.[52] Mercier lays bare the mind of the tyrant who finds it necessary to diminish the prosperity and happiness of a people in order to increase its diligence and submission.[53] Likewise in Wieland's novel the courtier Eblis is of the opinion that the crowd can only be held in check by hunger and blows. He thinks it useless to attempt to win the love of the "many-headed animal," since kindness merely arouses it to disobedience, and concludes that the people must be kept subservient by constant intimidation and punishment.[54]

There are further similarities. The Frenchman relates the story of the ass whose burden is continually increased by its villager owner until it falls to the ground and dies of exhaustion. He then points out the moral of the tale: the villager is the monarch and the ass the people.[55] Danischmend informs his sovereign of the belief of the despot that the ass can be loaded more and more heavily. Finally, however, it sinks to earth and perishes. Here again Wieland names his source. It is a "wonderful" book that will honor its author more in 2440 than it will be of value to him in 1772. While he considers the "honorable dreamer" to be a little too radical, he nevertheless finds it difficult not to esteem a man who loves his fellow beings so much that neither Bastille nor Bicêtre can keep him from saying what is in his heart.[56] This comment is characteristic of Wieland's attitude toward Mercier. He admires his enlightened views but looks askance at his revolutionary tendencies. Finally, in the throne room of 2440 there is a basket filled with bread to be given to the poor. It serves as a reliable thermometer of public misery.[57] Danischmend also wishes that a

[51] *L'An 2440*, p. 338.
[52] *Der Spiegel*, p. 84.
[53] *L'An 2440*, pp. 326nf.
[54] *Der Spiegel*, p. 172.
[55] *L'An 2440*, pp. 162nf.
[56] *Der Spiegel*, pp. 190, 190n.
[57] *L'An 2440*, p. 323.

political barometer could be invented to register the sum total of the abuses of a kingdom and the hour of its destruction.[58]

A summary of our discussion of *l'An 2440* and *Der goldene Spiegel* yields the following results. Wieland read *l'An 2440* at the latest toward the end of 1771, when he was writing the second part of *Der goldene Spiegel,* and mentions it twice in his novel. There are numerous close likenesses, almost all of which are to be found in the latter half of the German Staatsroman. We may conclude, then, that *l'An 2440* was an important source for Wieland. Both he and the Frenchman are saturated with the ideals of human progress. Both point to the evils of a selfish and despotic form of rule. Both advocate an enlightened and paternal monarchy. However, Wieland, as he himself admitted,[59] is much more conservative. The dictum of Goethe: "where the Frenchmen of the Eighteenth Century are destructive, Wieland teases,"[60] sums up well the essential difference between Mercier and the author of *Der goldene Spiegel* and *Agathon.*

It is typical of the age that *Der Spiegel* which contained the opinions of Mercier and other Frenchmen was translated into French shortly after its original publication.[61] Wieland was already known across the Rhine for his *Agathon,* a complete translation of which was to appear in 1774.[62] Mercier's "dramatic novel," *Jezennemours,* was published two years later, in 1776, and is in part a reworking of the first nine books of the German work. The similarity did not escape the notice of contemporary critics. Grimm wrote that the idea of *Jezennemours* seemed to be taken directly from Wieland's novel. He scored Mercier for having condensed the original, and indicated with perspicacity that the French tale grew worse in the second part, where it departed from it.[63]. Ten years later the resemblance of Monval in *Jezennemours* to Hippias in *Agathon* was pointed out by a German critic in the *Allgemeine Literaturzeitung.*[64]

[58] *Der Spiegel,* pp. 190f.
[59] Cf. above, p.
[60] Cited by Gervinus, *op. cit.,* IV, 341n., from *Maximen und Reflexionen über Literatur und Ethik.*
[61] Quérard, *la France littéraire,* X, 510.
[62] *Ibid.,* X, 509f., and *Allgemeine deutsche Bibliothek,* XXXII (1777), 127f.
[63] *Correspondance littéraire,* XI, 275f.
[64] May 22, 1786.

Monval, the freethinker in Mercier's novel, is indeed an exact copy of Wieland's Hippias, and his relationship to the hero, Jezennemours, is similar to that of Wieland's materialist to Agathon. Both support the young hero as a whim, both attempt to convert him to hedonistic doctrines. Both have a beautiful maid try to seduce him, and when this fails, both induce a former mistress to make him fall in love with her. Both arrange to have him meet her at a party. So it continues in the two novels. The guileless lad goes to the country to manage the estate of the mistress. He does not realize at first his fondness for her. She is in both cases a virtuous sinner who has lost her innocence in her fourteenth year. By the time he finally declares his affection she has fallen desperately in love with him. He relates to her the story of his youth, telling of his education by a religious order and of his love for a girl whom he saw for the first time at a religious festival. In both novels he flees after he is disenchanted by his patron as to the previous history of his beloved.

Mercier himself did not allow *Jezennemours* to be called a translation.[65] A translation it certainly is not in spite of the numerous similarities noted above. Many details in the two stories differ and the latter part of *Jezennemours* has no connection at all with *Agathon*. Mercier also omitted numerous long moral discussions and did not reproduce the sensuous atmosphere in which Wieland so excelled.

We see then a give-and-take between Mercier and Wieland. While the German borrowed many features of *l'An 2440* for *Der goldene Spiegel*, *Agathon* was adapted to French modes in Mercier's novel. Both Mercier and Wieland were moralists, and as far as it was possible in the Eighteenth Century, sociologists. Both were primarily interested in man and his relations to his fellows. While Mercier was for a Frenchman a surprisingly poor psychologist, Wieland was a German pioneer in the field of psychological portraiture. On the other hand, the author of *l'An 2440* was a more radical and a more manly advocate of reform and the new order than his rather spineless German contemporary.

---

[65] Cf. Béclard, *op. cit.*, 441n. Béclard refers to a statement in documents in possession of M. Duca, the grandson of Mercier, to which he had access.

VI

MERCIER AND GOETHE

SINCE THE discovery of *Wilhelm Meisters theatralische Sendung*
in 1910 and its publication in the following year,[1] there has been
much dispute whether the title should be taken in a literal or an
ironic sense. Scholarship has been largely occupied with the genesis and the relation of this early version to the *Lehrjahre,* while
ideas which it contains about the dramatist and his mission have received but little attention. They are, however, of great importance
since they represent the only discussion by Goethe of this problem
in the decade between 1775 and 1785. It is evident that Wilhelm's
mission is that of the playwright as well as the actor,[2] and indeed
Goethe speaks of his hero as his "beloved dramatic image."[3] In
his monograph on Mercier and the *Sturm und Drang,* San-Giorgiu
calls attention to a relationship between the dramatic conceptions
in the *Theatralische Sendung* and those in Mercier's *Nouvel essai
sur l'art dramatique* and suggests as a possibility that the former
may have sprung from a preoccupation of Goethe with the theater
which was due to the Frenchman's essay. San-Giorgiu states his
intention to make a comparative study of the ideas of the drama in
the *Nouvel essai* and the *Sendung*[4] and kindly informed me in the
spring of 1935 that he expected to publish his findings soon. The
present investigation, which takes account of his published re-
searches has proceeded quite independently. It is to be hoped that
when San-Giorgiu's results are available the two examinations of
Goethe's dependence on Mercier will make mutually supplemen-
tary contributions toward the solution of this interesting problem.

The present chapter will be found to deal mainly with this ques-

---

[1] *Wilhelm Meisters theatralische Sendung,* hrsg. von Harry Maync (Stuttgart und
Berlin, 1911). All references to the *Sendung* are to this edition.
[2] Cf. *Sendung,* pp. 182, 192, 198, 246, and excerpts of plays included.
[3] *Goethes Werke,* hrsg. im Auftrage der Großherzogin Sophie von Sachsen (Weimar,
1887-1919), *Briefe,* v, 352; in a letter to Frau von Stein, June 24, 1782.
[4] *Op. cit.,* pp. 48, 8.

tion.[5] As appears below, it was only through the *Nouvel essai*
that the French author exercised an influence on Goethe. Before
taking up the discussion of the relationship of this work to the
Theatralische Sendung, it will be of help to survey Goethe's acquaintance with Mercier's works so far as it can be documented.
We shall then examine his early contacts with the *Nouvel essai*
and the possible results of the impact of the ideas it contains on
him before he began work on the *Sendung.* The genesis of this still
presents some unsolved problems, and it will be necessary to
clarify these so far as possible before proceeding to our major
objective, the determination of the relationship between the conceptions of the drama as set forth in the two works. Finally, as a
matter of correlative interest, the chapter will conclude with a brief
review of Mercier's knowledge of Goethe's works.

Goethe's references to Mercier are neither numerous nor important, although they do span the last fifty-five years of his life.
A review of a theater almanac in the *Frankfurter* in 1773, if it can
be attributed to him, is the earliest known reference Goethe makes
to the Frenchman. Here the critic speaks of the impossibility before the year 2440 of having a stage on which only plays of Shakespeare and pieces like *Ugolino* and *Hermannsschlacht* will be
performed, an allusion to Mercier's utopian dream, *l'An 2440.*[6]
Some years later Goethe writes to Frau von Stein that he is sending
her the *Tableau de Paris* and some good peaches.[7] Not long after,
in 1784, he informs her that the picture of Paris both increased
and at the same time lessened his desire to see the French capital.[8]
His familiarity with the *Tableau de Paris* is further attested by the
fact that he appended a description of the two Rameaus in it to
his translation of Diderot's *Neveu de Rameau* (1805).[9] Goethe
also read *le Nouveau Paris,* having borrowed the entire work from
the Weimar library shortly after its appearance and kept it out

---

[5] Wilhelm's mission as a dramatist is no longer stressed in the *Lehrjahre* and many
of the passages which in the *Sendung* deal with the theory of the drama have been
either shortened or omitted entirely.

[6] *Werke,* XXXVII, 240; XXXVIII, 325.

[7] *Ibid.,* Briefe, v, 192; Sept. 19, 1781.

[8] *Ibid.,* Briefe, VI, 304; June 18.

[9] *Ibid.,* XLV, 230ff. The original is in Vol. XII of the *Tableau de Paris.*

for over two months.[10] Sartorius writes him early in 1802 that
Mme de Staël, Sieyès, and Mercier were not unfavorably impressed by Kant's philosophy, but Mercier alone was willing to
defend the German thinker in public.[11] As late as March of the
year before his death Goethe made an entry, "Diderot, Mercier,"
in his diary and crossed it out, thus signifying that he had completed the item.[12]

Goethe also alludes to Mercier as a dramatist. He describes to
Schiller a performance of *Der Essigmann* at Weimar in 1798 in
which Iffland played the vinegar merchant with what he considered great artistry and delicacy.[13] In the thirteenth book of
Dichtung und Wahrheit, written in 1813, he speaks of the time
when the growing bourgeois spirit was reflected by the popularity
of such family dramas as Diderot's *Hausvater, Der Essigmann,*
and others. A plan for this book of the autobiography contains
the entry, "Ekhof's personality—translation of French dramas—
Der Essigmann."[14] Besides this piece, which was performed again
on the Weimar stage under his direction in 1802,[15] Goethe may also
have known Mercier's *Déserteur.*[16]

Goethe may have learned of other works of Mercier through
the *Correspondance littéraire* of Melchior Grimm, which was designed to acquaint Germans with the outstanding literary events of
the French capital. It was, we know, received biweekly at Gotha,
and then passed on to Weimar.[17] It is also possible that his attention may first have been called to the *Nouvel essai* by Grimm's

[10] Cf. E. von Keudell, *Goethe als Benutzer der Weimarer Bibliothek* (Weimar,
1931), p. 41; from Dec. 6, 1800 to Feb. 7, 1801.

[11] Cf. *Goethes Briefwechsel mit Georg und Caroline Sartorius*, hrsg. von Else von
Monroy (Weimar, 1931), p. 9; Jan. 11. Mercier read a long paper on Kant to the
Institut de France in 1801. Cf. L. Wittmer, *Charles de Villers* (Genève, 1908), pp.
108f.

[12] *Werke*, Tagebücher, XIII, 267.

[13] *Ibid.*, Briefe, XIII, 124; April 25, 1798.

[14] *Ibid.*, XXVIII, 193f., 369f. Cf. also *Deutsches Theater Werke*, XL, 177.

[15] Burkhardt, *Das Repertoire des Weimarischen Theaters unter Goethes Leitung*,
p. 113.

[16] Cf. *Werke*, Tagebücher, II, 79; Aug. 5, 1797. This entry might, however, refer
to Sedaine's operetta. There is perhaps also a reference to Mercier's play in the
Campagne in Frankreich, Werke, XXXIII, 142.

[17] Cf. H. Morsch, "Goethes Festspiel: Des Epimenides Erwachen," *Goethe-Jahrbuch*,
XIV (1893), 221.

review written in July, 1774. Grimm was not too enthusiastic, but he did admit that Mercier's treatise contained several true and important ideas and showed a great love of humanity and an exaggerated youthful enthusiasm.[18] There is, to be sure, no evidence that Goethe read the *Correspondance* before he went to Weimar, although there is a mention of Grimm himself in that part of *Dichtung und Wahrheit* concerned with Goethe's stay in Strasbourg.[19] The task of discovering the "transmetteur" who conveys the literary product from the "émetteur" to the "récepteur," to use the terms coined by Van Tieghem,[20] is often very difficult, and it is not possible here to establish with any degree of certainty how Goethe became acquainted with the *Nouvel essai*.

The *Nouvel essai* was widely reviewed by German journals in the middle and late seventies. The conservative *Göttingische Anzeigen* in 1774 contains an objective summary of its contents, and stresses its ardor and its well-balanced thoughts.[21] In the following year the rationalistic *Neue Bibliothek der schönen Wissenschaften* devotes forty-five pages to Mercier's treatise, and justifies the length of its comment by the importance of his views and the warmth of his style. A chapter-by-chapter summary is given, accompanied by a few notes in which the validity of certain statements is questioned.[22] In 1777 the *Allgemeines Verzeichnis* considers the *Nouvel essai* so well known that it is not necessary to go into detail about it when speaking of the translation,[23] and the *Almanach der deutschen Musen* refers to its fiery declamations, its attack on the French classical stage, and its new, often paradoxical ideas as already familiar to Germans.[24] According to the *Allgemeine deutsche Bibliothek* in the next year, Mercier's work deserved to be more familiar in Germany, but its translator could have enhanced its value if he had added notes limiting its exaggerations and correcting its errors.[25] Mercier's essay became,

[18] *Correspondance*, x, 463f.
[19] Book xi; *Werke*, xxviii, 53. Cf. also *Werke*, xxix, 168.
[20] *La Littérature comparée* (Paris, 1931), p. 60.
[21] Oct. 22.
[22] xvii, 98ff.
[23] P. 132.
[24] Pp. 13f.
[25] xxxiv, 496ff.

then, very popular in Germany immediately after it appeared. It was also read throughout the rest of the century. Eschenburg's *Beispielsammlung zur Theorie und Literatur der schönen Wissenschaften* refers to it in 1793,[26] while the 1792-1799 edition of Sulzer's *Allgemeine Theorie der schönen Künste* finds that it sets forth many true, although often exaggerated rules.[27] Finally, in 1802, the *Allgemeine Literaturzeitung* alludes in a review of Mercier's edition of Schiller's *Jungfrau* to the French author's prejudice against the classical tradition as expounded in his *Nouvel essai.*[28]

However Goethe may first have learned of Mercier's treatise, whether it was from Grimm's *Correspondence* or from the early review in the *Göttingische,* it seemed in 1774-1775 so important to him that he induced his acquaintance Heinrich Leopold Wagner to undertake a translation of it. Toward the end of the year 1774 Wagner, whom Goethe calls "a member of the Strasbourg and later of the Frankfort group,"[29] came to the city on the Main, where he earned a scant living as translator and hack writer.[30] Born in Strasbourg in 1747, he had an excellent knowledge of French, had already translated Montesquieu's *Temple de Gnide* in 1770, and was also to make a German version of *la Brouette du vinaigrier* in his first year's residence in Frankfort. "Not without intelligence, talent, and learning,"[31] and extremely interested in things French, Wagner must have seemed to Goethe the ideal man to translate Mercier's disquisition.

The fortune of the translation of the *Nouvel essai* before it appeared in 1776 presents at least one interesting but probably insoluble problem. From the *Frankfurter gelehrte Anzeigen* in 1775 we learn that it is to be published at Easter of the same year with comments and additions by Goethe.[32] Contemporaneously, the *Neue Bibliothek der schönen Wissenschaften* states that the trans-

---

[26] VII, 217.
[27] Neue vermehrte zweite Auflage, I, 713b.
[28] May 26.
[29] *Dichtung und Wahrheit, Werke,* XXVIII, 251.
[30] For Wagner in Frankfort, cf. Erich Schmidt, *Heinrich Leopold Wagner,* 2d ed. (Jena, 1879), pp. 15ff.
[31] *Dichtung und Wahrheit, Werke,* XXVIII, 251.
[32] Cited by Schmidt, *op. cit.,* 1 ed. (Jena, 1875), p. 81n.

lation is being made under Goethe's supervision and that it will be published by Meyer in Lemgo.[33] Toward the end of this year, however, the *Frankfurter* notes that it is being printed by Schwikkert in Leipsic and not with notes and comments, but with contributions from Goethe's *Brieftasche*.[34] When it finally appeared in 1776 without the name of either the author or the translator, it was seen to contain, besides several poems and an article on art, a short introduction by Goethe. In this he confirms the report that he had promised to publish the translation and to supply it with comments. While admitting that in the meantime he had lost all desire to annotate it, since everybody was eager to do so, he nevertheless does not deny that there is in it much that is good, true, and noble, and that could be useful to Germany. The contributions from the *Brieftasche* were so evidently without connection with the translation that the *Göttingische* is unable to explain how they came to be added.[35] Two years later, in 1778, the *Allgemeine deutsche Bibliothek* states in quite unfriendly language that the "splendid remarks about dramatic art or lack of art" which had been promised, were replaced by the "most trivial stuff imaginable."[36]

It cannot be explained definitely why Goethe no longer wished to add notes to the translation. His own excuse is that everybody else was eager to comment on it, and the extensive review in the *Neue Bibliothek der schönen Wissenschaften* in 1775 may have seemed to him to obviate the necessity for further discussion. It has also been suggested that Goethe changed his mind because of the publication of Wagner's *Prometheus, Deukalion und seine Rezensenten*,[37] a satire directed against the critics of *Werther*, in which, for instance, Nicolai is represented as an orangutan and Claudius as "nightowls and frogs." *Prometheus* appeared in February, 1775,[38] and was at first attributed to Goethe himself.[39] Since

[33] XVII, 343. Cf. also M. Morris, *Der junge Goethe*, neue Ausgabe (Leipzig, 1909-1912), VI, 522.

[34] Cited by Schmidt, *op. cit.*, 1 ed., p. 81n.

[35] Oct. 31, 1776.

[36] XXXIV, 496ff.

[37] By Düntzer; cf. San-Giorgiu, *op. cit.*, p. 48.

[38] Schmidt, *Wagner*, 2d ed., pp. 32ff.

[39] By Merck. Cf. Morris, *Der junge Goethe*, V, 246f.; in a letter to Nicolai, May 6, 1775.

it tended to draw him into conflict with the men of letters who had been insulted, Goethe announced in April that not he, but Wagner was the author of the farce.[40] Wagner still visited the Goethe home as late as the thirtieth of March, that is, after the publication of the burlesque,[41] and we know that the two men were still in contact in August.[42] There is also record of a correspondence between them that lasted from early in September to the middle of October, while Wagner was staying in the neighboring village of Höchst.[43] This may indicate that they were still on friendly terms, which would invalidate the theory that Wagner's farce was the reason for Goethe's change of mind. On the other hand, the correspondence may just as well have been concerned with Goethe's new plan for his part of the translation. Still another possibility is that Goethe lost interest because of the numerous other projects which he had at the time. It hardly seems possible, however, that he altered his design because he wished to treat the problems of the poet and the actor at great length and in a more independent form.[44] All we can say with certainty is that when Goethe read the *Nouvel essai* in 1774 he found it valuable enough to have translated into German, and that scarcely a year later his enthusiasm for it had cooled.

The translation itself, attributed by Hamann to Lenz[45] and by Mercier to Schiller,[46] reproduces the original very exactly, adding only a few unimportant notes.[47] In one Wagner states his hope that Riccaut de la Marlinière might be banished forever from the German stage. In another he excuses Mercier for unfair criticism of the Homeric poems, because he was a "human being and a Frenchman." He also includes a letter from Lenz dealing with Goethe's *Prometheus*. Contemporary criticism seemed satisfied with the

[40] Morris, *Der junge Goethe*, v, 240.
[41] *Ibid.*, v, 26f., vi, 442.
[42] *Ibid.*, v, 469; letter of Miller to Kayser, Aug. 28.
[43] *Ibid.*, vi, 499ff. This is the last we hear of any personal relationship between Goethe and Wagner, although Goethe later unjustly accused his former friend of having plagiarized his plan for *Faust* in *Die Kindermörderin* (*Werke*, xxviii, 252). Wagner returned to Strasbourg in the summer of 1776 and died there in 1779.
[44] Suggested as a possibility by San-Giorgiu, *op. cit.*, p. 48.
[45] Gildemeister, *Hamanns Leben*, ii, 378.
[46] *Satires contre Racine et Boileau*, p. 45.
[47] Cf. Schmidt, *Wagner*, 2d ed., p. 132n., and Rosanow, *Lenz*, p. 480. Wagner's translation was not available to me.

quality of the translation. The *Allgemeines Verzeichnis* in 1777 finds it quite excellent despite several blunders.[48]

Goethe's *Brieftasche* contains five poems and two articles in prose.[49] These deal chiefly with the relation of the artist or sculptor to his work and, as was noted by contemporary criticism, have little or no connection with Mercier's treatise. Goethe admits this and calls them a collection of "whims of the moment." They were written between 1771 and 1775. The latest one which can be dated is the *Dritte Wallfahrt nach Erwins Grabe,* which has to do with the sentiments Goethe experienced as he climbed the cathedral tower in Strasbourg in July, 1775.[50]

The short introduction that precedes these contributions is of greater interest to us. We find here remarks about the stage that point toward the *Sendung* and at the same time seem to reflect the thoughts of Mercier. The French author advises the destruction of all treatises on poetry, among which he generously includes his own.[51] He protests against the tyranny of five acts and maintains that the breadth of the action and the subject should determine the length of the divisions and their number.[52] The unities are likewise of little importance, he contends, with the exception of the unity of action.[53] He also condemns the sacred rules of good taste, which conceal pettiness and coldness of ideas.[54] Similarly, Goethe states that it is almost time people stop discussing the form of dramatic pieces, and arguing about their length, their beginning, middle, and end, and about the unities. That is not the method of the author of the *Nouvel essai,* he continues, who drives directly at the content. Goethe also holds that it is better to throw away the rules even if a confused play should result rather than to compose a cold one.

The Frenchman remarks that style is to the soul what walking is to the body. He counsels the youthful author to avoid the style of others and to create his own. Style should be the "naïve expres-

---

[48] P. 132.
[49] *Goethes Brieftasche* is reprinted by Morris, *Der junge Goethe,* v, 344f.
[50] July 13. Cf. *Der junge Goethe,* v, 279.
[51] *Nouvel essai,* p. xiv.
[52] *Ibid.,* pp. 253, 254, 256f.
[53] *Ibid.,* pp. 145f., 147.
[54] *Ibid.,* p. vii.

sion of the soul."[55] Finally, Mercier wants everything that is even
faintly reminiscent of the novel to be avoided in the drama.[56]
Goethe's sentiments are again very similar. There is, he says, another form, an "inner form," which must not only be understood
but also felt with the heart. It contains every kind of form, is
granted to every true poet and cannot be learned. The term comes
from Shaftesbury, to be sure,[57] but the idea is to be found in the
advice Mercier gives to the young poet, cited above. Goethe is likewise disgusted that so many people, due to the lack of the sense of
inner form, break down novels into plays.

These opinions of Goethe, then, show a definite similarity to
those of Mercier. It seems as if he must have chosen certain sentiments from the *Nouvel essai* with which he was in accord and
expressed them in his own words. Even the French author's famous
line, "Fall, fall, O walls that separate the genres,"[58] seems to be
reiterated, with a broader significance to be sure, in his apologetic
hope that the *"salto mortale"* from the drama to art would not
hinder the enjoyment of his readers.

This consideration of inner form is the basis for the discussion
of the unities in the second chapter of the second book of the
Theatralische Sendung. It is followed in the *Brieftasche* by the
statement that he who really wants to work for the stage should
not concern himself with nature and should not plan anything
except "was sich auf Brettern zwischen *Latten, Pappen*deckel und
Leinwand durch Puppen, vor Kindern aufführen läßt." This seems
to point toward the *Sendung,* where a puppet show is presented
for the child Wilhelm and his brothers and sisters.[59] Later Wilhelm
uses *"Pappe,* Farbe und Papier" to aid him in his puppet plays.[60]
As a young man he enjoys standing for hours backstage in the
"Balken- und *Lattengerippe,*" where the "ausgestopften Lämm-
chen, Wasserfälle von Zindel," and the *"pappenen* Rosenstöcke"
charm his imagination.[61] It is possible, then, that Goethe may al-

[55] *Ibid.,* pp. 334, 331, 330.
[56] *Ibid.,* p. 106.
[57] "Inward form." Cf. *Der junge Goethe,* VI, 523.
[58] *Nouvel essai,* p. 105n.
[59] *Theatralische Sendung,* pp. 4ff. The italics here and in the following are mine.
[60] *Ibid.,* p. 17.
[61] *Ibid.,* p. 40.

ready have conceived the plan of the *Sendung* in 1775 at the
time when he came in contact with the *Nouvel essai*. It is therefore
of great importance to investigate the dramatic concepts in
Goethe's novel with reference to those in Mercier's work. If the
similarity proves to be great, then the probability of influence
cannot be denied.

Before undertaking this comparison, however, it will be necessary to consider the genesis of the *Sendung* in some detail. The
first definite proof we have that Goethe was working on it is a
note in his diary in February, 1777, that he had dictated some of
it in his garden.[62] The first book was ended early in the next year.[63]
The next part was not completed until four years later, in the
summer of 1782.[64] The work then proceeded more rapidly, the
third book being finished by November of the same year, and the
fourth a year later.[65] The last two books were brought to a close in
the fall of 1784 and 1785 respectively.[66] Goethe continues to refer
to work on *Wilhelm Meister,* but that does not concern us here.
It is, on the other hand, of some importance to us to discover if
there is any evidence to support the contention that he wrote any
part of the *Sendung* in his Frankfort days. The various references
that might lead us to conclude that he had put most of the first
book on paper between 1773 and 1775 prove to be false or not
pertinent.[67] On October 31, 1777, he wrote Frau von Stein that he
had taken a *"salto mortale"* over three fateful chapters of his
novel.[68] This can only allude to those chapters that make the
transition from the boyhood of Wilhelm to his affair with Mariane.[69] Now Goethe had already devoted himself to his novel three
times in 1777, before October, and it is consequently impossible
that more than the first few chapters could have been written
earlier than that. Hence, for instance, the report of Philipp Seidel

---

[62] *Werke*, Tagebücher, I, 34; Feb. 16.
[63] *Ibid.*, Tagebücher, I, 59; Jan. 2.
[64] *Ibid.*, Briefe, VI, 50; Aug. 29, to Frau von Stein.
[65] *Ibid.*, Briefe, VI, 88, 210; to Frau von Stein.
[66] *Ibid.*, Briefe, VI, 368, VII, 120; to Frau von Stein.
[67] For this and the following cf. W. Krogmann, "Die Anfänge des Wilhelm Meister,"
Zeitschrift für deutsche Philologie, LVII (1932), 56ff.
[68] *Werke, Briefe*, III, 182.
[69] There are really four chapters, x-xiii.

from the end of the year 1775, that he was copying a novel of which Goethe was the author,[70] cannot refer to the *Sendung*.

It is true, to be sure, that many of the views and events in the *Sendung* mirror earlier experiences and reading. Goethe's childhood preoccupation with puppets,[71] his youthful familiarity with the works of Corneille and Racine,[72] his interest in Shakespeare,[73] his acquaintance with Lenz's *Anmerkungen übers Theater*,[74] perhaps also with Diderot's *Paradoxe sur le comédien*,[75] his knowledge of the English comic novel,[76] all are reflected in the first version of *Wilhelm Meister*. The excerpts from Wilhelm's plays date back for the most part to Goethe's student days in Leipsic.[77] Many traits of the actress Corona Schröter have gone over into Mariane.[78] Goethe's activity as actor and manager of the amateur theater in Weimar, for which he wrote incidental pieces for birthday celebrations, planned scenery, and took care of other details, was likewise of importance for the conception of the *Sendung*.[79] Contact with such men of the theater as Schröder, Ekhof, and Dalberg also furnished him with information about the stage.[80] Goethe may have read Löwen's *Geschichte des deutschen Theaters* (1766), Schmid's *Chronologie des deutschen Theaters* (1775), and later Plümicke's *Theatergeschichte von Berlin* (1781).[81] The *Theatralische Sendung* contains ideas and experiences, then, which its author had in

---

[70] Cited by Krogmann, *op. cit.*, p. 60.

[71] Cf. *Dichtung und Wahrheit, Werke*, XXVI, 74f.

[72] *Werke*, XXVI, 167ff.

[73] *Cf. Zum Shakespears Tag* (1771), reprinted by Morris, *Der junge Goethe*, II, 137ff.

[74] Cf. Walzel in *Goethes Werke*, Festausgabe, hrsg. von Robert Petsch (Leipzig, 1926-1927), X, 343; and *Werke*, XXVIII, 75.

[75] Cf. C. A. Eggert, "Goethe und Diderot," *Euphorion*, IV (1897), 301ff.

[76] Of Goldsmith, Sterne, Fielding, and Smollett. Cf. Kurt Jahn, "Wilhelm Meisters theatralische Sendung und der humoristische Roman der Engländer," *Germanisch-Romanische Monatsschrift*," V (1913), 225ff.

[77] Cf. M. Morris in *Euphorion*, XIX (1912), 381f.

[78] Cf. H. Berendt, *Goethes "Wilhelm Meister"* (Dortmund, 1911), p. 16.

[79] Cf. *Werke*, Tagebücher, I, 117; May 13, 1780, and A. Diezmann, *Goethe und die lustige Zeit in Weimar* (Leipzig, 1857), pp. 155ff.

[80] Cf. A. Köster, "Wilhelm Meisters theatralische Sendung," *Zeitschrift für den deutschen Unterricht*, XXVI (1912), 219f., and *Werke*, Tagebücher, I, 41; July 3, 1777.

[81] Cf. B. Seuffert, *Goethes Theater-Roman* (Graz, Wien, Leipzig, 1924), p. 7: "Wie Berührungen vermuten lassen." I have found no direct evidence.

his youth and in his university and Frankfort days as well as later in Weimar. Goethe may have conceived the idea of composing the *Sendung* before 1777. Our examination has shown, however, that he could not have actually written much of it before that time, or some two years after he had read the *Nouvel essai*.

The *Sendung* gives a picture of the German stage from the days of Gottsched to a time shortly before the performance of Shakespeare in Hamburg in 1776. The second book and portions of the first and third books deal with the theory of the drama. In general, Wilhelm's beliefs are surprisingly conservative. They seem at times to represent Goethe's development before he became acquainted with Shakespeare rather than to give his position around 1782. Nevertheless, there are numerous opinions expressed that indicate more than a mere acceptance of the classical tradition. These are the concepts which resemble those to be found in the *Nouvel essai*.

We are now finally in a position to undertake the examination of the similarities in the two works. There are five aspects in which the dramatic notions in the first three books of the *Sendung* resemble those in the French author's discourse on the theater, while a large number of likenesses of lesser consequence can also be pointed out. In the first place, both authors emphasize the importance of the stage as a social force. For Mercier the stage is the place where legislation meets with the least resistance, where the viciousness of laws can be rectified, where all that can be accomplished which they leave undone.[82] The poet is a "lawgiver," the mouthpiece of virtue and the scourge of vice.[83] It is his task to make the spectator an instrument on which he can play and to inflame the crowd with his majestic thought.[84] He can engrave in the hearts of men respect for their fellow beings.[85] The theater, the "chef-d'œuvre of society," is the only place where men's voices may rise in concert and where men become aware of the divinity of their souls.[86] It develops the tenderness we have for our fellow

---

[82] *Nouvel essai,* pp. vi, 260.
[83] *Ibid.,* p. vi.
[84] *Ibid.,* pp. 234, vi.
[85] *Ibid.,* p. 8.
[86] *Ibid.,* pp. 3f.

beings and by accelerating the course of our ideas, perfects our reason and sensibility.[87] It should be a useful pleasure, a decent rest and recreation.[88] The state would be wise to supervise the pleasures of its citizens and to provide plays for their amusement.[89]

Compare Wilhelm's views on the social significance of the stage. In Chapter XV of the first book he expounds his views on the mission of the theater, attributing the effect of the drama, to be sure, to the actor rather than to the author. Wilhelm demands that the player should be as highly esteemed as the preacher, who is honored as the announcer of the word of God, for theater and pulpit are really complementary.[90] The actor reveals the voice of nature to the spectators, and attacks their hardened hearts with joy, seriousness, and pain in order to call forth the heavenly tone of relationship and love among them. At the theater, all men feel related and confess that they are brothers, as they are drawn upwards, touched by one common feeling.[91] The theater is a place of safety against boredom. The factory owner from whom Wilhelm collects a debt knows no better way to keep his workers out of trouble than to have them give plays.[92] The great influence of the stage on the culture of a nation and of the world as a whole is frequently the subject of conversation between Mariane and her friends.[93]

These speeches of Wilhelm occur at the beginning of his contact with the theater. They express his inner conviction of its value and intimate the method of its appeal.[94] This appeal is an emotional one; and that is our second point. That the theater is the most efficacious means of appealing to the innate sympathy of men is a keynote of the *Nouvel essai*. In the very first paragraph Mercier states that the purpose of the theater is to unite mankind by the

[87] *Ibid.*, p. 2.
[88] *Ibid.*, p. 216.
[89] *Ibid.*, p. 213n.
[90] *Sendung,* pp. 34f., 61.
[91] *Ibid.*, pp. 34f.
[92] *Ibid.*, p. 139.
[93] *Ibid.*, pp. 43f.
[94] The striking similarity of Schiller's *Schaubühne als eine moralische Anstalt betrachtet* (1784) to both the *Nouvel essai* and the *Sendung* in regard to the social value of the stage and its emotional appeal, points to the fact that these ideas were in the air at the time. Cf. below, pp. 139ff.

sentiment of compassion and pity: "que l'image qu'il (le spectacle) présentera serve à lier entr'eux les hommes par le sentiment victorieux de la *compassion* et de la pitié."[95] Its object is to exercise our sensibility and put into action the faculties of sympathy and commiseration: "Qu'est-ce que l'art dramatique? C'est celui qui par excellence exerce toute notre sensibilité, *met en action* ces riches facultés que nous avons reçues de la nature."[96] At the theater the souls of the spectators are enkindled by an electric movement. There one finds the truth by the electric shock of sentiment: "C'est là que la pensée majestueuse d'un seul homme irait *enflammer* toutes les âmes par une *commotion électrique*. C'est là . . . que l'homme . . . trouve le vrai, par un *coup électrique* du sentiment."[97] Mercier explains the Aristotelian purging of the passions. According to his interpretation the evil passions can be cured only by the strengthening of the emotions of pity and sympathy.[98] The effect of the theater, the French author maintains, consists in impressions rather than in precepts. The soul of the spectator rises to the level of the great action portrayed and is eager to imitate it. The soul becomes one with that of the tragic hero and suffers perhaps more than he does: "L'effet du théâtre consiste en *impressions*. Elle (l'âme) monte au niveau de cette grande et belle action, elle *brûle de l'imiter*."[99]

Wilhelm's views are couched in almost identical terms. After he sees the acrobatic stunts of the wandering troupe he exclaims: "What author, what actor would not feel happy if he could give the people the sentiment of compassion for humanity, if he could enkindle them with the idea of happiness and unhappiness, wisdom and stupidity, and bring their souls into a state of movement?"

Wenn man dem Volke oder den Besten daraus das *Mitgefühl* alles Menschlichen geben und sie mit der Vorstellung des Glückes und Unglückes, der Weisheit und Torheit, des Unsinnes und der Albernheit *entzünden* und erschüttern und ihr stockendes Innere *in Bewegung setzen könnte*.[100]

[95] *Nouvel essai*, p. 1. The italics in this and the following quotations are mine.
[96] *Ibid.*, p. 7.
[97] *Ibid.*, pp. vi, 8.
[98] *Ibid.*, p. 269.
[99] *Ibid.*, pp. 10f.
[100] *Sendung*, pp. 148f. This passage in a modified form is also in the *Lehrjahre, Werke*, XXI, 164f.

How satisfying it would be if he could spread good and noble thoughts by means of an electric shock: "Wenn man gute, edle, der Menschheit würdige Gefühle eben so allgemein durch einen *elektrischen Schlag* ausbreiten . . . könnte."[101] If the theater succeeds in these points, Wilhelm concludes, then perhaps the purging of the passions of which the Greek philosopher speaks will have taken place. Following the successful performance of his play Wilhelm is convinced that the good and noble deeds and the lifelike impression would be felt by everyone in the audience when he went back home to his family: "Daß jeder einzeln zu Hause mit den Seinigen und in den Seinigen die guten edeln Taten und lebendigen *Eindrücke* des Stückes *nachempfinden* würde."[102] Finally, we are told later that the effect of art is that each person experiences his own joy or sorrow in the fate of others.[103]

It is now evident that Goethe is operating in the same realm of thought as Mercier. The surprising similarity of their conception of the use of the stage and of the way in which it joins mankind together by the bonds of sympathy, and the fact that the ideas in the *Sendung* are occasionally expressed in the very terms of the Frenchman lead us to conclude that Goethe had the *Nouvel essai* clearly in mind when he wrote the passages we have just considered.

This conclusion becomes even more certain when we turn to our third point, the exalted position of the poet. In speaking of Corneille, Mercier remarks that the sublime is the image of a great soul.[104] Elsewhere he instructs the poet to arouse detestation for falseness, sordid self-interest, ingratitude, insolence, lack of sympathy, disdain, and prejudice.[105] He warns the poet that his work is not a thing to be performed in a routine fashion. "Do not profane a sacred art," he exclaims, "by transforming it into an unpleasant task."[106] The poet must possess the sacred ardor which is necessary for poetic composition, must be moved by all generous actions and

---

[101] *Sendung,* pp. 148f. The expression "elektrischer Schlag" is also to be found in Wieland's *Briefe an einen jungen Dichter.* Cf. above, p. 99n.

[102] *Sendung,* p. 209. A curious parallel is to be found in Iffland's *Theatralische Laufbahn,* cf. below, p. 200n.

[103] *Sendung,* p. 381.

[104] *Nouvel essai,* pp. 26f.

[105] *Ibid.,* pp. 127f.

[106] *Ibid.,* p. 192.

inspired by the desire for truth.[107] The ideas of the poet must flow
in a torrent. He must enjoy himself while creating, he must be
deeply interested in his subject and experience the same transports
as if he were in love.[108] Poetry must not be a relaxation or peaceful
enjoyment for him.[109] The poet must know his own soul and must
have established the correct harmony between himself and others:
"Il aura établi un *juste rapport* entre le monde et lui."[110] He must
have learned to rise above the petty and miserable passions of the
earth if he wishes to hover over the world and examine it from a
superior point of view. If he loves mankind and has the divine fire
of humanity which ennobles genius, then he is a benefactor of
humanity.[111] Humanity and universal benevolence must be en-
graved on his heart.[112]

Wilhelm's views are again very similar. A true poet, begins
Goethe's hero, following his discussion of Corneille and the unities with Werner, must have a great soul. Only such a man can
succeed in showing the passions that terrify us, the unhappy fate
that makes us feel pity. Only he can cause us to despise falsehood
and to hate wanton misuse of power.[113] Wilhelm tells his friend
that the work of the poet fills the whole soul and cannot be produced in a few random hours. The poet, he continues, is the re-
cipient of the most precious gifts of heaven and earth, and must
live in his subject and dwell in inner happiness with his treasures.
The poet already possesses and hence does not need to strive for
a harmonious adjustment to the world and his fellow men: "nach
dem Mitgefühl sein selbst in andern, nach einem *harmonischen
Zusammensein* mit vielen oft unvereinbaren Dingen." He must
also be like a god, above the petty worries and desires of the
average man. He sees the confusion of passions and the inexplicable
riddles of misunderstanding of others and experiences the joys and
sorrows of their fates. He is a teacher, a prophet, the friend of the
gods and of man at the same time.[114]

[107] *Ibid.*, pp. 318, 220.
[108] *Ibid.*, pp. 192f.
[109] *Ibid.*, p. 319.
[110] *Ibid.*, p. 185.
[111] *Ibid.*, pp. 183n., 8f.
[112] *Ibid.*, p. 220.
[113] *Sendung*, pp. 81f.
[114] *Ibid.*, pp. 87f.

The high position that both Mercier and Goethe give the poet, who, possessed of the divine gift, stands above mankind and leads it upward and onward, is another case of correspondence between the *Sendung* and the *Nouvel essai*. The similarity is much greater than that which has been suggested between Goethe's work and the chapter entitled "Dichter" in Sulzer's *Allgemeine Theorie der schönen Künste* (1771-1774)[115] or Wieland's *Briefe an einen jungen Dichter*.[116] The first two of these "letters" appeared in the summer and fall of 1782 in the *Deutscher Merkur*,[117] at a time when Goethe was completing the second and beginning the third books of the *Sendung*. They were intended as an answer to the many young poetasters who bothered the author of *Agathon* with poems and letters. Wieland shows at great length the difficulties that beset those who devote their lives to poetry alone, and emphasizes the necessity of earning a living.[118] Here we often find the viewpoint of Werner rather than that of Wilhelm. Both Wieland and Werner state, for instance, that the poet cannot live like a bird in carefree enjoyment of the world.[119] Wieland, to be sure, does express some sympathy for the person who wishes to dedicate his whole life to the muses.[120] Finally, the same words (*"unwiderstehlicher Trieb"*) are used by both Wieland and Werner.[121] Nevertheless, these similarities are slight, and although Goethe may have been familiar with the *Briefe*, they seem to have exercised no significant influence on the *Sendung*.

Our fourth topic is the similarity in the viewpoint of Goethe and Mercier toward the unities. The French author instructs the playwright to cast off every shameful yoke, to free himself from ancient slavery, to disdain restraint, even if Corneille did follow the bothersome rules. Although it is necessary to be of a definite height to join a certain regiment, the most courageous soldiers

---

[115] Sulzer's essay lacks the enthusiasm that is to be found in both Mercier's and Goethe's works. Sulzer also emphasizes the necessity for reason to control poetic creation. Cf. 2d ed. (Leipzig, 1778-1779), I, 335. Sulzer does, however, call the poet the "Prophet, Lehrmeister, Wohltäter seiner Nation"; I, 336.

[116] Suggested by Walzel in *Goethes Werke*, Festausgabe, x, 344.

[117] August, 3. Teil, pp. 129ff.; Oct., 4. Teil, pp. 57ff.

[118] *Deutscher Merkur*, 3. Teil, p. 135.

[119] *Ibid.*, 3. Teil, p. 135; *Sendung*, p. 89.

[120] *Deutscher Merkur*, 3. Teil, p. 137.

[121] *Ibid.*, p. 132; *Sendung*, p. 90.

are often shorter, and the leader is frequently the smallest man in the army, Mercier argues in support of his attack on petrified rules.[122] The Frenchman is against rigid categories in art. The poet, he thinks, must have an unobscured view and no longer feel his genius limited by the regulations of an attenuated art.[123] Mercier also rebels against the exact division of the tragic passions into terror and pity. He holds that they exist in infinite combinations, approach one another, subdivide, melt into each other. He claims, therefore, that they should have as many names as there are shades of meaning. It is useless, he concludes, to use the terms terror and pity in any restricted sense.[124]

One unity, according to the author of the *Nouvel essai,* must be scrupulously respected. That is the unity of action or "interest." It is the only essential rule, and it does not depend on man's caprices. Any play in which the chief interest is broken is an imperfect work. The true drama always tends toward one and the same effect, toward a completely unified action.[125] There must be a definite order, a just progression, and an imperceptible gradation of events. That is more important than the number of acts or their length.[126] The characters must be closely bound together without any one predominating, and they must not decide the action.[127] The word "drama," Mercier notes, comes from the Greek and means action. It is the most honorable title that can be given a piece, because without action there is neither interest nor life.[128] Mercier acknowledges Aristotle as an upholder of the unity of action, but condemns him for believing that customs and morals are not essential to tragedy.[129]

In regard to the other two unities the French author wishes greater leniency. He advises the playwright to enlarge his scene of action in so far as it is compatible with probability and provided that any change of location be made only between the acts.[130]

[122] *Nouvel essai,* p. 254.
[123] *Ibid.,* p. 105n.
[124] *Ibid.,* p. 281n.
[125] *Ibid.,* p. 147.
[126] *Ibid.,* pp. 256f.
[127] *Ibid.,* pp. 106f.
[128] *Ibid.,* p. 94n.
[129] *Ibid.,* pp. 265f.
[130] *Ibid.,* p. 146.

The limit of time may also be extended to three days, for a strict rule would make beauties of a new order impossible. Sixty hours may pass as quickly as twenty-four, since the spectator when moved or interested does not hold a watch in his hand.[131]

In general, then, Mercier prefers what he considers to be the principles of "good sense" to the theories of Aristotle. He instructs the poet to flee the critics who come forward as guides and imagine they can trace the course of genius with words. He has only condemnation for those men of letters who particularize that which should be generalized, who isolate related truths and hence shed only an equivocal and doubtful light on art.[132]

Wilhelm's approach to the problem of the unities is again not unlike Mercier's. Wilhelm and Werner discuss the unities in connection with the *Discours* of Corneille. While the common-sense merchant thinks that there are fixed precepts with which every author must comply, Wilhelm, while not denying the validity of the rules entirely, does not believe that they can be applied like weights and measures.[133] He then examines the unities in detail and in terms that remind us of Goethe's comments in the *Brieftasche*. Wilhelm is convinced that it is dangerous to enter the field of drama from the side of the unities. Although he does not condemn any rule that is taken from the nature of things, he considers such an approach awkward. In his opinion the drama is a whole and must not be broken into parts. If there are to be unities at all, why should their number be limited to three?[134] Just as Mercier suggests the existence of an infinite number of compounds of fear and pity, so Goethe-Wilhelm, perhaps having a passage of Lenz's *Anmerkungen übers Theater* (1774) in mind,[135] speaks of a dozen unities: those of custom, tone, language, character, costume, decorations, and lighting, which are of equal importance with the unities of time and place.

The unity of action, however, is more important than those of

---

[131] *Ibid.*, pp. 31n., 145f.
[132] *Ibid.*, pp. 96, 318.
[133] *Sendung*, pp. 67f.
[134] *Ibid.*, pp. 75ff.
[135] *Gesammelte Schriften*, hrsg. von Franz Blei (München und Leipzig, 1909-1913), I, 238: ". . . Hundert Einheiten will ich euch angeben, die alle immer doch die *eine* bleiben. Einheit der Sprache, Einheit der Religion, Einheit der Sitten."

time and place; it is indispensable.[136] It has been suggested that this view may reflect the memory of a phrase of Diderot, that nothing is beautiful that has no unity.[137] Still, there is no evidence that Goethe knew the theoretical writings of Diderot on the drama either in the original or in Lessing's translation, although he was acquainted with the Frenchman's narrative works and translated *le Neveu de Rameau* in 1804-1805.[138] Returning to our subject, we find Wilhelm maintaining that the drama must have continuous action and that the characters and sentiments must be subordinate to it.[139] Later, the hero's ability to keep dramatic action and descriptive and didactic passages separate calls forth approval from the circle of the count.[140] However, Wilhelm is in accord with the contention of the ancients that a play without either morals or true humanity could be successful if it contains sufficient action,[141] and in this differs fundamentally from the essentially moral author of the *Nouvel essai*.

Wilhelm finds a confusion in the use of the terms applied to the unities. Just as unity of action may be simplicity of action or the clever joining together of several threads, so unity of place may mean either that the location remains the same or that the distance between the scenes is not too great. Unity of time he considers an elapse of time that is probable. Wilhelm wants to abolish these terms when dealing with the drama and hopes to find a more natural and correct path of approach. He has taken care to discover what "thoughtful men" have written about the subject, even reading a translation of Aristotle's *Poetics*.[142]

It seems probable that Mercier was one of the "thoughtful men" to whom Goethe-Wilhelm refers, although there is of course no

---

[136] *Sendung,* p. 76.

[137] Cf. Seuffert, *Goethes Theater-Roman,* p. 14. Seuffert also points out that both Wilhelm and Diderot mention Charles XII and Henry IV in the same sentence.

[138] The relationship between Diderot and Goethe is traced carefully by R. Schlösser, *Rameaus Neffe.* "Forschungen zur neueren Literaturgeschichte," Nr. 15 (Berlin, 1900), pp. 75ff.

[139] *Sendung,* pp. 97, 106.

[140] *Ibid.,* p. 286.

[141] *Ibid.,* p. 142.

[142] *Ibid.,* pp. 76f. The ideas Wilhelm expresses on the unities are almost as conservative as those of Lessing's *Dramaturgie.* Goethe knew Lessing's work, but I have found no evidence that he was particularly influenced by it. Mercier did not know the *Dramaturgie* when he wrote the *Nouvel essai;* cf. below, p. 192.

mention of his name. In any case, there is a coincidence in his views on the technical rules of the drama and those of Wilhelm. Both object to the standardizing and categorizing of terms into rigid precepts. Both demand that the unity of action be held sacred, but are moderate in regard to the unities of time and place. If Goethe expresses ideas here which seem strangely conservative, is it due to the fact that he is proceeding historically in his novel, or may he not have recalled Mercier's comment in the *Nouvel essai* that the Germans should emphasize the rules, not as rigid laws, but to increase dramatic interest?[143]

Our fifth and last point is the similarity of Wilhelm's opinion of Corneille to that entertained by Mercier. The French author calls Corneille the restorer of the tragedy in France and praises *Cinna* and *le Cid* despite all their faults.[144] Mercier's approval of his countryman as a dramatic theorist, however, is qualified by censure. Corneille devoted himself too much to interpreting Aristotle, he believes, and while he made many corrections, he did not dare to set up new precepts. He is a timid lawgiver and his *Discours* contains a large number of false and puerile ideas.[145] The author of the *Nouvel essai* emphasizes the profundity of Corneille's poetry and admires in him not only the poet and the painter, but also the statesman.[146] The sublimity of his work is but the reflection of his soul.[147] He may lack grace and his style often may be incorrect and harsh, but nevertheless he is a man of bold ideas, who stimulates thoughts and dreams.[148] Mercier contrasts his elevation, force, majesty, and the grandeur of his characters with the discreet sorrow and subdued heroic outbursts of Racine.[149] Corneille's verses when recited on the stage stand out like virile and military music in a century of feminine taste, while Racine can only be preferred by an effeminate nation.[150] To sum up: Mercier admires the virility of Corneille and considers him, despite his

---

[143] *Nouvel essai*, pp. 108nf.
[144] *Ibid.*, pp. 24, 25, 98n.
[145] *Ibid.*, p. 255.
[146] *Ibid.*, pp. 283, 26.
[147] *Ibid.*, pp. 26f.
[148] *Ibid.*, p. 283n.
[149] *Ibid.*, pp. 283f.
[150] *Ibid.*, pp. 28, 27.

too close adherence to the rules, as a forerunner of the new era of the drama.

Wilhelm's views are surprisingly similar. He reads *Cinna* to Werner with great exultation, but does not dare to decide whether the "great" Corneille deserves his title. He is content to admire one who is far above him.[151] He also tells his friend that he considers the *Discours* to be a defense against too severe legislators rather than a code of laws which later dramatists must follow.[152] Wilhelm knows that Corneille has a great heart and a noble soul and that he portrays independent characters that are equal to all situations. He calls *Cinna* remarkable, simple, and beautiful. He lauds the French author for his ability to show with great power what we ourselves think and imagine. We feel for the characters he creates mixed feelings of delight and anxiety that are strange and new.[153]

Ja wenn der Autor Kraft und Saft hat, fähig ist, was wir uns allenfalls nur denken und vorstellen, lebendig hervorzuführen, wenn wir unsere Halbgötter jeden wichtigen Schritt gesetzt und fest tun sehen und eines jeden Betragen kernhaft und ganz ist in der schrecklichen Lage, wie befriedigt werden wir und wie dankbar vergnügt kehren wir zurück, wenn uns die Verlegenheiten, die *geteilten Gefühle* so lieblich ängstlich, so wohl zu dem Schrecklichen stimmend in unser Herz gelegt werden. Es mag nur einer nach etwas *Neuem* und Fremdem schnappen . . . er findet . . . immer seine Befriedigung.[154]

This is perhaps a recollection of certain thoughts expressed in the *Nouvel essai*. Mercier points out, in another context to be sure, that the sublimity of genius consists in finding and expressing what everybody would have said and done in a given situation. He also indicates that mixed sensations are the most agreeable of all.

Car si le sublime du génie est de trouver ce qui semble que chacun aurait dit, et dans le cours des événements de reconnaître ce que chacun aurait fait. . . .[155]

[151] *Sendung*, pp. 79f.
[152] *Ibid.*, p. 67.
[153] *Ibid.*, pp. 79f.
[154] *Ibid.*, p. 80. Italics mine.
[155] *Nouvel essai*, p. 52. Here Mercier is paraphrasing a thought of Diderot: "Ce qu'il faut que l'artiste trouve, c'est ce que tout le monde dirait en pareil cas; ce

Les *sensations mixtes* sont les plus agréables de toutes; elles apportent à l'âme une sensation *nouvelle* et plus délicieuse.[156]

Returning to Wilhelm's opinion of Corneille, we find him aware of the fact that the French author lost his versatility in his old age and that the products of his youth were often too grandiloquent.[157] Finally, he contrasts the great men pictured by Corneille with the merely distinguished characters of Racine.[158]

Both Mercier and Wilhelm speak of Corneille in terms of glowing admiration, although they do not overlook his faults. They consider him primarily as a man of great strength and deep thought. It has never been adequately explained why Goethe devotes these few paragraphs of praise to an author whose influence was already on the decline in Germany even before the vogue of Shakespeare began to make itself felt. We have seen that he read Corneille's *Discours* and some of his plays in his youth,[159] but there is no evidence to show that he had occupied himself with Corneille since that time. It has been suggested that Lessing's *Dramaturgie* may have induced Goethe to deal with Corneille.[160] Werner, for instance, states that some critics have questioned the validity for Corneille of the surname, "the great," which his countrymen had given him.[161] Lessing was, of course, foremost among those critics who wished to reduce his fame. Yet when we recall that there is no evidence that Goethe was particularly concerned with the *Dramaturgie* at this period, it seems more probable that his attention was called back to Corneille by the *Nouvel essai*, which appeared six years later than the work of the great German critic. In any case the similarity of Mercier's and Wilhelm's conceptions of the French author is very marked.

---

que personne n'entenda sans le reconnaître aussitôt en soi." (*Œuvres complètes*, éd. J. Assézat, [Paris, 1875-1877] VII, p. 104)

[156] *Nouvel essai*, pp. 67f.

[157] *Sendung*, p. 80. Here Goethe employs the word "rodomontade," which is also used by Mercier in connection with the abuses of the early Seventeenth Century French stage (*Nouvel essai*, p. 127). The word seems to be, however, quite common in Eighteenth Century German.

[158] *Sendung*, p. 315.

[159] Cf. above, p. 117.

[160] Seuffert, *Goethes Theater-Roman*, p. 14.

[161] *Sendung*, p. 80.

We have now examined the major resemblances in the conception of the drama in the *Nouvel essai* and the *Theatralische Sendung*. In addition there are also several minor similarities in the
two works. Of course, it is true that Goethe could have conceived
all the ideas we are going to treat without any knowledge of Mercier's treatise, but the large number of coincidences indicate the
contrary. However that may be, a discussion of these points will
be of a value in indicating how much alike were the conceptions
of poetry and drama on both sides of the Rhine in the last third of
the Eighteenth Century.

Among the similarities which we are going to indicate, one is
particularly striking. Mercier knows that a piece which is ap-
proved in the silence of the drawing room has passed the most
dangerous of all tests: "Le drame d'abord apprécié dans le silence
du *cabinet,* commence par l'épreuve la plus *dangereuse*."[162] Wilhelm also believes that it is more hazardous to present works in
the drawing room than on the stage: "Vor den Ohren solcher
geübter Kenner, im *Kabinette,* wo weiter keine Illusion dazu
kommt, ist ein weit *gefährlicherer* Stand als anderwärts."[163] The
same thought is expressed by Diderot in his *Entretiens sur le Fils
naturel:* "C'est dans le salon qu'il faut juger mon ouvrage."[164]
Goethe's statement, however, is expressed in Mercier's words and
not in those of the older Frenchman. This is certainly irrefutable
proof that similarity of idea in Diderot's theoretic writings on the
drama and in the *Sendung* does not indicate influence of the
former on the latter, but rather that occasionally Diderot's views,
often couched in more radical terms, became known to Goethe
through Mercier.

The venture announced by Mercier in the *Nouvel examen de la
tragédie française,* to make a philosophical investigation of a number of French, German, English, and Spanish plays,[165] recalls the
thought of the Legationsrat in the *Sendung* that the essence of the
drama could only be grasped through a study of its origin and an

---

[162] *Nouvel essai,* p. 337n. The italics are mine.
[163] *Sendung,* p. 297 (Book V). That Goethe uses the unusual word "Kabinett"
seems particularly significant.
[164] *Œuvres complètes,* VII, 92.
[165] Pp. 158f.

examination of the theaters of all nations.[166] Since, however, the *Nouvel examen* was not mentioned by Melchior Grimm nor well known in Germany,[167] it is hardly possible that Goethe was familiar with it. Perhaps he had in mind Lessing's *Beiträge zur Historie und Aufnahme des Theaters* or his *Theatralische Bibliothek,* both of which aimed to do that very thing. This project of Mercier and Goethe is cited only as further evidence of the remarkable likeness of their ideas.

A number of other similarities strengthen the argument for a relationship of Goethe's thinking to that of his French predecessor. Mercier claims that genius has always preceded schools of thought or disdained them.[168] "The poet came before the critic," echoes Wilhelm.[169] Mercier asks why youth prefers tragedy to comedy, and gives the reply that the goodness of children prevents them from seeing any exaggeration in that which seems to be great.[170] As a child Wilhelm thinks that it is easier to compose and play tragedies than comedies, since in the former the exaggerated and the affected seem exalted.[171] Mercier complains that the French actors appear in inappropriate garb and demands that each player be dressed according to his rôle. He understands also the significance of accessories and of decorations and hopes to treat them in a future work.[172] Wilhelm, on his part, is greatly taken aback by the poor and unsuitable clothes that are at the disposal of the actors in Madame de Retti's troupe, since he considers correct costume essential. That he contributes generously toward redeeming the costumes and repairing the decorations, shows that he too realizes the importance of scenery.[173] The French author notes that masks have a certain value and defends their use by the ancient Greeks.[174] Wilhelm is told by Madame de Retti of the advantages of Italian

[166] *Sendung,* p. 78.
[167] It is mentioned later by Sulzer, *Allgemeine Theorie,* neue vermehrte zweite Auflage, IV, 596a.
[168] *Nouvel essai,* p. 307n.
[169] *Sendung,* p. 77.
[170] *Nouvel essai,* p. 53n.
[171] *Sendung,* p. 24.
[172] *Nouvel essai,* pp. 139, 347ff.
[173] *Sendung,* pp. 167f.
[174] *Nouvel essai,* pp. 352, 353n.

masks.[175] In this connection it is interesting to recall the unsuc-
cessful attempt made by Goethe in 1801 to introduce masks on the
Weimar stage.[176] Again, Mercier suggests that the poet visit Lyon,
Marseille, Bordeaux, Nantes, and La Rochelle in order to famil-
iarize himself with the distinctive traits of these provinces.[177]
Similarly, Madame de Retti tells Goethe's hero of the plan of her
company to portray characters from various parts of Germany.
The comic figure was to come from Salzburg, the nobleman from
Pomerania, the doctor from Swabia, the lovers from Upper Saxony,
and the servant girl from Leipsic.[178]

Still further resemblances present themselves. Mercier inveighs
against the pomp of the French tragedy, which in his opinion has
become a serious farce, a phantom clothed in purple and gold, and
criticises those plays which portray only conspiracies, murders, and
tyranny. In addition he demands that the common man be the
subject of the drama rather than the king.[179] In Goethe's work exaggeration of sentiment, overabundance of scenes in which violent
death plays a part, portrayal of exalted deeds and feelings only
in haughty representatives of the nobility are characteristics of the
pieces that Wilhelm reads and performs as a child.[180] These are,
of course, outstanding abuses of the Eighteenth Century stage in
both France and Germany. Again, the author of the *Nouvel essai*
maintains that those pieces of poetry that the people do not understand are defective. Even if the voice of the people does not always
prove their excellence, its disapproval shows their weakness.[181]
Similarly, Wilhelm considers that writer insincere or extremely
conceited who dedicates his products only to connoisseurs, and
who calls all those who do not like them ignorant. Although the
best play must be tested by the expert, it is of equal importance
that it also appeal to those who are not in a position to pass a

[175] *Sendung*, p. 171.
[176] Cf. *Lessings Hamburgische Dramaturgie*, hrsg. von Petersen (Bong & Co.),
p. 487.
[177] *Nouvel essai*, pp. 110f.
[178] *Sendung*, pp. 171f.
[179] *Nouvel essai*, pp. 30, 30n., ix, 10, 158ff.
[180] *Sendung*, pp. 31, 41f.
[181] *Nouvel essai*, pp. 211, 205f.

critical judgment on its merits.[182] Finally, Mercier devotes a chapter of his essay to actors. He discusses at length the prejudice that they are not entitled to any social standing and concludes that it is just.[183] In Goethe's work the low social position of the actors of the wandering troupe that Wilhelm joins is stressed.[184] This is naturally a reflection of actual conditions in Germany throughout most of the Eighteenth Century.

In conclusion it may be of interest to indicate the appreciation of Shakespeare that Goethe shares with Mercier. It is not a question here of influence, but rather of similarity of view which reflects the spirit of the times in western Europe. The French author holds Shakespeare in great esteem without really knowing or understanding his genius. To Mercier the Englishman is a mixer of the comic and the serious, and along with Calderón, Lope de Vega, and Goldoni, the perfect exponent of the tragicomedy. Shakespeare is dear to his countrymen, Mercier contends, because he has found the secret of speaking to all the elements that make up his nation. His heroes are all real men, and the union of the simple with the heroic adds to the interest one feels for them. He is above all a national poet. The English theater is eloquent with the eloquence of the people and is for that reason so vehement and so singularly interesting. Poetry is made to stir the people, to control it, by borrowing its language, its passions, and even its rude and savage manner. That is poetry, that is Shakespeare, concludes Mercier with genuine enthusiasm.[185]

Wilhelm also becomes a fervent Shakespeare enthusiast. At first he shares the prejudices of the time and considers him a senseless monster who sins against the rules of probability and decency. When finally he reads his plays he is carried away by the storm of moving life and the naturalness of the characters. He reads *Henry IV* and arrays himself as Prince Hal. He reads *Hamlet* and tries to penetrate to the very core of the hero's soul.[186] Goethe had,

---

[182] *Sendung*, p. 98.
[183] *Nouvel essai*, pp. 355f., 362.
[184] *Sendung*, especially p. 202.
[185] *Nouvel essai*, pp. 96f., 206, 207nff.
[186] *Sendung*, pp. 316, 326f., 335f., 369ff.

of course, a much deeper understanding of the great Englishman than Mercier showed here or elsewhere in his writings.

We have come to the conclusion of our discussion of the similarities between *Wilhelm Meisters theatralische Sendung* and the *Nouvel essai sur l'art dramatique*. It must be taken into account that Mercier's lengthy treatise deals with many problems with which Goethe's novel is not concerned. Also, it is obvious that striking differences exist. Goethe could have no sympathy with the French author's contention that the *raison d'être* of a play was to teach a moral lesson, nor with his demand that the drama should become entirely bourgeois. Many of the likenesses pointed out seem quite incidental, others are not very exact, while still others are ideas common to the period in both France and Germany and can be found, for instance, in the writings of Diderot, Lessing, Lenz, or Wieland. However, the conception of the stage as an important social force which operates by creating a feeling of sympathy and brotherhood among the spectators, the high ideal of the poet's mission, a disregard for the unities as something destroying the real unity of the play, the appreciation of Corneille, and a number of minor traits are very similar in the two works. Occasionally even the same words are used. In light of the evidence both external and internal presented above, the conclusion seems justified that Goethe had the *Nouvel essai* in mind when he wrote the first three books of the *Sendung*.[187]

In conjunction with our discussion of the influence of Mercier on Goethe and his dramatic novel it is interesting to note that the French author was familiar with at least two of Goethe's works. He read *Werther* with the greatest delight and enthusiastically annotated the margins of a French translation of it.[188] In addition, he left in manuscript form a play entitled *Romainval, ou le Poète vertueux*, which is nothing more than an adaptation of *Werther* with a different conclusion. Characteristically, Mercier alters the tragic fate of his hero and has him, after four acts of lamentation, saved from committing suicide by a friend.[189] Mercier also knew

---

[187] This chapter in condensed form was read at the Modern Language Association meeting in Chicago in 1937.

[188] Cf. Béclard, *op. cit.*, p. 424.

[189] *Ibid.*, pp. 223, 326nf.

Götz von Berlichingen, which he planned to translate, although he did not rate it so high as Schiller's *Räuber.*[190] At the end of *Montesquieu à Marseille,* an edition of Mercier's works is announced for the next year, 1785. Among the historical dramas "la Main de fer, pièce imitée de l'allemand, en 5 actes" is listed. An edition of *les Tombeaux de Vérone* published in 1785 also speaks of this projected play.[191] However, we hear nothing more about it and must conclude that the plan was never carried out.[192]

[190] *Briefe von und an Klopstock,* p. 368; Cramer to Klopstock, March 14, 1796.

[191] Cf. Béclard, *op. cit.,* p. 223.

[192] "La Main de fer" should not be confused with *l'Homme de fer, songe,* which appears at the end of the third and last volume of the 1786 edition of *l'An 2440.*

VII

MERCIER AND SCHILLER

ALMOST ALL German men of letters of the last quarter of the Eighteenth Century were familiar with some phase of Mercier's multifarious works. Schiller was no exception. We find evidence of his knowledge of the French author in his correspondence and also in his dramaturgical essays, his historical writings, his poetry, and in his plays, both completed and fragmentary. It is the purpose of this chapter to investigate in detail this relationship of Schiller to Mercier. Finally, a brief consideration of the latter's attempt to popularize the German author west of the Rhine will be added.

Schiller's correspondence contains several brief allusions to Mercier. Despite their intrinsic unimportance, they are of some moment to us here, showing for want of other evidence that during the latter half of his short life his attention was occasionally directed to Mercier. In a letter to Dalberg written in 1783 the Swabian playwright notes that he has already experienced all the power and the nourishment for the heart and the eye that Spiess's *Schlenzheim* offers in the otherwise wretched *Graf Walltron* and "Mersier's" *Déserteur*. Plays of this kind, he adds, are probably so popular on the boards because they deal with more obvious subjects than the court intrigues of an *Emilia*.[1] Schiller's opinion of the French dramatist rose in the next few years, perhaps due to the fact that he became acquainted with the *Portrait de Philippe II,* of which he translated the preface.[2] When he hears from Dalberg in 1787 that Mercier has seen *Die Räuber* in Mannheim, and wants to have his dramas translated into French and to write a preface to them, he exclaims that that would be "splendid." Further, he tells Huber that the Mannheim theater manager was delighted with the idea and wished to translate the pieces literally before

---

[1] *Schillers Briefe,* hrsg. von Fritz Jonas (Stuttgart, Leipzig, Berlin, Wien, Einleitung: 1892), I, 157; Sept. 29.
[2] See below, pp. 147ff.

giving them to the French translator to revise.[3] A few months
later Schiller writes his friend Körner that he has read Mercier's
article in the *Journal de Paris* in which he describes his visit to the
city on the Rhine.[4] A decade later Wilhelm von Humboldt writing
from Paris informs him that a new play by Lemercier, "not by the
prominent Mercier," has achieved undeserved popularity in the
French capital.[5] Karoline von Wolzogen announces to Schiller and
his wife in 1802 that the "ass Mercier" has translated *Das Mäd-
chen von Orleans*.[6] Finally, Körner writes Schiller in the last year
of the poet's life that Iffland surpassed his highest expectations
in *Der Essigmann* and in other rôles.[7] Add to these references
Schiller's review in the *Allgemeine Literaturzeitung* of 1788 of
Hoff's *Historisch-kritische Enzyclopädie* which quotes from the
Tableau de Paris and mentions Mercier by name,[8] and we arrive
at the conclusion that Schiller knew the Frenchman as a dramatist,
as the author of a description of Paris, and as a cosmopolitan
spirit interested in German literature.

There is no direct evidence that Schiller read the *Nouvel essai*,
which, as we have seen, was reviewed by a number of German
journals in the seventies and was translated into German by Wagner in 1776. However, the similarity between the views in Mercier's
treatise on the drama and those in the dramaturgical writings of
the young Schiller is quite clear and invites a thorough investigation. The examination of the French scholar Léon Mis, which is
intended as a supplement to the work of Rosanow on Mercier and
the *Sturm und Drang*,[9] is not altogether satisfactory. Mis does not
specify whether Schiller knew of Mercier or of his essay on the
drama. He does not state why he limits his study to a certain few
discourses of the German author. The categories of his compari-

[3] *Briefe*, I, 430; Oct. 26.
[4] *Ibid.*, I, 445; Dec. 19, 1787.
[5] *Neue Briefe Wilhelm von Humboldts an Schiller*, hrsg. von F. C. Ebrard (Berlin, 1911), p. 182; Dec. 7, 1797.
[6] Cf. *Charlotte von Schiller und ihre Freunde*, hrsg. von L. Geiger (Berlin, preface:
1908), p. 52; June 5.
[7] Cf. *Schillers Briefwechsel mit Körner*, hrsg. von K. Goedeke, 2d ed. (Leipzig,
1878), II, 481; Feb. 25, 1805.
[8] Cf. *Schillers Werke*, hrsg. von Boxberger (DNL), VIII, 209ff. cf. also below, p. 154.
[9] *Lenz*, chaps. v, vi.

son are often confused and confusing. In the following analysis I shall attempt to throw the similarities between the theories of the two into clearer relief. I have received, to be sure, several hints from Mis's confused but not entirely valueless article.[10]

Schiller's early dramatic theories are to be found in his comments on *Die Räuber* (1781-1782) and *Fiesko* (1783-1784) and in the essays *Über das gegenwärtige deutsche Theater* (1782) and *Was kann eine gute stehende Bühne eigentlich wirken* (1784).[11] The *Briefe über Don Carlos,* which appeared in Wieland's *Deutscher Merkur* in 1788 and offer a defense of the character of Posa and of the unity of the piece, and the reviews of Goethe's *Egmont* (1788) and *Iphigenie* (1789) do not deal primarily with the theory of the drama. Two later discourses, *Über den Grund des Vergnügens an tragischen Gegenständen* (1792) and *Über die tragische Kunst* (1792), show particularly the influence of Kant and so do not concern us here.[12] Since those treatises that interest us appeared within a period of four years, and since there is no perceptible change in Schiller's attitude to the theater during that time, we need not concern ourselves further with their chronology, but can proceed at once to a discussion of the similarity of the ideas they contain with those in the *Nouvel essai.*

The conception of the stage as an institution that serves morality and promotes the love of virtue and the hatred of vice was especially popular among the critics and dramaturgists of Eighteenth Century Europe. Gottsched and Lessing in Germany and Diderot in France[13] wished to utilize the theater in their struggle against the darkness of ignorance and iniquity. No one, however, stressed the moral purpose of the drama more strongly or at greater length than Mercier. The dramatic art, he declares in the *Nouvel essai,*

[10] I am in accord with Mis's conclusion, *op. cit.,* p. 202: "Die Ähnlichkeit . . . ist zu schlagend, als daß man nur zufällige Übereinstimmung annehmen sollte."

[11] Republished in 1802 with the title *Die Schaubühne als eine moralische Anstalt betrachtet.* I shall call it by this title for the sake of convenience.

[12] Schiller's essays dealing with the theater are conveniently assembled by Otto Falckenberg, *Schillers Dramaturgie* (München und Leipzig, 1909).

[13] Diderot's ideas are very similar to those of Mercier and Schiller in this respect. Cf., "Tout passe; mais la vertu et la vérité restent" (éd. Assézat, VII, 127); "O quel bien il en reviendrait aux hommes, si tous les arts d'imitation se proposait un objet commun, et concouraient . . . avec les lois pour nous faire aimer la vertu et haïr le vice (Assézat, VII, 313).

if properly employed can aid in the enlightenment of humanity, cultivate public reason, and lead mankind back to the simple, clear, and intelligible elementary notions of true morality and sane politics. It is the quickest and most efficient method of arming invincibly the forces of human reason in the fight for a national awakening.[14] The question to be posed in the criticism of a literary work is always: what is its use?[15] Mercier asserts that the men of letters of the world will dictate the laws that will ensure a period of public felicity: "Enfin, le corps des gens de lettres . . . dictera nécessairement aux hommes d'état et aux rois les leçons qui doivent commencer la *félicité publique.*"[16] That Schiller is operating in the same realm of thought is shown by a statement in *Die Schaubühne als eine moralische Anstalt betrachtet,* that the highest objective of philosophy is the furthering of general happiness: "Die höchste und letzte Forderung, welche der Philosoph und Gesetzgeber einer öffentlichen Anstalt nur machen können, ist Beförderung *allgemeiner Glückseligkeit.*"[17]

Both Mercier and Schiller stress the social and moral value of the stage. The importance which both attribute to this aspect makes a detailed discussion desirable. The French author advocates that the theater be an object of instruction for the people, a decent relaxation, a useful pleasure, and not just a distraction, or a means of keeping the crowd from serious and patriotic reflection. For the poet to misuse it, is to profane an instrument of public felicity which completes what the laws leave undone and which rectifies their viciousness.[18] In the theater legislation for the benefit of the people would meet the least resistance and achieve the greatest success, entirely without violence.[19] Mercier asserts that the stage is made to supplement the lack of experience of youth, to right what youth has seen wrongly, to aid the intelligence of the mediocre, and to teach men, whose ideas are often vacillating, what they should hate, love, and esteem. The drama instructs man

[14] *Nouvel essai,* pp. iv, vf.
[15] *Ibid.,* p. 140n.
[16] *Ibid.,* p. 2n. The italics in this and the following citation are mine.
[17] *Schillers sämtliche Schriften,* hrsg. von Goedeke (Stuttgart, 1867-1876), III, 510. All references to Schiller are to this edition unless otherwise noted.
[18] *Nouvel essai,* pp. 216, 259f.
[19] *Ibid.,* p. vi.

how to deal with his fellows. It can likewise correct the pettiness of his ideas and his exaggerated self-love in such a way that his blush and his cure are not visible to others.[20] The stage would also be of value in enlightening kings and in revealing to them a truth of which they are too often ignorant, that they are dependent on others.[21] Again, Mercier contends that the poet must always be the mouthpiece of virtue. However, he does not demand that the playwright invariably reward innocence and punish vice as long as he arrays the former in all its divine traits and detests the latter. The author who merely recompenses goodness and castigates wickedness does not always depict the theater of the world in a natural fashion.[22] The French author warns the poet not to forget that the characters of men are mixed and that too decided colors are harsh and incorrect. In his opinion, not enough attention has been paid to these mixed types which represent all humanity. Men whether good or bad are not entirely abandoned to virtue or vice, for they have moments of repose as well as of action. The gradations of virtue and vice are infinitely varied. Who knows how depravity and sublimity, ferocity and compassion are linked together in the same person? Who can penetrate the soul of the coward who becomes brave, of the proud man who stoops to subserviency, of the tyrant whose ambition causes him to act justly?[23]

Schiller's attitude toward the contemporary German stage is similar. It has become, he contends in *Über das gegenwärtige deutsche Theater*, less a school than a pastime, a way of avoiding the boredom of long winter nights and a means of amusing the great army of the idle with the froth of wisdom, the counterfeit of sentiment, and gallant indecencies.[24] In *Die Schaubühne* the German dramaturgist maintains that the influence of the stage begins where that of the law ends. If justice is perverted and fear binds the arms of authority, then the theater seizes the scale of justice

---

[20] *Ibid.*, p. 15f., 2.

[21] *Ibid.*, p. 36n.

[22] *Ibid.*, pp. 250f., 247.

[23] *Ibid.*, pp. 52, 107. In the case of the tyrant one thinks involuntarily of Fiesko. Cf. also Schiller of Franz Moor: "Stirbt er nicht bald wie ein großer Mann, die kleine kriechende Seele!" (*Selbstrezension, Schriften*, II, 365.)

[24] *Schriften*, II, 343.

and the sword and flays evil before a redoubtable tribunal.[25] The
authorities could use the stage as an organ of government to deal
with the crowd. Schiller thinks that they could maintain their laws
and extend their influence over the people by this means,[26] and
hence differs from Mercier, who, we know, wishes the control to
be in the hands of the middle class. Schiller considers the stage not
only a general cure for injustice, but also a school for practical
wisdom, a guide for the bourgeoisie, and an infallible key to the
human soul. It can also cure the errors of education. The drama,
here the comedy in particular, can heal our silly faults without
making us blush.[27] Schiller contends that the stage is also useful
because the rulers may become familiar there with truth and with
mankind, which they otherwise seldom or never encounter.[28] An
announcement of *Die Räuber* directed to the public (1782)
stresses the moral purpose of the play. Schiller demands here a
stricter morality than even Mercier. He intends to show in his
piece that the invisible hand of fate punishes unbridled profli-
gacy.[29] The *Erinnerung an das Publikum* (1784) which accom-
panies the stage version of *Fiesko* takes cognizance, however, of
the fact that virtue is not always recompensed. Its author realizes
that often the noblest impulses and the best seeds of greatness and
goodness are buried by the pressure of daily life and by ridiculous
conventions.[30] In the second preface to *Die Räuber* (1781) Schiller
states that he wished to show the fall of wickedness and to exalt
religion, morality, and bourgeois laws, but in doing so has drawn
characters that are neither completely good nor entirely bad,
"ganze Menschen," he calls them. He believes that an entirely
vicious person is quite unartistic, since even the worst man is not
without redeeming features.[31] Again, in the preface to *Fiesko*
(1783) Schiller expresses the hope that he has drawn his hero

---

[25] *Ibid.,* III, 514.
[26] *Schaubühne, Schriften,* III, 522.
[27] *Ibid.,* III, 518, 521.
[28] *Ibid.,* III, 520.
[29] *Schriften,* II, 337.
[30] *Ibid.,* III, 350f.
[31] *Ibid.,* II, 9ff. Cf. also the first preface to *Die Räuber, Schriften,* II, 5f., and
Diderot, "Un ouvrage sera romanesque . . . si l'on y voit les dieux ou les hommes
trop méchants, ou trop bons" (éd. Assézat, VII, 330).

as much a human being as a political figure, in order that the audience may be moved.[32] However, in practice neither Schiller nor Mercier applies the theory of mixed characters. What Mme de Staël wrote in de l'Allemagne about Schiller—that when he depicts the wicked, who appear to him in his imagination as an obstacle, as a physical scourge, it is with greater exaggeration and with less depth than if he had really known them[33]—is true also of Mercier.

It is interesting in connection with the characters of Die Räuber to note the death of the arch-villain, Franz Moor. We are reminded of a suggestion of Mercier. The French author would like to see a tyrant, especially Nero, abandoned to the terrible realization of his crimes, not wishing to live, but afraid of death. He would implore a slave to kill him, and struggling horribly in mortal agony, would realize that justice must punish him for the wrongs he has inflicted on mankind.[34] In Schiller's play Franz is shown half-crazy from the visions of his evil deeds. He mocks at the thought of death, nevertheless he fears it. Moser, the pastor whom he summons, says he would like to see him die like a tyrant and calls him a Nero without a kingdom. Moser asks him if he thinks he can be pardoned for the injustices he has done others. After the pastor's departure, Franz falls into a chair with convulsive movements, and later tumbles to the floor in order to pray. Finally, he begs his servant to stab him and when he refuses, takes his own life.[35]

For Mercier and Schiller the stage is a great social and moral force. In addition, they believe it achieves its effect by appealing to the emotions. The French author maintains that the theater is the only place where men may assemble and where their voices may rise in concert. There the soul realizes its divinity.[36] The theater also develops the natural tenderness that we have for our

[32] Schriften, III, 6.

[33] De l'Allemagne, 2d ed. (Paris, 1814), I, 245.

[34] Nouvel essai, pp. 50nf.

[35] Reynaud, Histoire générale de l'influence française en Allemagne, 2d ed. (Paris, 1915), p. 436, speaks of the general resemblance of Die Räuber to le Déserteur. Both Karl Moor and Durimel become outcasts from society partly through the fault of another.

[36] Nouvel essai, pp. 3f.

fellow men.[37] The writer, however, must be inexorable and reveal all the calamities that await us, must strengthen our courage against impending misfortunes and accustom our eyes to the somber touches of the portrait of the human condition: "Il faut que l'écrivain soit inexorable . . . qu'il *roidisse notre courage* contre les malheurs imminents."[38]

Schiller's views are very similar. In the final words of *Die Schaubühne* he depicts with great ardor the emotional appeal of the stage. What a triumph, he exclaims, when people from all classes and regions, free from the fetters of artificiality and fashion, made brothers by all-encompassing sympathy, forget themselves and the world, and approach their heavenly origin! Each enjoys the rapture of all to a heightened degree, each has room for only one feeling in his heart, that he is a human being![39] Further, in *Das gegenwärtige deutsche Theater* Schiller praises the stage which allows a friend of truth to dream of his own fate in that of another and to harden his courage through the sight of the misery and sufferings of others: "wenn hie und da ein Freund der Wahrheit . . . *seinen Mut* an Szenen des Leidens *erhärtet.*"[40]

The rôle of the theater for Mercier and Schiller, then, is to promote human happiness and to improve society morally by means of an emotional appeal. In addition, the playwright becomes in their eyes the teacher and patriotic leader of his land. Mercier acclaims the eloquent poet who is enkindled with a truly patriotic spark as the master of public opinion, of an invincible force that rules even those who do not believe they obey it. It is his duty to speak to the multitude, to show himself as a lawgiver. He is the singer of virtue, the castigator of vice, the man of the universe. The stage can inflame the people with the simple eloquence and the majestic thought of a single person.[41]

Schiller shares this view of Mercier. In *Das gegenwärtige deutsche Theater* he despairs because the playwrights of his native country lack the patriotic vanity to be teachers of the people.[42]

[37] *Ibid.*, p. 4n.
[38] *Ibid.*, p. 248. The italics here and in the following citation are mine.
[39] *Schriften*, III, 524.
[40] *Ibid.*, II, 348.
[41] *Nouvel essai*, pp. x, vi, 205, vf.
[42] *Schriften*, II, 343.

The stage, he remarks elsewhere, is the canal through which the light of wisdom pours from the intellectual few into the whole state. Improved ideas, tested principles, and purer feelings flow from it through the veins of the people.[43] The artist is the intermediary between the All Powerful from which he learns and humanity whom he is to teach.[44]

Both Mercier and Schiller are patriotic and realize the importance of the stage for their countries. The French author defines the true tragedy: it is understood by all classes of people, it has an intimate connection with political affairs, it informs the masses of their real interests, it causes an enlightened patriotism in the breast of the spectator and makes him cherish his native land. Mercier stresses the connection between the Greeks' love of country and their theater. It was concerned with Greece and its history and was interesting because it was an affair of state.[45]

Again Schiller's views coincide with Mercier's. Schiller insists on the importance of a permanent theater for Germany. If all German poets were in agreement, he thinks, and would dedicate themselves to matters that concern the people, then there would be a national stage and a nation. The German author also notes the patriotic tone of the Greek drama. What is it, he asks, that united Greece so closely, that attracted the people so irresistibly to its stage, if not the patriotic content of the plays, the Greek spirit, and the great interest of the state?[46]

Both Mercier and Schiller score the exaggerations of the English and the unnaturalness of the French stage. The author of the *Nouvel essai* has little sympathy for those dramas in which the extravagant and the romanesque appear, where coarse nature prevails. It is not enough to copy nature, he contends, but the objects and traits which are to be imitated must be so chosen that a picture results which disguises deformity and shows only that which contributes to the general effect.[47] On the other hand, Mercier calls the traditional theater of his nation an unreal phantom

---

[43] *Schaubühne, Schriften,* III, 521.
[44] *Vorrede zu Fiesko, Schriften,* III, 6.
[45] *Nouvel essai,* pp. 39f. 19ff.
[46] *Schaubühne, Schriften,* III, 522f.
[47] *Nouvel essai,* pp. 140, 140n.

clothed in purple and gold. Since Corneille, French writers have
fashioned their plays for a feminine public. Racine is the worst
offender in this respect. "The lover and his beloved sigh melodi-
ously to Racine's flute," Mercier remarks scornfully.[48]

Schiller also inveighs against the monstrosity of the English
theater and protests against its popularity in Germany. He maintains that the artist must not copy nature directly, but reduce it
to a harmonious and symmetrical miniature. Likewise he raises
objections to the adoration of the antithesis of Shakespeare, French
taste. The German author, doubtless as a result of reading Lessing's unjust polemics,[49] disparages le Cid and Corneille, and
not Racine as Mercier had done. He feels that the characters of
the French classical tragedy are nothing but smooth, elegant puppets and that the plays themselves can only please delicate noble-
women.[50]

Another weakness of the stage on both sides of the Rhine was
poor acting, and this was scored by both our authors. Mercier finds
three-fourths of the actors in the French capital mediocre. They
are unable to vary their play. They believe erroneously that they
have a personal existence on the boards, and hence the spectator
sees them distinct from the parts they are giving.[51] Schiller, in
turn, pours out invective against the actor who wishes to usurp
all the honors at the expense of the drama, who plays his part with
many conventional and mechanical gestures, who declaims too
much. He scores the player who is more interested in the audience
and its reactions than in his own rôle. In Schiller's opinion the best
actor conducts himself as if he were a sleepwalker, living the
part and only vaguely conscious of the spectators.[52]

So far we have been concerned with a comparison of Mercier's
and Schiller's views in regard to the content of the drama. We
have seen that both insist on the social and moral purpose of the
theater and stress its emotional appeal. Both hold an exalted opin-

[48] Ibid., pp. ix, 28f.
[49] The influence of the Dramaturgie is unmistakable. Another unfavorable comment on Corneille is in the first preface to Die Räuber, Schriften, II, 4.
[50] Das gegenwärtige deutsche Theater, Schriften, II, 343ff.
[51] Nouvel essai, pp. 351f.
[52] Das gegenwärtige deutsche Theater, Schriften, II, 343ff.

ion of the mission of the poet, emphasize his patriotism, and desire freedom for him, as Mis points out,[53] only that he may serve humanity. Both castigate the exaggerations of the English and of the French classical traditions. Both score poor acting. Finally, as we shall now see, both express a similar opinion about the form of the drama.

We have examined Mercier's attitude toward the formal rules governing the drama at great length above[54] and consequently will give here only a brief summary. The French author wants the poet to shake off every painful yoke, free himself from ancient slavery, and disdain compulsion. He is the avowed enemy of Aristotle, whose poetic treatise he says has been as fatal to the progress of literature as his dialectics have been to that of philosophy. Mercier is in favor of greater leniency in regard to the rules. While maintaining that the unity of action, of "interest," be held inviolate, he allows more than twenty-four or the thirty hours of Corneille, if necessary, and permits a change of scene, to be sure, only between the acts.[55] Turning to Schiller, we find a similar attitude. In the second preface to *Die Räuber* he explains why he has not followed the rules in his piece. He had so much material that it was impossible to jam it all into the straitjacket of the precepts of Aristotle and Batteux. He also protests against the unity of time. It is a contradiction to demand that a drama in which the motives of three extraordinary persons are laid bare be limited to twenty-four hours.[56] It was, of course, by no means unprecedented in the Germany of 1781 to defend the overthrow of the established rules. Here Schiller is following in the footsteps of young Goethe and other dramatists of the *Sturm und Drang* as well as in those of the author of the *Nouvel essai*.

Such are, in brief, the points which the dramaturgical writings of Schiller up to 1784 and Mercier's *Nouvel essai* have in common. It must be kept in mind, of course, that Schiller does not treat

[53] *Op. cit.*, pp. 202f.

[54] Cf. "Mercier and Goethe," p. 123ff.

[55] *Nouvel essai*, pp. 267n., 145ff.

[56] *Schriften*, II, 8. Mis (p. 201) calls Schiller in respect to the composition and form of *Die Räuber* a "weniger treuer Schüler Merciers." Perhaps Schiller did go further than Mercier would have advised. Still it seems to me that he has just drawn the logical conclusions from the Frenchman's theories.

the theory of the drama at the same length as Mercier, and that there are consequently many ideas in the French treatise that find no echo in the German essays. Likewise, there are matters on which the two authors differ. While the Frenchman, for instance, maintains that it is prostitution of the poet's mission to be concerned with the ridiculous as long as there are vices to be punished, Schiller believes in the use of satire and scorn in dealing with the foolish and their inane antics.[57] Then, too, it is evident that Mercier is everywhere more sentimental than the German writer. We must also remember that there is no definite proof that Schiller read the *Nouvel essai* at all. Again, we must consider that Schiller was open to ideas from a number of sources, both French and German. Many of his theories have parallels, for instance, in Diderot's writings on the drama.[58] Finally, we must not overrate the whole matter of influence, and must credit Schiller with some originality. However, the similarity of his views and Mercier's on the purpose and form of the drama is very striking. In at least two cases verbal similarity seems to exist. It appears, then, in the light of the evidence produced that we may assume with some certainty that the *Nouvel essai* had an influence on the German dramaturgist.

We have noted in passing that Schiller was acquainted with Mercier's *Portrait de Philippe II, roi d'Espagne*. It appeared at Amsterdam in 1785 in at least two editions, preceded in both by a *Précis historique,* an essay of some fifty pages dealing with the villainy of the son of Charles V.[59] Schiller's translation of the *Précis* appeared, along with the second act of *Don Carlos,* in *Thalia* in 1787. It was entitled "Philipp der Zweite, König von Spanien, von Mercier," with a footnote, "Précis historique zu

---

[57] *Nouvel essai,* pp. 55, 61f.; *Schaubühne, Schriften,* III, 517f.

[58] Especially in regard to the moral value of the drama. I have called attention to some of the likenesses in my notes in passing. So far as I know there is no evidence that Schiller had read at this time the discourses appended to Diderot's plays. For Diderot and Schiller, cf. L. Geiger, "Schiller und Diderot," *Marbacher Schillerbuch,* I (Stuttgart und Berlin, 1905), pp. 81ff., and E. Eggli, "Diderot et Schiller," *Revue de littérature comparée,* I (1921), 68ff.

[59] *Portrait de Philippe* II, *roi d'Espagne,* par M. Mercier, auteur du Tableau de Paris. . . . Copy in the Universitätsbibliothek, Hamburg.—(anonymous), cf. *Schriften,* IV, 88n. References to the former edition.

seinem Portrait de Philippe second." In general the translation reproduces Mercier's original quite exactly as the following comparison indicates:[60]

Qu'étaient les Hollandais vers le milieu du xvi⁰ siècle? Leur subite éléva-
tion est peut-être le fait le plus étonnant de l'histoire moderne. Des
matelots et des pêcheurs, occupant un petit pays marécageux, luttent
contre la mer qui menace de les engloutir, et se défendent contre les
meilleurs soldats de l'Europe, que l'Espagne payait avec l'or du Mexique
et du Pérou.

Was waren die Holländer in der Mitte des sechzehnten Jahrhunderts?
Ihre schnellwachsende Größe ist vielleicht die bewundernswürdigste
Begebenheit in der neuen Geschichte. Ein Haufen Matrosen und Fischer,
Bewohner eines sumfigen Landes, kämpfen mit dem Meere, das sie zu
verschlingen droht, und wehren sich gegen die besten Krieger in Europa,
die Spanien mit dem Golde von Mexico und Peru besoldete.

However, Schiller does make some omissions and changes. He
leaves out Mercier's footnotes, a few longer passages that have to
do with French policies or Spanish internal affairs,[61] and several
of his protests against tyranny which destroy the unity of the
portrait.[62] The German author also makes the content clearer by
the insertion of an occasional explanatory word or phrase drawn
from his reading in Watson's *History of the Reign of Philip II*
(1777).[63] In addition, he softened the empty pathos of Mercier
and toned down his characteristically exaggerated picture of the
wretched, tyrannical king.[64] On the whole, Schiller's version reproduces the French original with artistry and accuracy, although not
slavishly. A more unified and better organized portrait of Philip
and his rule is given, without, however, the enthusiastic note of
the *Précis* having disappeared.

Incorporated in the translated essay is the poem, "Die unüberwindliche Flotte." It paraphrases a footnote of Mercier that pictures the destruction of Spain's proud Armada by the storm gods.

---

[60] *Portrait*, p. 33; *Schriften*, IV, 102.
[61] *Portrait*, pp. 8-10; 19-24; 44-50; also the complete conclusion giving a discussion of the historical drama, pp. 50-52.
[62] *Ibid.*, pp. 4-5; 24; 31; and especially p. 36.
[63] Pointed out by Bellermann in his edition of Schiller, XIV, 492; *Schriften*, IV,
91, l. 9; 92, l. 5-6.
[64] *Portrait*, p. 4, *Schriften*, IV, 89, l. II; *Portrait*, p. 37, *Schriften*, IV, 104, l. 14.

Schiller changed the comment of the original, "voici de quelle manière un poète a peint cet événement," to "diese merkwürdige Begebenheit hat ein Dichter jener Zeit in folgender Ode besungen" (later, "nach einem ältern Dichter").[65] It has been pointed out that Mercier's source was a passage from the prose book of devotion, *Der Christ in der Einsamkeit*, by the contemporary German writer and court chaplain, Martin Crugot (1725-1790).[66] Crugot's work had twelve editions between 1756, when it first appeared, and 1799, and was translated into French in 1770.[67] It is, however, doubtful that Schiller knew *Der Christ*.[68] His poem is in any case closer to Mercier's note than to the German passage, as the following comparison indicates:[69]

Une flotte formidable fait mugir les flots. C'est plutôt une armée de châteaux flottants; on l'appelle l'invincible, et la *terreur* qu'elle inspire, *consacre* ce nom.

Crugot: Sie braust durch die Fluten daher, jene schreckliche Flotte, oder vielmehr das furchtbare Heer schwimmender Schlösser. Sie heißt auf Erden die Unüberwindliche, und sie heißt es dem Ansehn nach mit recht.

> Sie kommt—sie kommt, des Mittags stolze Flotte,
> Das Weltmeer wimmert unter ihr,
> Mit Kettenklang und einem neuen Gotte
> Und tausend Donnern naht sie dir.
> Ein schwimmend Heer furchtbarer Citadellen
> —Der Ocean sah ihresgleichen nie,
> Unüberwindlich nennt man sie—
> Zieht sie einher auf den erschrocknen Wellen;
> Den stolzen Namen *weiht*
> Der *Schrecken,* den sie um sich speit.

The fourth stanza of the poem (beginning, "Wer hat das hohe Kleinod dir errungen") stresses the importance of the English victory more than Mercier's version perhaps, but in general the

---

[65] *Portrait*, p. 7n.; Schiller, *Schriften*, IV, 91n.

[66] Cf. Berger, *Schiller*, 7 ed. (München, 1912), I, 632. Boxberger in his edition of Schiller (I, 245n.) quotes Crugot's passage and refers to Manchot, *Martin Crugot, der ältere Dichter der unüberwindlichen Flotte Schillers* (Bremen, 1886).

[67] Cf. Berger, *op. cit.*, I, 632.

[68] Bellermann in his edition of Schiller, I, 320.

[69] *Portrait*, p. 7n.; *Der Christ*, p. 40; Schiller, *Schriften*, IV, 111. The italics are mine.

verses follow this original in sense and emphasis. The note Schiller appended to his poem concerning the English medal that Elizabeth struck off to commemorate the great sea triumph ("Afflavit Deus et dissipati sunt") is taken from the *Précis* and like its source is not entirely accurate.[70]

A trace of the influence of the *Portrait* can still be noticed in the *Geschichte des Abfalls der vereinigten Niederlande* which appeared a year later, in 1788. In the introduction Philip is shown as having the same despicable character as in Mercier's work.[71] Further, as Bellermann indicates,[72] an occasional sentence in the *Geschichte* is strikingly reminiscent of the *Précis*. Mercier, for instance, says of the Dutch: "Des matelots et des pêcheurs, occupant un petit pays marécageux, luttent contre la mer qui menace de les engloutir," while Schiller remarks: "Hier ein friedfertiges Fischer- und Hirtenvolk, in einem vergessenen Winkel Europas, den es noch mühsam der Meeresflut abgewann."[73]

The similarities of *Don Carlos* to the *Portrait* are greater than those in the *Revolt of the Netherlands*. They are due partly, to be sure, to the fact that both authors used the same sources, Saint-Réal's *Don Carlos, nouvelle historique* (1672) and Watson's *History of the Reign of Philip II*. A contemporary critic in the *Göttingische* pointed out that Schiller had accomplished a difficult undertaking and left behind two competitors, Saint-Réal and Mercier. He praised the *Nouvelle historique,* but commented that the *Portrait* showed it was easier to see the advantages of a dramatic treatment of the theme than to carry it out. Schiller took only a few hints from Saint-Réal and nothing at all from Mercier, the critic states.[74] It is not my purpose to discuss the sources of Schiller's play.[75] I shall confine myself to indicating the similarities that escaped the eye of the commentator in the *Göttingische* but which do exist between the French piece and the *Thalia Don Carlos.* (1785-1787).

---

[70] Bellermann in his edition of Schiller (1, 320), points out that the medal was made in Holland and ended "dissipantur."

[71] Cf. Berger, *op. cit.*, II, 89f.

[72] In his edition of Schiller, XIV, 492.

[73] *Portrait*, p. 33; *Schriften*, VII, 9.

[74] Feb. 2, 1788.

[75] For this, cf. Kontz, *les Drames de la jeunesse de Schiller* (Paris, 1899), pp. 400ff.

Since the first act of *Don Carlos* was finished in 1784 and published early in 1785, the likeness of the scene between the Prince and Elizabeth in the two plays is due to a common source, here probably Otway's *Don Carlos* (1676).[76] In the course of the year 1785, however, Schiller doubtless read Mercier's drama along with its preface which he translated into German, for similarities in his second and third acts become more numerous. The hermit Hyacinthe may have served as a model for the German Prior. Both ask the monarch not to disturb their contemplative life:[77]

". . . N'est-ce pas assez d'avoir si longtemps troublé le monde, sans venir encore interrompre le repos de ceux qui en sont séparés?"

> —Zu was Ende?
> Erlassen Sie mir's lieber, Prinz. Die Welt
> Und ihr Geräte liegt schon lange Zeit
> Versiegelt da auf jene große Reise.
> Wozu die kurze Frist vor meinem Abschied
> Noch einmal es erbrechen?

Again, in the fourteenth scene of the *Portrait* the hero menaces the cardinal with the threat of destroying some day the merciless priests who are even more cruel than savages.[78] In the scenario of the first scene in the second act of the early *Don Carlos* the Cardinal informs the king of the minatory remarks directed by the prince against the Inquisition, a detail that is not to be found in the *Nouvelle historique* nor in Watson's *History*.[79] Further, when Don Carlos asks his father to give him the command in Flanders, the similarities are so striking, with no basis in Saint-Réal's account, that a definite borrowing from Mercier may be assumed:[80]

Philippe: Les passions qui dominent votre âme l'entraînent à sa perdition.

[76] *Portrait*, Sc. 2, pp. 66ff.; Schiller, *Schriften*, v¹, 34ff. Cf. Kontz, *op. cit.*, p. 442n.
[77] *Portrait*, p. 59; Schiller, *Schriften*, v¹, 154. Cf. also Lessing's Klosterbruder, *Nathan*, l. 2448ff.
[78] *Portrait*, p. 126.
[79] *Schriften*, v¹, 65. Cf. Zollinger, *Beziehungen*, p. 99.
[80] *Portrait*, Sc. 5, pp. 81f.; Schiller, *Schriften*, v¹, 76ff. Cf. Zollinger, *Beziehungen*, pp. 99ff. The italics are mine.

Philippe: Vous croyez qu'il suffit de votre air de *jeunesse* pour en
                imposer à des rebelles.

Don Carlos: Confiez-moi le soin d'aller en votre nom apaiser les troubles
                de la Flandre; je promets de vous y faire aimer. J'y ferai,
                par mon exemple, respecter et observer avec empressement
                vos volontés et vos loix.

Philipp: Geduld!
                Zu heftig braust das Blut in deinen Adern,
                Du würdest nur zerstören.

Philipp: Du redest wie ein Träumender. Dies Amt
                Will einen Mann und keinen *Jüngling* . . .

Karlos: Schicken Sie
                Mich mit dem Heer nach Flandern. Wagen Sie's
                Auf meine weiche Seele. Schon der Name
                Des königlichen Sohnes, der voraus
                Vor meinen Fahnen fliegen wird, erobert,
                Wo Herzog Albas Henker nur verheeren.

In both plays, then, the father speaks of the passionate character
of the son and emphasizes his youth, which would make it difficult for him to cope with the situation in Brabant. Again, Don
Carlos in both dramas wants to emulate his famous grandfather.[81]
The note that Schiller took from the *Précis* and appended to *Die
unüberwindliche Flotte* served perhaps also as the basis for the
last scene of the *Thalia Don Carlos* in which the king pardons the
luckless Medina Sidonia whose fleet was destroyed when God let
the winds loose.[82]

Further resemblances can be found in the last acts of *Don
Carlos,* not contained in the *Thalia* version. The great scene between Posa and Philip is in the spirit of tolerance with which the
Portrait begins. Both plays set forth conceptions of the duties of
the monarch in terms of the enlightened Eighteenth Century
rather than of the Spain of Philip II.[83] The words of the dying

---

[81] *Portrait,* p. 82; *Schriften,* v[1], 77.

[82] Cf. above p. 150. F. W. C. Lieder points out in a note to his edition of *Don
Carlos* (New York and London, 1912), p. 486, the following passage of Watson's
History (II, 270) which may also have served as a source for Schiller's scene: Philip
to Medina Sidonia, "that no man could answer for the success of an enterprise,
which like that wherein the duke had been engaged, depended on the winds and
the waves."

[83] According to Kontz, *op. cit.,* pp. 434f., Montesquieu's *Esprit des lois* is of greater
importance for this scene than Mercier's play.

queen in the Portrait (p. 271), "On placera votre image auprès de celle des Tibère et des Néron," seem to be echoed in a line that Posa speaks to the king (l. 3191f.), "Zu einem Nero und Busiris wirft Er Ihren Namen."[84] Finally, it is possible that the change of Schiller's' play from a family to a political drama may have been due to his preoccupation with Mercier. In an epilogue to the *Précis* the French author praised the political piece as a means of interesting the spectator in public and national affairs (pp. 50ff.).[85]

We see that Schiller knew Mercier's play and made use of it for several details, although it is by no means a principal source for *Don Carlos*. There is, however, no truth in the assertion that the character of the king is in any way influenced by the Frenchman's conception of him.[86] In the French play he is an out-and-out villain, the embodiment of those qualities that the enlightened Mercier despised. In Schiller's opinion, on the other hand, Philip is not completely bad. If he were, the German author believes his play would be worthless.[87]

Finally, it is not entirely impossible that Schiller may have received the idea of writing a Tell play from Mercier, who was an ardent partisan of the Swiss champion of freedom.[88] In fact, he suggests in the *Nouvel essai* that if the Swiss ever want to establish a theater of their own, they should begin with Wilhelm Tell.[89] However, plays on this subject had already appeared in both French and German before Schiller wrote his version.[90] In addition, Goethe also called his attention to the Swiss hero in

[84] Kontz, *op. cit.*, pp. 193f. Again, in the *Portrait* the king states that Abraham sacrificed his son and that the guilty Don Carlos is therefore to be abandoned to the Inquisition (p. 200). In the next-to-the-last scene in the finished *Don Carlos* the Großinquisitor uses a biblical figure, the death of Christ, whereupon Philip gives up his function as a judge over his son (l. 5269f.).

[85] Witkowski in his edition of Schiller, v, 17: "schwerlich," which is also my opinion.

[86] Kontz, *op. cit.*, 432, finds a "certaine grandeur d'âme" in Mercier's Philip which I was unable to discover.

[87] *Schriften*, v¹, 3.

[88] Cf. *l'An 2440*, pp. 157f.

[89] *Nouvel essai*, p. 40n.

[90] French versions by Henzi (1762), Lemierre (1766); German versions by Bodmer (1775), Zimmermann (1779), Ambühl (1791). Cf. E. Merz, *Tell im Drama vor und nach Schiller.* "Sprache und Dichtung," Nr. 31 (Bern, 1925).

1797.[91] The most that can be said is that Schiller's interest in Tell might have been aroused by Mercier's writings. In any case we have here another example of the similarity of interest of the two authors.

Mercier's influence is particularly strong in the fragment, *Die Polizei*. The German author's interest in Paris was due in part to accounts of Wilhelm von Wolzogen, Bode, Friedrich Schulz, and Wilhelm von Humboldt. He was also familiar with *Nicolas, ou le cœur humain dévoilé* (1796-1797) of Mercier's friend, Restif de la Bretonne, doubtless too with the latter's *Nuits de Paris* (1788-1794). Schiller also knew the *Causes célèbres* of Gayot de Pitaval, for he wrote an introduction to Niethammer's German translation of it, which appeared from 1792 to 1795.[92] The chief source for *Die Polizei*, however, is the *Tableau de Paris* (1781-1789).

Stettenheim's monograph, *Schillers Fragment: "Die Polizei,"* gives a detailed account of the relationship of Schiller's play to the *Tableau de Paris*.[93] The German author doubtless became acquainted with the description of Paris when he reviewed Hoff's *Historisch-kritische Enzyclopädie* for the *Allgemeine Literaturzeitung* in 1788.[94] Hoff includes Mercier's account of d'Argenson, Parisian chief of police at the end of the Seventeenth and the commencement of the Eighteenth Century, and as we have noted above, mentions Mercier by name. Schiller may have used the copy of the *Tableau de Paris* that belonged to the Duchess Anna Amalia. The edition he consulted was the new, augmented one which began to appear in 1782.[95]

The plan for *Die Polizei* was made after March, 1799,[96] and indicates that Schiller intended to write a tragic and a comic version. The tragedy was to show a monstrous, complicated crime involving many families. D'Argenson was to be the hero and

---

[91] *Goethes Werke,* Briefe, XII, 328; Oct. 14.

[92] Cf. Schiller, ed. Bellermann, X, 73f., and *Schillers dramatische Entwürfe und Fragmente,* hrsg. von G. Kettner (Stuttgart, 1899), p. 23. Mercier lauds Gayot de Pitaval in the *Nouvel essai,* pp. 154nf.

[93] Cf. pp. 41-48, 57-73.

[94] April 30.

[95] Cf. Stettenheim, *op. cit.,* pp. 35, 43. Cf. above p. 137.

[96] *Goethes Werke,* Tagebücher, II, 238; March 22, 1799.

Paris and its police were to be exhaustively portrayed. Schiller drew the material for this plan from the *Tableau de Paris*. The characterization of the chief of police, the duties of the police, the minor characters that are to appear, the hour-by-hour description of life in the French city are taken directly from Mercier's work.[97] A single example must suffice to indicate this similarity. The *Tableau de Paris* gives an account of the duties of the lieutenant of police. He must see that there is always an adequate food supply on hand and must check the tyrannical power of the merchants but at the same time encourage their trade. He must set limits to the necessary abuses and keep them from coming to the attention of the public. He must be ubiquitous without being noticed, and ignore that which is best left unpunished. He penetrates into the interior of families by subterranean passages and keeps their secrets: "pénétrer par des conduits souterrains dans l'intérieur des familles et leur garder les secrets qu'elles n'ont pas confiés."[98] Schiller also lists the duties of the police. They have to regulate the food supply of the city and keep the merchants from charging exorbitant prices but at the same time aid industry. They must regulate vice and prevent scandal from becoming public. They must be able to see everything and to act quickly in any locality. The police lieutenant knows, like a confessor, the weakness of many families and must therefore exercise great discretion: "Der Polizeiminister kennt, wie der Beichtvater, die Schwächen und Blößen vieler Familien und hat, ebenso wie dieser, die höchste Diskretion nötig."[99]

It is clear, then, that Schiller found his material for *Die Polizei* in the *Tableau de Paris*. However, the spirit of the fragment is his own. Schiller used what Mercier had to offer, in his youthful dramaturgical theories, in certain of his historical writings, and in *Don Carlos* and *Die Polizei*, never following him slavishly

---

[97] Stettenheim, *op. cit.*, pp. 47f. The plan for the tragedy is conveniently reprinted in *Schillers dramatische Entwürfe*, pp. 252-258.

[98] *Tableau de Paris*, VIII, 98f. Cf. the *Nouvel essai*, p. 181: "Je ne connais pas de livre plus nouveau, plus moral, plus instructif, plus intéressant, plus curieux à faire . . . qu'un livre sur Paris. Ce serait à un lieutenant de police à en fournir les matériaux. . . ."

[99] *Die Polizei, Schillers dramatische Entwürfe*, p. 255.

but always exercising critical discrimination and selectivity. We
are struck again and again by the similarity of interest of the
two writers. This becomes even more evident when we turn to
Mercier's knowledge of Schiller and his attempt to popularize
him in France.

Mercier's acquaintance with Schiller's literary productions
dates from the visit he paid to Mannheim in 1787. There he saw
a presentation of *Die Räuber*. He tells us in a letter to the *Journal de Paris* in the same year that he did not know one word of
German, but that kind neighbors and his general knowledge of
the theater enabled him to follow the action of the piece. He
praises the "pathetic, terrible, and tender" scenes of this extraordinary" play.[100] Mercier's letter also became known in Germany, being reproduced by H. A. O. Reichard in the *Cahiers de
Lecture* in 1787.[101] It came, too, as we have seen, to Schiller's attention in the same year.[102] Mercier's praise also gratified the
actor who performed the part of Franz Moor, none other than
the versatile Iffland.[103] In addition, it is possible that the French
admirer of *Die Räuber* assisted Lamartelière and Beaumarchais
in their adaptation of the play, which was produced at the Théâtre
du Marais in 1792 with the title, *Robert chef de brigands*.[104]

The proposal that Mercier made to Dalberg during this visit
to Mannheim, to have Schiller's plays translated into French,
bore fruit some fifteen years later with the appearance of a prose
translation of *Die Jungfrau* by K. F. Cramer, the translator of
le Nouveau Paris.[105] It was edited and supplied with a preface
by Mercier. In this he welcomes the opportunity to publish a
tragedy, which by its interest, gravity, and rare historical fidelity,

---

[100] Cf. E. Eggli, *Schiller et le romantisme français*, 1, 79f.

[101] Cf. *Frankfurter gelehrte Anzeigen*, Feb. 15, 1788.

[102] See above, p. 137.

[103] *Über meine theatralische Laufbahn*, pp. 76f.

[104] Cf. G. Isambert, *la Vie à Paris pendant une année de la Révolution* (Paris,
1896), p. 214. Eggli, *op. cit.*, 1, 96: "S'il est vrai que Mercier ait été l'un des
conseillers du directeur Langlois, on peut conjecturer avec quelque vraisemblance . . .
qu'il fut l'une de ces personnes qui s'intéressèrent . . . à cette adaption." It is interesting to recall that Mercier rated *Die Räuber* higher than *Götz*, cf. above, p. 135.

[105] *Jeanne d'Arc, ou la Pucelle d'Orléans*, tragédie en 5 actes, auteur Schiller, tra-
ducteur Cramer, éditeur Mercier (Paris, 1802).

leads to a veneration of Jeanne and gives her the respect due her by all of her countrymen who are not depraved or prejudiced by Voltaire's *Pucelle*. Schiller's tragedy, he continues, is not that of Racine, but such as he, Mercier, esteems and would like to see naturalized in France. He speaks also of Schiller's success in Germany, of which he has heard enthusiastic reports. Incidentally, we encounter here a line that is typical of Mercier and the nascent liberalism of the early Nineteenth Century: "Heureux qui connaît le cosmopolitisme littéraire."[106] The translation may also owe something to the Frenchman, for Cramer informed Charles de Villers in the year of its publication that Mercier had taken over the duties of a colorist and given it all the services of an excellent midwife.[107] The translation itself is mediocre and uninspired, and is inclined to be more wordy than the original. It does, however, reproduce accurately the thought of Schiller's play.[108] The preface which won for Mercier the name of "le Saint-Jean du romantisme français,"[109] only set public opinion against *Die Jungfrau,* and after the first storm of disapprobation passed, it slipped quickly into oblivion. Villers wrote seven years later, in 1809, that in all France only twelve copies had been sold.[110]

The fact that Mercier himself wrote a *Jeanne d'Arc* is another instance of the similarity of his and Schiller's interests. He pro-

---

[106] *Jeanne d'Arc,* pp. iiiff., viii.

[107] Cf. *Merciériana,* xxix; Eggli, *op. cit.,* 1, 251.

[108] Cf. the following passage:

Johanna: Er ist gerührt, er ist's! Ich habe nicht
    Umsonst gefleht, des Zornes Donnerwolke schmilzt
    Von seiner Stirne tränentauend hin,
    Und aus den Augen, Friede strahlend, bricht
    Die goldne Sonne des Gefühls hervor.
    —Weg mit den Waffen—drücket Herz an Herz—
    Er weint, er ist bezwungen, er ist unser! (l. 2370ff.)

Jeanne: Je l'ai touché . . . oui il l'est; ce n'est point en vain que j'ai supplié; la tempête fulminante du courroux s'est brisée sur son front; ses larmes coulent ainsi que la rosée des champs naguères embrasée; le sentiment l'emporte. . . . Vous! cessez le combat, pressez-vous tous cœur contre cœur. . . . Il pleure, il est subjugué! il est à nous. (pp. 87f.)

The *Allgemeine Literaturzeitung,* May 26, 1802, gives a detailed account of the preface, points out a few poor translations, praises Cramer highly, and rejoices that neither Mercier nor any other Frenchman undertook the translation.

[109] Eggli, *op. cit.,* 1, 251, refers to the *Courrier français,* March 17, 1825.

[110] Eggli, *op. cit.,* 1, 255f., quotes from the *Lübeckische Anzeige,* May 3, 1809.

posed to read his play at the Comédie-Française in 1789, but it has not come down to us.[111]

Cramer also planned to put *Maria Stuart* into French, and wrote to Fauriel in 1804 that his translation had been in Mercier's hands for some time in order that he might polish the style.[112] There is, however, no further trace of this *Marie Stuart*, which was to follow Gerstenberg's *Ugolino* in a "Théâtre étranger" projected by Cramer and Mercier.[113]

Mercier never lost his admiration for Schiller. In his *Satires contre Racine et Boileau* (1808) he praises him as a man of genius and calls the dramatic muse his "wife."[114] In an "Épitre à Lemercier" published in the *Journal de Paris* two years later, he condemns the prevailing "goût" which classes Shakespeare and Schiller as fools.[115]

Mercier and Schiller knew, then, of each other, translated each other's works and had a large number of projects in common. In fact, one French critic wrote a few years after Mercier's death that he was held in great veneration by the Germans, who found a striking resemblance between him and their Schiller.[116] They moved largely in the same realm of thought, in that of the didactic Enlightenment that prevailed in western Europe in the last quarter of the Eighteenth Century. Mercier, however, with all his ideas and ideals was quite devoid of artistry. Schiller, on the other hand, happily combined idealism and artistry to produce literary products of world renown.

[111] Cf. Béclard, *op. cit.*, pp. 223, 227n. Mercier's attitude toward Jeanne is shown by a statement in his *Portraits des rois de France* (1783), III, 8f.: "Ses mœurs étaient sans reproche; elle ne donna jamais aucun soupçon sur sa vertu."

[112] Cf. Eggli, *op. cit.*, I, 256. Cf. also a letter of Cramer to Villers in 1802, Eggli, I, 256n.

[113] *Ibid.*, I, 256f. Béclard, *op. cit.*, pp. 223, 228n., speaks of a five act *Marie Stuart* of Mercier which he was unable to find and concludes: "Il y a apparence qu'elle devait quelque chose à Schiller." Berger, *op. cit.*, II, 486, speaks of a French translation of *Maria Stuart* made by Cramer in 1802, "mit einer begeisterten Einleitung des französischen Dramatikers Sébastien Mercier." He has evidently confused this with the translation of the *Jungfrau* that appeared in that year.

[114] Pp. 5f., 45.

[115] Cf. Eggli, *op. cit.*, I, 347f.

[116] Zollinger, *Beziehungen*, p. 115, quotes from Lepeintre, *Suite du répertoire du théâtre français*, XXXIV (Paris, 1822), 285.

VIII

MERCIER AND THE *STURM UND DRANG*

THE *Sturm und Drang* in Germany is the literary form of the social, political, and spiritual forces of protest and liberalism that
were in operation in western Europe in the latter half of the
Eighteenth Century, and that culminated in France in the great
Revolution. The term *Sturm und Drang* is generally applied to
that movement of German literature which, inaugurated in 1767
by Herder's *Fragmente über die neuere deutsche Literatur*, domi-
nated thought and letters east of the Rhine until about 1786
when, with Schiller's *Don Carlos* and Goethe's Italian journey,
it gave way to the classicism of Weimar. Its slogans were nature,
feeling, passion, freedom, and social reform. Its theoretical basis
was laid by Herder, Merck, Gerstenberg, Wagner, Lenz, Klinger,
Hahn, Bürger, Goethe, and Schiller. To it belong plays by Gerstenberg, Wagner, Lenz, Klinger, Leisewitz, Goethe, and Schiller. The Ritterdrama of Törring and Babo and the "family
plays" of Schröder, Iffland, Grossmann, and others contain many
of its characteristics. In the novel it is represented by *Werther*,
the *Theatralische Sendung, Ardinghello,* and *Anton Reiser*, while
the poetry of the Göttingen group and the verse of Lenz and
young Goethe gave lyrical expression to its sentiments and aspi-
rations.

The significant works of the French champion of freedom,
Mercier, are contemporaneous with the literary products of the
German movement. It is, then, not at all remarkable that numerous and often very striking resemblances are to be found between
his dramaturgical views and his plays and those of the German
literary rebels. The present chapter will deal mainly with this
question. First, a comparison of the dramatic theories of Mercier with those of the *Stümer und Dränger* will be given, which
it is hoped will shed light on the general trend of thought in
Continental Europe at the time. This will supply the necessary

background for the following analysis of the French author's influence on individual members of the group.

The most pronounced of these general likenesses perhaps is the vigorous attack launched by Mercier and the German "geniuses" upon the French classical drama. In the *Nouvel essai* Mercier points out the inability of the classicists to portray lifelike characters. Their heroes march along pompously, their hats decorated with plumes. They are exaggerated in their pride and their language. These monsters of the imagination who never could have existed are drawn from the library rather than from the open book of the world.[1] Mercier ridicules the deifying of good taste. Good taste, he believes, is usually only an expression of weakness, a term invented to conceal pettiness and frigidity of ideas. In fact, he finds the whole classical drama of his native land cold. Its sentiments are false, extravagant, and unnatural; the terms "nature," "humanity," "the gods," "terror," "vengeance," "tyrant," "horror" occur with great frequency, but lack sincerity.[2] These plays, pervaded with the atmosphere of pomp and ceremony, are really serious farces that have nothing to contribute to the nation. Their unreality is attributable to their lack of popular appeal, to the fact that they were composed for a select circle and not for the multitude.[3]

The assault of the *Stürmer und Dränger* on the classical drama of France is just as vehement as Mercier's. Here the "geniuses" are also following in the footsteps of Lessing whose *Dramaturgie* dealt a severe blow to French literary prestige in Germany.[4] For Herder the French heroes are "dramatic fictions who outside the theater would be called fools," for Hahn they are "artificial fools" and "painted dolls."[5] Gerstenberg finds no characters in the French plays, only passions that are declaimed.[6] Herder

---

[1] *Nouvel essai*, pp. 30f., viiif.
[2] *Ibid.*, pp. vii, 51.
[3] *Ibid.*, pp. 30, 22f.
[4] For Mercier and Lessing, see below, pp. 192ff.
[5] *Shakespear, Herders sämtliche Werke*, hrsg. von Suphan, v, 214; for Hahn, cf. R. M. Werner, *Hahn*, p. 57.
[6] Cited by S. Melchinger, *Dramaturgie des Sturms und Drangs* (Gotha, 1929), pp. 10f., from *Anm. zur Braut*, p. 192, which was not available to me. Melchinger's excellent survey has been of great use to me in this part of my chapter.

has nothing but derision for the "goût" that allows only gallant heroes and well-dressed ladies and gentlemen on the stage. The piece in which good taste predominates in his opinion is merely an "academy of moral propriety."[7] Wagner speaks of the "sweet-sounding Racine" and of the "gilt paper manikins" of the French theater.[8] The *Stürmer und Dränger* consider the classical stage "unnatural and disgusting" (Herder), "ornate and beautified beauty, fanciful machinery" (Heinse), "showy and affected" (Gerstenberg), "without action or strength" (Hahn).[9] It possessed "sociability and good taste," Herder admits, but it had no popular appeal and was intended only for a small group.[10]

In their condemnation of French tragedy Mercier and the Germans deny that it can be defended as the successor of the Greek drama, and they make an onslaught on the time-honored unities, generally supposed to be sanctified by Aristotle and the ancient tradition. Mercier finds the French imitations of classical plays artificial. They have no connection with contemporary life. They are neither fish nor fowl but a mixture of the past and the present in which moderns answer to Greek names.[11] While he admits the undeniable excellence and the patriotism of the tragidies of Sophocles and Euripides, he objects to them as patterns for French plays.[12]

The author of the *Nouvel essai* is a rebel against strict classification and hence protests against Aristotle's four divisions of tragedy on the grounds that there are as many genres as there are subjects.[13] In general, he has little esteem for the Stagirite, whose *Poetics*, he believes, contains only dry categories, subtle distinctions, obscurities, and platitudes.[14] Mercier prefers the

[7] *Shakespear, Werke*, v, 215.

[8] Cited by Melchinger, *op. cit.*, p. 13, from a review in the *Frankfurter gelehrte Anzeigen*, 1774.

[9] *Shakespear, Herders Werke*, v, 216; *Briefe über das italienische Gedicht, Ricciardetto, Heinses sämtliche Werke*, hrsg. von Schüddenkopf, III[11], 469; for Gerstenberg, cf. *Rezensionen*, hrsg. von O. Fischer. "Deutsche Literaturdenkmale des 18. und 19. Jahrhunderts," Nr. 128 (Berlin, 1904), p. 77; Werner, *Hahn*, p. 57.

[10] *Über die Wirkung der Dichtkunst, Werke*, VIII, 412n.

[11] *Nouvel essai*, pp. 22, 285f.

[12] *Ibid.*, pp. 19ff.

[13] *Ibid.*, p. 267.

[14] *Ibid.*, p. 266.

"canons of good sense" to Aristotle and counsels the young poet to obey his own inspiration rather than the rules.[15] Further, he expresses the hope that the walls that separate the genres will fall, and following Diderot and others, actively sponsors the "drame," which is to be born from the mixture of tragedy and comedy.[16] He has, of course, little sympathy for the unities. We have seen that he demands leniency in regard to the unities of time and place, while insisting that the third unity be strictly observed. In addition, Mercier advises the poet to take nature as his model.[17] This leads in his own practice to the external realism that marks *l'Indigent* and *la Brouette du vinaigrier*. He does not, however, advocate an absolute naturalism. He realizes that it is not enough to copy nature. The objects must be chosen with care and embellished by the magic brush of art, or a drab reproduction will be the result.[18]

Like Mercier, Herder and the other *Stürmer und Dränger* consider the plays of the French classical tradition artificial imitations. Herder in his essay on Shakespeare denies that the copies of ancient manners and actions can lay claim to greatness. The French works may well serve as a school of national wisdom, give a picture of heroic conduct, and generally speaking be quite excellent, but by no means do they achieve the purpose of the Greek theater. Herder does not underestimate the ancient plays. He realizes that they had a definite relationship to the period and the conditions under which they were written, and that the rules which they followed were the natural result of an organic development.[19]

In the minds of the critics belonging to the revolutionary generation, Aristotle was responsible for straitjacketing the drama with rules, particularly with the canon of the so-called unities. Hence in general they do not hold him in high esteem. Gerstenberg maintains that the Stagirite wrote for his own time and not for the present and that the *Poetics* is not one of his best thought-

---

[15] *Ibid.*, pp. 96, 318.
[16] *Ibid.*, pp. 105n., 17f.
[17] *Ibid.*, p. 124.
[18] *Ibid.*, p. 142.
[19] *Shakespear, Werke*, v, 216, 215, 211.

out works.[20] Goethe's brother-in-law, Schlosser, calls him a "cold barbarian."[21] Lenz, who likewise had no great respect for Aristotle, protests against his unities and suggests that there might be a hundred instead of three.[22] Gerstenberg, inveighing against the conventional genres exclaims "away with the classification of mere names." He also attacks the unities, finding it hardly possible that significant events can take place on a single spot in a short period of time.[23] Herder has just as little sympathy for the dramatic theorist and his maxims. The unities of time and place are for him mere shadows in comparison with the action and the development of the soul, the shell around the kernel. He pokes fun at those who consult their watches after every scene to assure themselves that the action could have taken place in that amount of time.[24] The disregard of the *Stürmer und Dränger* for the established rules is complemented by an emphasis on realism. Merck discovers the essence of the epic and the dramatic in the commonplace scenes of family life, while Lenz has Goethe express the hope in *Pandämonium Germanikum* that he has not strayed far from nature.[25] It is, however, not a strictly photographic reproduction that these "geniuses" desire, but like Herder they know that something more than just the ability to describe accurately is necessary for the successful play.[26]

Not only did Mercier and the *Sturm und Drang* cast off the fetters of the established rules, they also strove to widen the scope of the drama, to increase its popular appeal, and to give it social import. The ire of the French author is aroused because tragedy is now intended not for the multitude but for the select few. He wants the small theaters enlarged, the number of benches doubled, and the loges opened to the general public.[27] The drama

---

[20] *Etwas über Shakespeare, Vermischte Schriften* (Altona, 1815-1816), III, 266, 263.

[21] Cf. Erich Schmidt, *Lenz und Klinger* (Berlin, 1878), p. 25.

[22] *Anmerkungun übers Theater, Gesammelte Schriften*, hrsg. von Blei, I, 238.

[23] *Etwas über Shakespeare, Vermischte Schriften*, III, 268; *Rezensionen*, p. 103.

[24] *Shakespear, Werke*, V, 228, 222. Cf. *Nouvel essai*, p. 146.

[25] *Allgemeine deutsche Bibliothek*, XXVI (1775), 104, Melchinger, *op. cit.*, p. 35; for Lenz, *Gesammelte Schriften*, III, 11.

[26] *Haben wir eine französische Bühne, Werke*, II, 227.

[27] *Nouvel essai*, pp. vii, 214f.

should be played rather than read. To attain popularity, it must cease dealing with figures of antiquity and treat the problems of modern times. It should have a present utility for society.[28] That means to Mercier, of course, that the theater must be dedicated to the interests of those of humbler birth, more particularly the bourgeosie. His own "drames," we have seen, are propaganda pieces in favor of the middle class. The stage, he demands in words that are echoed by Schiller, must supplement the laws of the nation and serve as a school of morality for the spectator.[29] While the moral purpose is one of the pillars on which the author of the *Nouvel essai* bases his conception of the theater, he does not wish it to become unpleasantly noticeable. He orders the "cold moralist" whose dry aphorisms are insignificant compared with the colorful picture of the eloquent artist, to withdraw and take his thick book with him.[30] Mercier does not insist that virtue always be rewarded and vice castigated. It is sufficient for the poet to show the beauty of goodness.[31] Scorning the theory that the characters of a play should be either all good or all bad, he argues for the mixture that is to be found in nature itself.[32] In short, then, Mercier advocates a more popular drama, which, although relegating the moral purpose to a subordinate position,[33] is to treat modern problems and solve them in the spirit of social equity.

A similar desire to reach wider circles with the drama is manifested by the *Stürmer und Dränger*. Lenz, for instance, wrote his plays with an audience of common people in mind, while Bürger planned a bourgeois tragedy that would be as effective in the village as on the court stage.[34] The "geniuses" also intend their plays to be produced. Lenz wants "terribly to be performed."[35] Wagner praises Klinger for having given attention in his piece *Sturm und*

[28] *Ibid.*, pp. 293, 149.
[29] Cf. above, pp. 140f.
[30] *Nouvel essai*, pp. 10f.
[31] *Ibid.*, pp. 250f.
[32] *Ibid.*, p. 52.
[33] This is not true of his practice, however.
[34] *Briefe von und an Lenz*, hrsg. von Freye und Stammler, I, 115; *Briefe von und an Bürger*, hrsg. von Strodtmann (Berlin, 1874), I, 176.
[35] *Briefe von und an Lenz*, I, 164.

Drang to the requirements of the theater, and Merck finds it preferable for a drama to be seen rather than read.[36] There is, however, no unanimity in the ranks of the *Stürmer und Dränger* on the score of the social mission of the theater. While Herder, subordinating all to the genial portrayal of character and event, launches a vigorous attack on the stage as a school of morals,[37] Lenz, Klinger, Wagner, and Schiller believe that it can benefit society. Lenz recognizes the influence the theater can have on the nation; Klinger's stated purpose in *Das leidende Weib* is to show the worth of innocence; and both Wagner and Schiller call the stage a school of morals.[38] The "geniuses" favor the bourgeoisie; and their plays, especially those of Wagner and Lenz, give sympathetic treatment to the lower classes. Even these young writers, however, are averse to the usurpation of the stage by formal morality, and like Merck would not wish the moral lesson to disturb the audience's enjoyment of the piece.[39] There is also a general dislike of characters who are spotlessly perfect. The *Stürmer und Dränger* seek to reach a broader circle of people with the presentations of their plays. While Herder and also Heinse recognize only the rights of genius, the others of the group are intent upon laying bare and ameliorating the existing social order.

It is now apparent that the attitude of Mercier and of the *Stürmer und Dränger* toward the drama is quite similar. These points of likeness, as we have sketched them, fall under three general headings. Both the French author and the Germans attacked French classicism, both advocated a new form freed from the shackles of past tradition, both favored a more popular drama with social significance. Before turning, however, to the investigation of the actual influence of Mercier on his contemporaries

---

[36] Melchinger, *op. cit.*, p. 105, quotes the *Seyler-Briefe*, p. 133, which were not available to me. For Merck, cf. Melchinger, p. 105.

[37] *Shakespear, Werke*, v, 215.

[38] For Lenz, *Rezension des Menoza, Gesammelte Schriften*, ii, 334; for Klinger, cf. a letter to Deinet, August, 1775, cited by M. Rieger, *Klinger* (Darmstadt, 1880-1896), i, 378; for Wagner, cf. *Die Kindermörderin*, hrsg. von Erich Schmidt. "Deutsche Literaturdenkmale des 18. und 19. Jahrunderts," Nr. 13 (Heilbronn, 1883), p. 109.

[39] Cf. Merck in a review of *Die Waisen* in the *Frankfurter*, 1772, ascribed to him by Melchinger, *op. cit.*, p. 29.

across the Rhine, we must discuss briefly several other points of agreement.

The *Stürmer und Dränger* had their Shakespeare enthusiasm in common with Mercier. To be sure, to the latter, the Englishman was little more than a name, a symbol for a national and more popular theater,[40] while for the Germans he embodied the spirit of the new drama of northern culture, and served as an unfailing source of inspiration. However, Mercier's vague appreciation of the "proud and independent" genius of the British poet was for Eighteenth Century France even more revolutionary than the unqualified acceptance of him in Germany.

More striking perhaps than this manifestation of a European vogue is the coincidence of Mercier's and Herder's view of the dependence of the drama on specific location and time. The French author objects to the personages of French tragedy who do not belong to any country. It is not "man in general," he says, "who is to be drawn but man in a certain time and place."[41] The author of the famous Shakespeare Essay of 1773 points out that an English dramatist necessarily writes in a different tradition from that of an ancient Greek, and asks scornfully if the time and place of life are matters of no concern.[42]

Finally, Mercier and the German literary rebels have to a certain extent their conception of genius in common. Mercier seeks to remove the obstacles that hinder the flight of genius. Nevertheless, although he admits the rights of inspiration and stresses the necessity of an individual style,[43] he is both unwilling and unable to detach himself from the didacticism of the Enlightenment. Not only are all his plays dramatized moral lessons, but even in theory he holds that the title of "good man" is higher than that of "man of genius."[44] That the poet is free, but at the same time obligated to serve humanity is a paradox shared, as we have seen, by Schiller and to some extent by others of the

---

[40] Cf. above, "Mercier and Goethe," p. 133.

[41] *Nouvel essai*, pp. 48, 150n. Cf. also Rousseau, *Lettre à d'Alembert, Petits chefs-d'œuvre de J.-J. Rousseau* (Paris, 1870), p. 388.

[42] *Shakespear, Werke*, v, 217, 222.

[43] *Nouvel essai*, pp. 244, 321nf.

[44] *Ibid.*, p. 187n.

Sturm und Drang group. The Germans emphasize the freedom of genius and see in its intensity and dynamic power the *raison d'être* of the drama, which then may be used for social purposes. On the other hand Mercier—and here lies an essential difference —was more intent upon the effect of the play than on the process by which it came into existence. Still the *Nouvel essai* does contain passages in which is to be found a doctrine of the supremacy of original genius like that of the *Sturm und Drang,* incipient in form and muffled in tone, to be sure, but all the more remarkable coming from the France of the 1770's.[45]

The problem of determining influence is always a delicate one. The very evident similarity of the dramaturgical views of Mercier and the Germans of the *Sturm und Drang* does not in itself permit the assumption that the German movement was in any way affected by the theories of the *Nouvel essai.* For coincidence of idea can well be the result of a great historical force that manifests itself independently in two lands. The critics who have considered the relationship of Mercier to the *Stürmer und Dränger,* however, all assume a relation of some kind. Rosanow, who first (1909) called attention to the debt of these men to the *Nouvel essai,* maintains that their love of Shakespeare, their realism, and their social and patriotic conception of the drama reflects a knowledge of the French work.[46] Both Köster (1912) and Petsch (1921) point to an influence of Mercier's social criticism on the *Sturm und Drang* drama.[47] San-Giorgiu, to whose careful monograph (1921) I am greatly indebted for part of the present chapter, investigates the relationship of Wagner, Lenz, and Klinger to the theories of the *Nouvel essai.*[48] Clara Stockmeyer (1922) and H. Ulmann (1923) again call attention to the similarity of

---

[45] Cf. the following (p. 192): "Tout ce qu'on ne fait pas avec une *volupté secrette,* avec une *inspiration forte,* active, permanente, on le fait mal"; for it is wrong to make "un métier de l'art d'écrire," and to produce "chaque matin sa besogne, sans éprouver ni *flamme* ni *transport.*" Then *"le feu sacré* s'éteint," and "on perd ces grands traits qui distinguent le génie." (The italics are mine.)

[46] *Lenz,* p. 142.

[47] Köster, "Die allgemeinen Tendenzen der Geniebewegung im 18. Jahrhundert," reprinted in *Die deutsche Literatur der Aufklärungszeit* (Heidelberg, 1925), pp. 278f.; Petsch, *Deutsche Dramaturgie,* 2d ed. (Hamburg, 1921), I, xix.

[48] *Sébastien Merciers dramaturgische Ideen im Sturm und Drang.*

the social views of the French author and the *Stürmer und Dränger*.[49] The French scholar Mis estimates (1928) that Mercier was for the German "geniuses" and in particular for Lenz's *Anmerkungen* what Diderot was for Lessing and his *Dramaturgie*.[50] Melchinger's excellent *Dramaturgie des Sturms und Drangs* (1929), the most recent treatise to discuss this subject, also maintains the obligation of the German playwrights to Mercier's doctrine of a popular theater with a moral purpose.[51] The whole problem, how far the young "geniuses" followed Mercier consciously or at second hand and how far they were carried along in the same direction by the spirit of the time, is purposely left undecided by Walzel (1914).[52] There is a bit of timidity but a great deal of sagacity in this critic's conclusion. We, too, must leave the question of general influence open and content ourselves with the investigation of specific instances, with the examination of the relationship between Mercier and certain of the *Stürmer und Dränger*.

It will be recalled that Mercier enjoyed an immense popularity in Germany just at the time when the *Sturm und Drang* was at its height. A large number of his works were translated into German, at least seventy-five editions appearing between 1770 and the turn of the century. His plays were performed repeatedly on the German stage. German periodicals devoted many a page to the criticism of his various works. Thus he was in the foreground of discussion in Germany at a period when a new, revolutionary movement was on foot. In fact, his dramaturgical treatise and several of his dramas are, in translation, themselves a part of the German literary upheaval.

Now, as will be seen, it was primarily the *Nouvel essai* that attracted the attention of the *Stürmer und Dränger*. It is not

---

[49] Stockmeyer, *Soziale Probleme im Drama des Sturmes und Dranges.* "Deutsche Forschungen," Nr. 5 (Frankfurt am Main, 1922), pp. 8f.; Ulmann, *Das deutsche Bürgertum in deutschen Tragödien des 18. und 19. Jahrhunderts* (Elberfeld, 1923), p. 20.

[50] "Sébastien Mercier, Schiller und Otto Ludwig," p. 191.

[51] *Op. cit.,* pp. 104, 113n., and elsewhere.

[52] "Das bürgerliche Drama," *Vom Geistesleben alter und neuer Zeit* (Leipzig, 1922), p. 194.

possible to ascertain just when in 1773 it came from the press, but internal evidence leads to the belief that it appeared early in the year.[53] Our inquiry is thus logically restricted to those German works that were written subsequent to its appearance. To Goethe and Schiller we have already devoted separate chapters. Herder, Merck, and Gerstenberg will not be treated further in the present study, it being felt that the similarity of their ideas to those of Mercier was too general to warrant a detailed investigation.[54] Consequently, the following pages will deal only with the debt of Wagner, Lenz, and Klinger, who were familiar with Mercier's works, to the French dramaturgist and playwright. Mercier's influence on the actor playwrights, Schröder, Iffland, Grossman, and others, will be studied in the concluding chapter.

It is to be expected that Mercier's influence on Heinrich Leopold Wagner, who of the *Stürmer und Dränger* was the most closely in contact with France, would be particularly noticeable. Born and reared in Strasbourg, where he died in 1779 at the age of thirty-two, Wagner owed a part of his cultural background to France. In addition, he was the most realistic and with Lenz the most democratic of the "geniuses." His literary fame, such as it is, rests upon two plays that evince these qualities, the naturalistic and socialistic *Reue nach der Tat* (1775) and *Kindermörderin* (1776). They were written in Frankfort at a time when Wagner was engaged in translating Mercier.

It is not clear just how Wagner became acquainted with *la Brouette du vinaigrier*. Perhaps his attention was first called to it by the half-French, half-German Ramond de Carbonnières (1755-1827), who became a member of the Salzmann group in Strasbourg in December, 1775, and whose writings show traces of a knowledge of the *Nouvel essai*.[55] It is possible that Ramond

---

[53] Cf. *Nouvel essai*, xiv, 349n.

[54] If Max Morris is correct in his determination of the authorship of the reviews in the *Frankfurter gelehrte Anzeigen* in 1772, then Herder was familiar with Mercier's *l'An 2440*. I have found no indication that Merck knew Mercier's writings, while Gerstenberg's critical works fall in a period before the Frenchman's influence began to make itself felt.

[55] Cf. Rosanow, *Lenz*, pp. 489nf., and Heymach, "Ramond de Carbonnières," *Jahresbericht des Fürstlich Waldeckschen Gymnasiums zu Corbach* (Mengeringhausen, 1887), p. 11.

may have met Wagner earlier in that year and have spoken to him about *la Brouette du vinaigrier*. However, this assumption is highly uncertain, and it seems more probable that Grimm's review of it (June, 1775) which, although scoring its bad taste, speaks of its "candor and verity," induced the German to undertake the translation.[56] In any case, *Der Schubkarn des Essighändlers* appeared in 1775. It was, we remember, an accurate and adequate rendering of the original.

The following year saw the publication of Wagner's translation of the *Nouvel essai*, begun, as we have seen, late in 1774, at the instigation of Goethe. As in the case of *la Brouette du vinaigrier*, the translator worked with great care and reproduced Mercier's French with exactness, adding only a few unimportant notes and comments.[57] Thus Wagner was gaining an intimate knowledge of Mercier's theory and practice that was likely to be reflected in his own independent plays.

The first of these, *Der wohltätige Unbekannte*, appeared in 1775 and gave dramatic form to a widely circulated story, according to which Montesquieu is supposed to have aided an indigent family to buy back its father from captivity in Africa.[58] Wagner's one-act play is not without merit. It received favorable criticism from literary journals, appeared on the stage in Hamburg, and was translated into French by the author himself.[59] Mercier used the same story for his three-act *Montesquieu à Marseille*, published in 1784. This, of course, can have nothing to do with *Der wohltätige Unbekannte*, but it bears witness to the similarity of interest of the two authors.

Even the subtitle of this play, "eine Familienszene," points toward Mercier. We recall that the French author defines the "drame" as "a fine moment of human life that reveals the interior of a family";[60] and he illustrates his theory in *le Faux ami*

---

[56] *Correspondance*, XI, 84f.
[57] Cf. above, "Mercier and Goethe," pp. 113f.
[58] Cf. Schmidt, *Wagner*, 2d ed., pp. 59, 132f., and *Deutscher Merkur* (1775), 4. Vierteljahr, pp. 74ff.
[59] Cf. *Wagner*, 2d ed., pp. 132f., and 1 ed., p. 17; cf. also the *Göttingische Anzeigen, Zugabe*, 1776, ccccliv.
[60] *Nouvel essai*, p. 106.

(1772), *l'Indigent* (1772), and other plays. Although the eight-year-old daughter in Wagner's work reminds us slightly of little Merval in the former, the German drama has much more in common with *l'Indigent*. In both, a brother and sister begrudge themselves the necessities of life in order to effect the release of an imprisoned father. In both, the parent refuses his freedom if it must be secured by dishonorable means. The stage setting of *Der wohltätige Unbekannte* has certainly been influenced by that of *l'Indigent*. In the latter work the abode of Joseph and Charlotte is a "misérable salle basse," the "tabourets sont dépaillés," the "meubles sont d'un bois usé," and in the background a "morceau de tapisserie cache un grabat." The Robert family in the German drama inhabits a "kleines armselig möbliertes Zimmer" that has as its furniture "vier hölzerne Stühle, einen alten Schrank und im Grund ein Bett mit ganz schlechten Vorhängen." Furthermore, a similar atmosphere of poverty and hunger, and of tears and virtue prevails in the two pieces. Finally, the preeminence accorded money matters in *Der wohltätige Unbekannte* is to be encountered in Mercier's *Brouette du vinaigrier*. While Wagner's source was a newspaper story, his choice of subject and his treatment of it were most certainly influenced by his knowledge of Mercier's plays and dramatic theories.

Wagner's next piece is characterized by a disregard for the established rules and a marked democratic tendency. *Die Reue nach der Tat,* written in 1775, was produced by Schröder in Hamburg and by Grossmann in Kassel.[61] It pictures the love of an assistant judge, Langen by name, for the daughter of a coachman, Walz, and the thwarting of this love by the machinations of Langen's fanatically aristocratic mother. The form of the play is not conventional. It has six acts, it lasts several weeks, and its scene is shifted, but never within an act. This technique seems to be a direct reflection of Mercier's precepts. It will be remembered that the French author found it only reasonable that a piece have two, four, or six acts, depending entirely on its subject.[62] As for the unity of time, Wagner has gone beyond Mercier's outer limit,

---

[61] Schmidt, *Wagner,* 2d ed., p. 133.
[62] *Nouvel essai,* pp. 253, 257.

but he adheres to his restrictions on the unity of place, that while the scene may be altered the change may be made only between the acts.

Wagner's play reproduces the bourgeois family life which the Frenchman advocated as subject matter and is hence according to his definition a "drame" in content as well as in form. The coachman Walz, a "guter Alter," with his brusque demeanor and his kind heart represents just as Dominique, the vinegar merchant in *la Brouette du vinaigrier*, the best of the lower middle class. Like him, he is proud of his humble calling and very solicitous of the welfare of his dependents. Further, *Die Reue nach der Tat* is a *Tendenzstück*. It contains an attack on the prejudice of social distinctions, an appeal for the right of marriage between persons of different ranks, a characteristic that caused a contemporary reviewer in Nicolai's conservative *Allgemeine deutsche Bibliothek* to remark with some apprehension that an imitation of Langen's behavior might endanger the present "sensible" social arrangement.[63] We have seen that in general Mercier's plays are propaganda pieces in favor of the common people. *La Brouette du vinaigrier*, in particular, deals with this problem, earlier brought to the attention of the public by Richardson and Rousseau, the relationship of a man and woman of different stations in life. Wagner wrote, then, a "drame" according to Mercier's directions. Following the dramaturgical theories of the *Nouvel essai*, he disregarded the classical rules, and in imitation of the French author's practice, he introduced class struggle into his play. The bourgeois milieu, the type character Walz, are reminiscent of *la Brouette du vinaigrier*. Only the passionate outbursts of Langen and the horrible conclusion point rather to the North than to the West.

Die Kindermörderin, written in the year following *Die Reue*, is likewise a "drame" in Mercier's sense of the word. Similar to the older play and in agreement with the Frenchman's suggestion, it has six acts. The unity of time is greatly extended, but the scene is shifted only to nearby localities and only between the

[63] XXVII (1775), 499.

acts. This play is characterized by a naturalism far more extreme than that of Mercier's most realistic drama, and exceeding his most radical demands. Once having received sanction and example from the author of the *Nouvel essai,* Wagner proceeded further in the direction indicated, until he produced a work that his authority scarcely would have greeted with much enthusiasm.

Die Kindermörderin treats a contemporary problem that was much in the air in the last decades of the Eighteenth Century. We need only to recall Bürger's ballad, Maler Müller's idyl, *Das Nußkernen,* or Schiller's youthful poem, or examine the learned journals of the day to realize the attention that socially-minded Germans were giving to the question of infanticide in those years.[64] Like *la Brouette du vinaigrier* and *Die Reue, Die Kindermörderin* is a *Tendenzstück* in defense of the bourgeoisie. In the person of von Hasenpoth it scores class prejudice which prevents the marriage of an officer, von Gröningseck to Evchen, the daughter of Humbrecht, the butcher. Wagner's play attests his acquaintanceship with Lenz's *Soldaten* and perhaps with Goethe's plans for *Faust.*[65] There are also a number of aspects in which it resembles Mercier's *Déserteur.* The situation in the French play is similar. A young officer, Valcour, takes up quarters in a family in which there is a young and attractive daughter. He immediately tries to take liberties with her, but is told by the major not to molest an honest family, and finally learns to respect the bourgeois girl. His cynical observation on woman's nature may perhaps be reflected in the words von Hasenpoth directs to his friend to induce him to desert Evchen:[66]

Toutes ces femmes, au premier abord s'effarouchent, crient, tempêtent; peu à peu elles s'humanisent, s'apprivoisent, deviennent douces.

Ich hab' wenig Frauenzimmer angetroffen, die nicht sehnlichst wünschten, bestürmt zu werden, und noch die erste zu sehen, die nicht nach der Niederlage ein paar Krokodilstränen geweint hätte.

[64] For an exhaustive treatment of this subject, cf. O. H. Werner, *The Unmarried Mother in German Literature* (New York, 1917).

[65] In *Dichtung und Wahrheit* Goethe unjustly accuses Wagner of plagiarism, *Werke,* XXVIII, 252.

[66] For Mercier, cf. *Œuvres dramatiques* (Amsterdam, 1776), I, 194; for Wagner, cf. *Sturm und Drang,* hrsg. von K. Freye (Bong & Co.), II, 491.

Wagner could hardly have been ignorant of *le Déserteur,* since it was so extensively translated, performed, and reviewed in Germany. It seems highly probable that he had it in mind, along with other works, to say nothing of actual conditions, when he wrote his play.[67] In addition, the butcher Humbrecht is a representative of the tradesman as paterfamilias that we have encountered in Dominique and Walz. The bourgeois father type is not new, to be sure, but Mercier was the first to democratize it to the rank of vinegar merchant. Humbrecht, however, does not entirely conform to type, since he is more than a man of sweet sentiment. He is able to experience deep feeling and real passion. Further, while the same air of virtue and morality prevails in *Die Kindermörderin* as in *la Brouette du vinaigrier,* the lachrymose sentimentality of the French piece has been replaced by a genuine sense of the tragic.

A less crassly realistic version of *Die Kindermörderin* was prepared by Wagner for the stage in 1779 with the title *Evchen Humbrecht oder Ihr Mütter merkts euch.* In an introduction, the author makes a few general remarks about the theater which may reflect his reading of the *Nouvel essai.* He wonders how in such days of hypocrisy the theater can become a school of morals. That would be too much to expect, he thinks, until we return to unspoiled nature which we have left so far behind. Still he hopes that this will be possible and that in the end real virtue will be triumphant. That Mercier wishes the theater to become an instrument of instruction has often been stated. In his opinion the drama is advantageous and necessary for a people that needs to be led back to the primitive and holy laws from which it has strayed.[68]

[67] An interesting parallel to the opening scene of *Die Kindermörderin* is to be found in *le Nouveau Paris,* III, 144, where it is stated that middle-class balls only succeed in filling the rooms of the foundling homes.

[68] *Nouvel essai,* p. 6: "Mais pour un peuple qui a besoin d'être ramené à ces loix primitives et saintes dont il s'est prodigieusement écarté, à ce sentiment naturel que les préjugés ont éteint; le spectacle lui est avantageux et nécessaire." *Die Kindermörderin,* hrsg. von E. Schmidt, pp. 109f.: "In unsern gleißnerischen Tagen . . . kann die Schaubühne . . . keine Schule der Sitten werden; dies von ihr zu erwarten müssen wir erst dem Stande der unverderbten Natur wieder näher rücken, von dem wir weltenweit entfernt sind." Both Mercier and Wagner may have Rousseau's *Lettre à d'Alembert* in mind.

We have little else from Wagner on dramatic theory. Passing over a review or two in the *Frankfurter,* which cannot be attributed to him with any degree of certainty, we need take into consideration only his eighteen letters on Seyler's troupe and its performances at Frankfort on the Main in 1777. These take no particular point of view on art, but contain for the most part only summaries of plays presented and eulogies of actors. Wagner, however, does assail the modernized ancient heroes of the French tradition, in particular those of Voltaire's *Mérope.*[69] He is merely continuing here the attack on the French classics that Lessing had begun ten years before and that Mercier had now undertaken in France. The similarity is much too vague to permit the assumption of any definite influence by the author of the *Nouvel essai.*

Not only does Wagner express his disapproval of *Mérope,* but he also satirizes its author in a dramatic sketch, *Voltaire am Abend seiner Apotheose* (1778). He brings before us the great French writer after the successful presentation of his last piece, *Irène.* Voltaire wishes to see into the future and falls into a stupor. A ghost, the spirit of the Nineteenth Century, appears and presents him with a dictionary of French literature, dated Paris, 1875. He reads in it an estimation of his life and works. His philosophy is called illogical, his history uncritical, his plays excellent only in style and execution. For his "would-be" epic on Henry IV he will receive in Purgatory the cruel punishment: "sich seine *Henriade* in der lateinischen Übersetzung so viele Jahr lang, als Verse oder gereimte Zeilen drin sind, von einem Ende bis ans andre vorlesen zu lassen."[70] He has *esprit,* the book admits, but he has used it against morality and religion. He has persecuted Rousseau and sinned against Shakespeare. His works have been collected into two volumes, the first of which contains his masterpiece, the *Traité sur la tolérance.*[71] The use of a dream of the future to criticize the present is found in *l'An 2440,* with which Wagner must have been acquainted. The reduction of Voltaire's

---

[69] Cf. Schmidt, *Wagner,* 2d ed., p. 51. The *Briefe* were not available to me.

[70] *Voltaire am Abend seiner Apotheose,* hrsg. von B. Seuffert. "Deutsche Literaturdenkmale des 18. und 19. Jahrhunderts," Nr. 2 (Stuttgart, 1881), p. 16.

[71] *Ibid.,* pp. 18f.

voluminous work to a few volumes seems to be modelled on a similar procedure in Mercier's utopia. Here in the king's library only a half of Voltaire's works has been preserved. The citizens of Mercier's ideal world also realize that he lacked depth, that he "faisait du génie avec de l'esprit."[72] They despise him for his treatment of Rousseau, but admire him as a lover of humanity and a great poet. Mercier, however, is not so severe as his German follower, and speaks highly of the *Henriade* and the tragedies.[73]

The probability that the similarity between Wagner's plays and the theories and examples of Mercier is more than a coincidence is increased by the fact that the German author was busy translating *la Brouette du vinaigrier* and the *Nouvel essai* at a time when he composed his own dramas. The latter are in Mercier's terminology "drames" in form, subject matter, and characterization. On the one hand, their disregard for the classical rules and their external realism, and on the other, their bourgeois atmosphere of virtue and tears and their social and revolutionary tendencies may well have been determined by their author's acquaintance with Mercier's plays and dramaturgical writings. This is supported by the resemblance between Wagner's few comments of a theoretical nature and the opinions set forth in the *Nouvel essai*. More than any other of the "geniuses," Wagner turned to Mercier, the French *Stürmer und Dränger,* for inspiration, patterns, and confirmation of his own ideas.

Lenz did not have recourse to foreign and indigenous models to the extent that Wagner did, and hence, although he had an excellent knowledge of French and was acquainted with Mercier's works, received from them only a few suggestions and an encouragement and confirmation of his own ideas. This is also San-Giorgiu's conclusion[74] and presents, as we shall see, a fairer view of the matter than that of Rosanow, who sees an influence in

---

[72] *L'An 2440,* p. 236.

[73] *Ibid.,* pp. 235ff. That Wagner owed something to Mercier was pointed out by a contemporary reviewer in the *Literatur- und Theaterzeitung;* cf. H. Korff, *Voltaire im literarischen Deutschland des 18. Jahrhunderts.* "Beiträge zur neueren Literaturgeschichte," N.F., Nrs. 10, 11 (Heidelberg, 1917-1918), II, 651.

[74] *Op. cit.,* p. 86.

every similarity of these "spiritually related men,"[75] or that of Kindermann who in his otherwise excellent book on Lenz gives the Frenchman scant attention.[76]

There is little external evidence that Lenz was acquainted with Mercier's works. In his essay on *Hamlet* (1773 or 1774) he cites in French a comment of Mercier directed against unjust satire.[77] Later, in 1776, as we have seen, he receives a copy of *l'An 2440*, "Sébastien Mercier's revelation" from Wieland.[78] Finally, in an *Entwurf einiger Grundsätze für die Erziehung überhaupt*, written later in Russia, he alludes to the opinion of the French author that the study of history is dangerous to youth.[79] These references are, to be sure, few, and of little intrinsic importance.[80] It is clear, however, that Lenz knew Mercier's writings at a time when he was revising and completing his *Anmerkungen übers Theater*.

This work, which Goethe cites along with Herder's essay on Shakespeare as the foundation of *Sturm und Drang* theory, contains the most significant of Lenz's dramatic views. Its rhapsodic and confused nature, due in part to the author's undisciplined thinking, reflects the circumstances of its origin. Lenz maintains that he read the *Anmerkungen* to a group of friends two years before the appearance of *Götz von Berlichingen* and the Shakespeare treatise, while Goethe later discounted the idea that the essay could have been composed in 1771.[81] In the light of the

---

[75] *Lenz*, p. 73, etc.

[76] *Lenz und die deutsche Romantik* (Wien und Leipzig, 1925).

[77] *Gesammelte Schriften*, IV, 216: "Tout homme est en butte aux traits de la satire, sagt Mercier, mais l'honnête homme se tait et la satire périt bientôt d'elle-même." I have not been able to locate the source of the quotation. A similar thought is to be found in *l'An 2440*, p. 244.

[78] *Briefe von und an Lenz*, II, 43.

[79] *Gesammelte Schriften*, IV, 326; cf. *l'An 2440*, pp. 67ff., *Nouvel essai*, pp. 46ff.

[80] In a short definition of the drama, headed *Für Wagnern* (1776), Lenz compares two types of plays to two gardens, a figure that seems to be borrowed from the *Nouvel essai;* cf., *Gesammelte Schriften*, IV, 286f.: "Es gibt zweierlei Art Gärten, eine, die man beim ersten Blick ganz übersieht, die andere, da man nach und nach, wie in der Natur, von einer Abwechslung zur andern fortgeht. So gibt es auch zwei Dramata. . . ." *Nouvel essai*, p. 97n.: "Nos tragédies ressemblent assez à nos jardins; ils sont beaux, mais symmétriques, peu variés, magnifiquement tristes. Les Anglais vous dessinent un jardin où la manière de la nature est plus imitée."

[81] *Dichtung und Wahrheit*, *Werke*, XXVIII, 251.

conscientious and detailed investigation of Theodor Friedrich[82] it becomes clear that a part of Lenz's work dates back to that year, while other parts were added in 1773 and 1774. Perhaps it is not entirely justifiable to assign an exact time to the composition of every page and to assume a definite number of revisions, as Friedrich does, but his hypothesis, which attributes the introduction, part of the body, for instance the criticism of Voltaire, and the conclusion to a time following the publication of Herder's essay in May, 1773, is very convincing, and will be used as a basis for the following comparison of the *Anmerkungen* with the *Nouvel essai*.

San-Giorgiu's study of the similarity of thought in those divisions of Lenz's work that were written in 1773 or in the next year and in Mercier's essay is thorough and comprehensive. My own investigation has failed to bring to light any material that would modify to any great extent his conclusions, and the summary that follows will be found to deviate from his only here and there in emphasis.[83]

In the first place, I can no more than San-Giorgiu discover any phrase or sentence that Lenz took directly from the *Nouvel essai*. Only the exclamation of the French author: "Il n'est pas difficile de trouver un versificateur exact, élégant, châtié, harmonieux; j'en connais cinq ou six. Mais le poète! le poète!" may be reflected in Lenz's comment: "Daher sehen sich die heutigen Aristoteliker . . . genötigt, eine gewisse Psychologie für alle ihre handelnden Personen anzunehmen . . . die im Grunde . . . nichts als ihre eigene Psychologie ist. Wo bleibt aber da der Dichter, Christlicher Leser! wo bleibt die Folie?" It is evident that the context is not exactly the same, and hence it would be a bit too bold to maintain that Lenz borrowed the expression, "wo bleibt aber da der Dichter," from Mercier.[84]

---

[82] *Die "Anmerkungen übers Theater,"* "Probefahrten," hrsg. von A. Köster, Nr. 13 (Leipzig, 1908); cf. the review of Hermann Schneider, *Anzeiger für deutsches Altertum,* XXXIII (1909), 295ff.

[83] My study was undertaken independently of San-Giorgiu's, but confirms his conclusions in almost every respect.

[84] *Nouvel essai,* p. 298n.; *Anmerkungen,* reprinted in Friedrich, *op. cit.,* p. 121. References to the *Anmerkungen* are to this edition unless otherwise noted.

There are, however, a number of striking points of likeness in the *Nouvel essai* and the *Anmerkungen*. In the first place, Lenz makes an attack on the French classical drama for its subservience to good taste, its monotony, its ungenuine imitation of antique and earlier models. However, we know that this is common to Mercier and Lessing and the entire *Sturm und Drang*. Here there is only a possibility that Lenz's views may have been strengthened by the French essay.

More probable is our second point, the influence Mercier may have exerted on Lenz's criticism of the preponderance of the love element on the French stage. The author of the *Nouvel essai* brings the matter up repeatedly. He chides Corneille, Crébillon, Racine, and Voltaire for having made sacrifices to this prejudice. Lenz, on his part, holds up to ridicule the French stage, where everybody is in love and everybody expatiates on his passion in the most elegant expressions.[85] Now Rousseau, in the *Lettre à d'Alembert*, had protested against the gallantry and effeminacy of Racine's elegant, sweet, and tender heroes, and refused the foremost position in a play to the element of love, holding that its excesses are dangerous and inevitable.[86] Lenz had great esteem for the Geneva philosopher, and just as well may have had in mind these comments of his as those of Mercier.

Thirdly, both Mercier and Lenz voice objection to the dramatist's portraying his own thoughts and sentiments rather than natural characters. Mercier believes his "drame" will be free from this fault and never tires of condemning both tragedy and comedy for showing the physiognomy of the author. Lenz also inveighs against the French masterpieces for presenting the writer's soul rather than a true picture of nature. His comment on this lack of objectivity is couched in terms similar to Mercier's:[87]

Mercier: J'ai voulu dire que presque tous les personnages de nos tragédies ont reçu du poète, ou leur existence, ou leur caractère.

Lenz: Ich sage, der Dichter malt das ganze Stück auf seinem eigenen Charakter.

---

[85] *Nouvel essai,* p. 245; *Anmerkungen,* p. 112.
[86] *Petits chefs-d'œuvre,* p. 479.
[87] *Nouvel essai,* pp. 48, 166; *Anmerkungen,* p. 130.

As San-Giorgiu, who also noticed this likeness, suggests,[88] the German author may here, too, have received stimulation from Rousseau. Nevertheless, it seems more probable to me that he had Mercier in mind, especially since the *Nouvel essai* is replete with allusions to this matter, and is also much closer to him in time.

An aversion to the French drama on still another score is shown by the German and French literary rebels, and this is our fourth point. Mercier, we remember, recognizes the intrinsic value of the Greek theater but objects to the imitation in modern times of its oracles and vows. Just as he censures the "dangerous doctrine of fatalism" as foreign to French character,[89] so Lenz in the conclusion to the *Anmerkungen* stresses the "blind and servile fear of the gods" as characteristic of the ancient drama and condemns the French author of tragedy for having his hero suffer not in expiation of his own misdeeds but as a victim of some higher power.[90] Although Lenz's discussion of the Greek theater otherwise has little in common with Mercier's,[91] this criticism of the use of fate in the French tragedy is similar enough to justify the conclusion of a very probable influence.[92]

Not only in their negative reaction to prevailing literary conventions do the ideas of the two men coincide, but also in their positive demand that the stage become popular and national (*volkstümlich*). The French author, we recall, maintains that real tragedy will be understood by all classes of citizens, that it will be concerned with the problems of the nation and inspire an enlightened patriotism in the breast of the spectator; in a word, that it will be national.[93] Lenz, faced with a different problem, to be sure, demands a national theater as an antidote to the vogue of imitation that had produced "German Sophocles' and Shakespeares." He wants the taste of the people and its traditions taken into consideration rather than Aristotle's rules.[94] Again, when he

[88] *Op. cit.*, p. 71.

[89] *Nouvel essai*, pp. 21, 32.

[90] *Anmerkungen*, p. 136.

[91] Here San-Giorgiu finds a greater similarity than I do. The parallels he quotes, however, do not seem very exact.

[92] The parallel in Rousseau's *Lettre à d'Alembert* is not very exact, cf. *Petits chefs-d'œuvre*, p. 402.

[93] *Nouvel essai*, pp. 39, 45.

[94] *Anmerkungen*, pp. 112f., 136f.

champions Shakespeare enthusiastically as a poet who writes for all humanity from the most exalted to the lowliest, he reiterates the thought of Mercier that the great Englishman had found the secret of speaking to all the people of his nation.[95] As far as our fifth point is concerned there is some probability that Lenz's conception of popular drama was influenced by the *Nouvel essai*.

Lenz thus concurs with Mercier in approving the "volkstümlich" nature of Shakespeare's plays. In the sixth place, he also joins the French author in extolling the lifelike characters of the British genius. For Mercier, Shakespeare's personages are real men who unite the simple and the heroic,[96] while to the German, they seem as little ashamed as the rabble that warm blood pulsates in their hearts, for as real human beings, they are not subject to fainting spells and do not die before our eyes uttering idle formulas.[97] This likeness, however, is of a general nature, and no definite influence need be assumed.[98]

Finally, a similarity may also be noted in the definition of dramatic genres. In contrasting comedy with tragedy, the author of the *Anmerkungen* holds that while the mainspring of the latter is the person, the chief interest in the former is in the event (*Sache*). In the comedy, a general understanding of the characters is quite sufficient; it is not necessary to know them thoroughly. Likewise Mercier, who devotes several chapters of his essay on the drama to Molière and the comedy, utters a protest against the "comédie de caractère." He objects to the subordination of everything in the comedy to the principal personage. The character must have its origin in the subject (*sujet*) and not be its pivot.[99] The probability that Lenz had in mind Mercier's conception of the comedy seems strong, especially in view of the fact that Lessing had expressed a contrary opinion in the *Hamburgische Dramaturgie*.[100]

---

[95] *Ibid.*, p. 139; *Nouvel essai*, p. 206.

[96] *Nouvel essai*, p. 206.

[97] *Anmerkungen*, p. 139.

[98] San-Giorgiu, *op. cit.*, p. 73: "probable." Gerstenberg and Herder both stress the real personalities in Shakespeare.

[99] *Anmerkungen*, pp. 138f.; *Nouvel essai*, pp. 68f.

[100] *Hamburgische Dramaturgie*, hrsg. von Petersen (Bong & Co.), p. 222: "und da in der Komödie die Charaktere das Hauptwerk, die Situationen aber nur die Mittel sind . . ." Cf. also p. 484n.

A summary of the investigation of the influence of the *Nouvel essai* on the *Anmerkungen* yields the following results. Although all the similarities of thought we have noted occur in the introduction, conclusion, or other parts of Lenz's essay which almost certainly were composed after the publication of Mercier's work, there are no verbal parallels or other points of likeness close enough to justify the assumption of literal borrowing. Indeed these resemblances are in several cases quite general in nature and not restricted to the two men. The attack on French tradition, the protest against the preponderance of love in the French drama, the plea for objectivity in a play, and the enthusiasm for Shakespeare's characters Lenz has in common with Mercier and others. The degree of possibility of influence will vary according to the personal feeling of the investigator and will have little scientific value.[101] In condemning the element of fate in the French tragedy, in vindicating a national and more popular stage, and in demanding a comedy of event, Lenz was probably under the influence, perhaps only confirmatory, of Mercier. That these three points are contained in the latest part of the *Anmerkungen,* written when Lenz knew of the author of the *Nouvel essai,* lends added credibility to such a contention. Here as elsewhere in this chapter, however, it is of far greater significance to have shown the great similarity of views on the part of the French and the German critic in their attack on the ruling dramatic conventions. Step by step as we have followed their advance against the classical tragedy, we have seen more clearly the identity of idea underlying the literary revolution on both sides of the Rhine.

It is also possible to point out the probability of Mercier's influence on other essays and on letters of the same period that deal with the theater but have a lesser intrinsic and historical value than the *Anmerkungen.* The essay, *Von Shakespeares Hamlet,* which we have seen quoted Mercier, discusses Shakespeare and the rules. Lenz comes to the conclusion in accord with the

---

[101] I agree with San-Giorgiu in finding probable an influence in regard to the popular and national stage and the comedy of event. While he includes the relationship to Shakespeare as probable, I am inclined to lay more emphasis on the condemnation of the fate element in the French tragedy. For the influence of Herder's Shakespeare essay on the *Anmerkungen,* cf. Friedrich, *op. cit.,* pp. 27f.

example of the great British dramatist that the unities of time and place must be subordinate to the interest. It will be recalled that Mercier allows leniency in regard to the same precepts and demands that the unity of interest—the term used by Lenz—be held inviolate.[102]

In a review of his own *Neue Menoza* in 1775, Lenz supplements the remarks made in the *Anmerkungen* about comedy. He defines it here not as a presentation that merely causes laughter but as a picture of human society designed for everybody. Calling the distinction between laughter and tears an invention of later critics, he asks how a comedy can be gay if it portrays a serious society, and concludes that Terence and Molière were more humorous than Destouches and Beaumarchais. This interpretation is similar to Mercier's conception of the "drame." That genre, as we know, is to represent in a serious fashion a "fine moment of human life," and to appeal to all classes. The French author also stresses the fact that laughing and crying have the same origin, and contends that if Molière returned to the world in 1773, he certainly would not be so gay.[103]

In a letter to Sophie von Laroche from the same year, 1775, Lenz speaks of the effort he made in *Die Soldaten* to portray realistically the various social ranks as they are, not as aristocrats imagine them. He considers the entire people to be his public. His purpose, he contends, is to acquaint the common man with the ugliness of evil and to work against the depravity of morals.[104] Here we recognize at once parallels to Mercier's and Diderot's plea for a realistic picture of the various "conditions," to Mercier's desire for a popular drama, and above all to his wish that the theater give instruction, spread useful principles, and cultivate public reason. Finally, in the *Verteidigung des Herrn W. gegen die Wolken* (1776) Lenz reiterates this view that the whole people, with the exception of the rabble, should judge a literary work. At the same time he also maintains that the philosopher must lead the common people to a better culture. Again the German author is giving

---

[102] *Gesammelte Schriften,* IV, 217; *Nouvel essai,* p. 147.
[103] *Gesammelte Schriften,* II, 333f.; *Nouvel essai,* pp. 67n., 68n.
[104] *Briefe von und an Lenz,* I, 115.

voice to Mercier's ideas. The Frenchman, while he distinguishes between the most "vile populace" and the "people," puts great faith in the critical discrimination of the masses, and also indicates the importance of the scholar and man of letters as leader of his nation.[105] Mercier's influence, then, seems to be just as strong in the several essays just traversed as in the *Anmerkungen*.

Lenz's plays also show that he has not read Mercier's treatise and "drames" in vain. The German's drama, generally speaking, is characterized by a disregard of outer form, a realism approaching naturalism, and an interest in moral and social problems. Although Lenz gives a picture of the lower classes of society, on whose side his sympathy undoubtedly lies, he did not write his plays primarily as protests against the established order *per se,* but rather as exposés of particular abuses. *Der Hofmeister,* published in 1774, but written in the two years preceding, is devoted to an attack on one of these evils, as the title indicates, the position of a private tutor in a noble family. The employment of the theater for or against some feature of the social order is very characteristic of Mercier. Adopting Rousseau's ideas to Diderot's technique, he denounces in *le Déserteur* the too severe punishment of fugitive soldiers, and in *le Faux ami* argues for a more sacred conception of matrimony. Now Lenz was among the first in Germany to make the drama a vehicle for modern social problems, and in that respect *Der Hofmeister* may well owe something to Mercier.[106] It gives a contrasting picture of the various conditions of society, in accord with Mercier's precept, and ends with one of those sentimental scenes of reconciliation that are so characteristic of the "drame." Furthermore, Wenzeslaus' defense of matrimony as an institution of God has a counterpart in scenes of *le Faux ami.*[107] However, the whole technique, the coarseness of the comedy, and the almost Zolaesque naturalism are Lenz's own, and the plot points to Rousseau rather than to the author of the *Nouvel essai.*

[105] *Gesammelte Schriften*, IV, 301; *Nouvel essai*, X, 1, 202n., etc.

[106] Cf. Hettner, *Geschichte der deutschen Literatur im 18. Jahrhundert*, hrsg. von Witkowski (Leipzig, 1929), III, 140: *"Der Hofmeister . . .* stark beeinflußt von den Dramen des Franzosen Mercier und von dessen *Nouvel essai."*

[107] This was a popular theme in the pathetic comedy of the Eighteenth Century. Cf. F. O. Nolte, *The Early Middle Class Drama* (Lancaster, Pa., 1935), pp. 121nf.

Die beiden Alten (1775), however, shows undeniably the influence of the Frenchman. This dramatic sketch relates how a young nobleman, enticed by a seductive woman and aided by a villainous servant, incarcerates his aged father in order to get possession of the estate. His uncle, sister, and brother-in-law visit him, the father gains his freedom, and pardons his repentant son. To this play, that was supposedly taken from a newspaper story, Lenz gave the subtitle "Familiengemälde." The appellation, as in the case of Wagner's *Reue nach der Tat,* reminds us of Mercier, and the division into three acts recalls the form of *le Faux ami, Jean Hennuyer,* and *le Juge.* The atmosphere is that of the lachrymose French comedy, the characters all have their prototypes in Mercier's "drames." In Belloi, the brother-in-law, we recognize the brave officer of bourgeois heritage, such as the major in *le Déserteur.* The venerable white haired father and the virtuous and weeping daughter are to be found both in Diderot and Mercier. The hero, St. Amand, not really a bad fellow, but led from the path of virtue by his love of women, recalls de Lys of *l'Indigent* or Jenneval in the play of that name. His conduct like that of Jenneval results less from innate badness or greed than from succumbing to the charms of an avaricious woman of easy virtue. As a matter of fact, as San-Giorgiu indicates, *Die beiden Alten* has much in common with *Jenneval.*[108] Lenz's adventuress has practically the same name as Mercier's (Mercier: Rosalie; Lenz: Rosinette), and the conclusion of the drama seems to be a direct imitation of the last scenes of the French piece. In both the hero is on the point of killing a close relative, but listens to the voice of conscience and hastens to save him. Both humble themselves and are forgiven in a happy and *attendrissant* conclusion. *Die beiden Alten,* in contrast with *Der Hofmeister* and *Die Soldaten,* reflects no personal experience of its author. It derives its very existence from the tearful, sentimental comedy of France, its characters from Mercier, and incidents of its plot from the latter's first play.

Die Soldaten (completed in 1775), on the other hand, mirrors a definite experience in Lenz's life. It is not necessary to enter here into the details of the "affaire Fibich"; suffice it to say that Lenz

[108] *Op. cit.,* p. 78n.

had ample opportunity in Strasbourg for firsthand observation of the conduct of troops. His play is in the tradition of the Soldatenstück which became popular with *Minna von Barnhelm* and took on a lachrymose and sentimental character with *le Déserteur* and its many German translations, adaptations, and imitations. While, however, it has nothing in common with *Minna*, it is slightly similar to Mercier's work. It gives dramatic expression to the problem of the relation of the soldier to women, which Lenz treated in a more general way in his essay *Über die Soldatenehen* (1776). The theme is not new, but in *Die Soldaten* it became for the first time in Germany the subject of a drama of protest.

Let us now examine *Die Soldaten* in greater detail in regard to points of likeness it may have with Mercier's play on the same theme. Rosanow points out certain resemblances of plot of a general nature.[109] Both pieces are laid in the border region between France and Germany, both show the relation of French officers to the indigenous middle class. The officers' cynical observations, like those of von Hasenpoth in *Die Kindermörderin,* have a pattern in Valcour's contemptuous utterances about women; their actions, in his plan to defile Clary; while the restraining voice of the chaplain brings to mind the words of the major, whom Valcour calls the "old preacher of the regiment." However, Lenz has gone further and has not like Mercier merely played with the theme of seduction, but actually portrayed it. Here as elsewhere in his "drames" the Frenchman was unable to free himself from the shackles of the Rococo which he cast aside in his dramaturgical essay. Again, Lenz does not deify the middle class to the degree that is characteristic of Mercier. While Marie's father, Wesener, belongs to the bourgeois paterfamilias type of the vinegar merchant, he is not without blame for the tragedy. Nowhere in the play does its author expatiate on the rights of the middle class as do Mercier and in his train Wagner and Grossman. When we take into account the similarities discussed above, and also the fact that there is a reference to *le Déserteur* in Lenz's play,[110] a certain influence of

---

[109] *Op. cit.,* pp. 301f.

[110] Act I, Sc. 3; it is not possible to determine definitely whether the allusion is to Sedaine's operetta or Mercier's "drame."

Mercier on *Die Soldaten* cannot be denied, although it should not be exaggerated. Here again the German author received suggestions and confirmation of his own views from his French ally and proceeded to exploit the ideas in his own manner.

In several cases, where there can be no question of influence, it is of value to note the similarity of interest of the two men. Lenz's *Tankred an Reinald* (1769), based on an episode in Tasso's epic, is a "heroid," a form in which Mercier published a number of poems in 1764. The German's *Über die Soldatenehen* espouses a point of view which Mercier touches upon in a chapter of the *Tableau de Paris*, that soldiers should be allowed to marry, since married men are more courageous and more deeply attached to their country.[111] Finally, Lenz's interest in his mother tongue, as evinced by the two lectures he delivered in Strasbourg in 1775, finds an interesting parallel in Mercier's plea in the *Nouvel essai* for a more picturesque and less restrained language,[112] and his effort with the *Néologie, ou Vocabulaire des mots nouveaux* (1801) to increase the French vocabulary.

Sharing a number of interests and often devoting themselves to the same problems, Mercier and Lenz present together a complementary picture of the French and German *Sturm und Drang*. A more independent genius and a thinker less given to imitation, Lenz was necessarily not affected by influences from without in the way that Wagner was. Lenz knew French well, must have been familiar with Mercier's early plays that flooded the German stage in the 1770's, and was occupied with the author of the *Nouvel essai* in 1773 or 1774. As San-Giorgiu indicates, the influence of the French treatise on the theater on those portions of the *Anmerkungen* that were written in these years is very probable, while various other theoretical works also show its effect. In his plays Lenz brought the social problem on the stage, picturing the various classes according to the Frenchman's precepts, realistically and with moral intent. While *Der Hofmeister* and *Die Soldaten* show traces of Mercier's practice and theory, *Die beiden Alten* is undeniably modeled on one of his "drames." Our examination of

[111] *Tableau de Paris*, IV, 25.
[112] *Nouvel essai*, p. 335.

these plays in their relation to Mercier leads to a fuller realization of the individual characteristics of the German author. Indeed, the very resemblances tend at times to bring Lenz's originality into view. In Mercier, Lenz found an ally whose stimulation and confirmation were all the more significant because they came from a nation from which the *Stürmer und Dränger* were endeavoring to liberate themselves.

One of the best estimates of Mercier's appeal to Germany is to be found in Klinger's *Betrachtungen und Gedanken*. This collection of maxims and discussion of the "world and literature" did not appear until the third year of the new century when its author had long since abandoned his *Sturm und Drang* enthusiasms. It contains the following note: "Mercier strayed to France; to judge by many of his works, old and new dramas, moral teachings, and stories, he was really meant to be an author for the whole German public. Then, too, he had a larger following in Germany than in his native land."[113] This appreciation of Mercier's foreign popularity is interesting in comparison with the opinion of a French critic writing for the *Année littéraire* in 1782, that the Germans had no tragedy or comedy due to the fact that Mercier's theories had led them astray.[114] It is, however, the only allusion we find in Klinger to the author of the *Nouvel essai*. In addition, in view of the importance of Shakespeare and Rousseau for the German author's early development, we cannot expect to discover that Mercier exerted a great influence on him, although similarities of theory and parallels in plot can be pointed out.

The few remarks that Klinger makes during his *Sturm und Drang* period about the nature of the theater are contained in a letter to Deinet (1775) and in the introduction to the edition of his works that appeared in 1786. The former contains a defense of his play *Das leidende Weib*. In this drama, he writes, he wished to show the value of innocence, the penitence and punishment of the wrongdoer, and the triumph of virtue over vice.[115] Klinger wrote his piece, then, with an eye to its moral purpose and its

---

[113] (Köln, 1803-1805), II, 433.
[114] Cited by Zollinger, *Beziehungen*, p. 115.
[115] Cf. Rieger, *Klinger*, I, 377ff.

instructive effect on the spectator. That is, of course, one of the cardinal points of the doctrine of Mercier and Diderot. However, it would be too bold and not at all necessary to assume that Klinger borrowed directly from either of them, although the possibility cannot be rejected entirely, especially since the play under consideration is a "drame." We come to a similar conclusion in regard to the introduction to his works. There he joins Mercier in castigating the classical French dramas for their lack of objectivity and the gallantry of their heroes. He also raises his voice in favor of a national and popular theater that will appeal to the heart of the German people.[116] Still all this had become by 1786, due to some extent to the *Nouvel essai* itself, part and parcel of the *Sturm und Drang*. We cannot assume here any influence of Mercier, other than an indirect one, perhaps through Wagner and Lenz.

There is nothing in the majority of Klinger's plays—"explosions of a youthful spirit and dissatisfaction," he calls them—that suggests a knowledge of Mercier. Nevertheless, certain similarities between the writers may be noted and at least one possible borrowing by Klinger can be documented. *Das leidende Weib* (1775) with its portrait of family life and its emphasis on virtue stands fairly close to the Frenchman; there are, however, no similarities in plot. To be sure, the scorn of the tempestuous youth, Franz, for poetic systems and his opinion that those who build them without feeling are fools, bring to mind Mercier's paradoxical exhortation that every treatise on poetics should be consigned to the flames, beginning with his own.[117] Otherwise there is no evidence that Klinger had here the author of the *Nouvel essai* in mind. In fact the outbursts of passion, the romantic scenes, and the picture of a decadent society point rather to Shakespeare and to Klinger's idol, Rousseau.

That Klinger wrote "many a comedy" exactly in accord with Mercier's rules is one of those unsubstantiated generalizations that unfortunately haunt the pages of even the best doctoral

---

[116] Cf. San-Giorgiu, *op. cit.*, p. 83. This was not available to me.

[117] *Das leidende Weib, Sturm und Drang*, hrsg. von Freye (Bong & Co.), III, 35f.; *Nouvel essai*, xiv.

dissertations.[118] *Der Schwur gegen die Ehe* (1797), for instance, is a "comédie gaie," a genre quite foreign to the serious-minded Mercier, and is a parody on conventional morality rather than a serious appeal for virtue. However, one comedy seems to reflect an acquaintance with the French author. *Die falschen Spieler* (1781), which mirrors actual experiences of Klinger in Prague, relates the story of a prodigal son's return to virtue and the bosom of his family. The figure of the goodhearted father, von Stahl, a rôle after the heart of the Mercier enthusiast Schröder,[119] recalls the vinegar merchant. Further, von Stahl's son, getting into a dispute with his major, challenges him, and is forced to leave the regiment. It will be remembered that because of a quarrel with a superior, Durimel likewise deserts his flag and takes refuge in a foreign land. Now *Die falschen Spieler,* despite the fact that it is a Familiengemälde with an evident moral purpose, contains quite a bit of gay humor, and occasionally even pokes fun at a too narrow conception of virtue. Further, certain scenes show the influence of *Minna* and *Die Räuber.* Thus all we can say with certainty in regard to influence is that the dismissal of an officer because of a disagreement with his superior may have been taken by Klinger for his family comedy from *le Déserteur.*[120]

The relationship may be summarized as follows: Klinger knew various of Mercier's works and recognized his German appeal. While exact parallels in their theories do not exist, general similarities suggest the probability of an indirect influence of the *Nouvel essai.* Although most of the German author's plays, with the exception of *Das leidende Weib,* have nothing in common with Mercier's rules and "drames," *Die falschen Spieler* contains, as we have just seen, an incident perhaps taken from the Frenchman's plays. Thus, while Mercier's influence on Klinger is comparatively slight, it cannot be rejected entirely.[121]

---

[118] San-Giorgiu, *op. cit.,* p. 84.

[119] Rieger, *Klinger,* II, 17.

[120] It is also possible that Klinger may have received this idea from one of the various German imitations of Mercier's play.

[121] The dramatic sketches of Leisewitz, *Die Pfandung* and *Der Besuch um Mitternacht* (both 1775) offer in a spirit akin to Mercier's, protests against tyranny and court abuses. However, the German author's more famous *Julius von Tarent*

We are now in a position where we may sum up Mercier's relationship to the *Sturm und Drang*. The parallels that have been noted in him and in the German literary rebels attest the similarity of thought which prevailed on both sides of the Rhine during the last third of the Eighteenth Century. The attack on the French tragedy, which was the embodiment of aristocracy in form and subject matter, the plea for a national and more popular drama, and the advocacy of greater freedom and realism in composition are nothing more or less than manifestations in the field of literature of the social, political, and spiritual changes that were taking place in Europe. We have passed in review these general resemblances, have indicated that they were often shared by other Frenchmen, by Diderot and Rousseau, and also by the German, Lessing. With Walzel, we have left undecided the degree of Mercier's influence on the *Sturm und Drang* and have been content to try to determine what specific "geniuses" owe to him. We have, however, always indicated similarity of idea even when no influence could be documented and have called attention to this similarity as significant of the progress of European thought at the time. We have found that Wagner, the Mercier translator, stood completely under the French author's influence; that Lenz's dramatic views and his plays were affected by his critical writings; that Klinger appreciated Mercier's popularity and may have borrowed an incident from *le Déserteur* for his own use. The *Stürmer und Dränger* found in Mercier confirmation of their ideas and new suggestions to aid them on the path that they had already begun to follow. It was particularly significant to them that this assistance came from an ally among the ranks of the enemy.

(1776), although known to the Frenchman (cf. Danzel und Guhrauer, *Lessing, neue Ausgabe*, Leipzig, prefaces: 1849-1853, II[11], Beilage, p. 7) shows no trace of his influence.

IX

MERCIER, LESSING, AND THE GERMAN MIDDLE-CLASS DRAMA

THE FINAL phase of our investigation is a consideration of Mercier's relationship to the German middle-class drama, a genre that was popular contemporaneously with the more spectacular outbursts of the *Sturm und Drang* and that continued to delight the German public long after the last embers of protest had died away. The discussion will be introduced by a comparison of the dramatic theories and the bourgeois plays of the French author and of Lessing, who really paved the way for this genre in Germany.

Lessing's *Dramaturgie*, the culmination of over fifteen years of preoccupation with the theater, was essentially conservative in nature. Still, it launched a powerful attack on the French classical tradition, and thus set the stage for the more radical theories of the *Sturm und Drang*. It is similar in some respects to Mercier's *Nouvel essai*. Since Lessing's treatise appeared five years before the French essay, it of course can owe nothing to it. It is not even certain that the German critic knew Mercier at all. He never mentions him by name in his works. However, his attention was called to him several times in the later years of his life.[1]

It is more to the point to investigate whether Mercier may not have felt the effect of Lessing's dramatic views and plays. There are no grounds for assuming that Mercier had read the *Dramaturgie* when he wrote his *Nouvel essai* in 1773. He could not read German, and Lessing's work was not translated into French until 1785. Again, considering his high opinion of foreign and German literature, he certainly would have referred to the German critic as an ally if he had known him.[2]

[1] By Ramler in 1772, cf. Danzel und Guhrauer, *Lessing*, 2d ed., hrsg. von Maltzahn und Boxberger (Berlin, 1880-1881), II, 661f., 318; by Karl Lessing in 1774, cf. *Lessings sämtliche Schriften*, hrsg. von Lachmann und Muncker (Göschen, 1886-1924), XXI, 44; by Nicolai in 1777, cf. *Lessings sämtliche Schriften*, XXI, 160f.

[2] According to Gaiffe, *le Drame en France au xviii° siècle*, p. 444, the *Dramaturgie* may have influenced the *Nouvel examen de la tragédie française* (1778). Gaiffe,

Mercier was called the "French Lessing" by J. H. Campe, the German pedagogue.[3] In addition, a report from Paris published in Bertram's *Annalen des Theaters* in 1796 states that the French author recalled Lessing, even in his facial expression.[4] The justification for Campe's epithet lies in the fact that Mercier, like Lessing, was an opponent of French classical tragedy and its narrow requirements. However, while Lessing proceeded in a scientific and rational fashion, basing his theories on the precepts of Aristotle, Mercier followed a more emotional method and considered the influence of the Greek philosopher pernicious to the modern theater. The similarity and the dissimilarity of the two dramaturgists is put into clear relief by a contemporary French and German review of the translation of the *Dramaturgie*. When the author of *la Brouette du vinaigrier* said the same thing as Lessing about the imperfections of the French stage, a critic commented in the *Année littéraire* in 1785, people just shrugged their shoulders. Mercier's "unfortunate dramas," which were beginning to rot in the bookstores, did not win anybody for his paradoxes; but a man of the merit of M. Lessing deserved all the more attention because he drew his principles from the very nature of art and from the poetic treatise of Aristotle.[5] Likewise, a German reviewer in the *Allgemeine deutsche Bibliothek* in 1788 contrasted Lessing's systematic criticism with the sporadic protests, the fervid expressions of discontent of Mercier and Rousseau.[6]

Similarly, a glance at the practice of Lessing and Mercier reveals the conservatism of the former and the progressiveness of the latter. Both write serious plays in which the chief rôles are not taken by legendary heroes or kings. Both compose social dramas

---

however, does not support this view by any evidence. The publication of the French translation of the *Dramaturgie* in 1785 was formerly ascribed to Mercier, and he may have been indirectly interested in the venture. However, if the German treatise was translatd by Cacault as is generally assumed, and as the title page reveals, revised, corrected and published by Junker, who was professor of German at the royal military school in Paris, what was Mercier's rôle? Cf. Béclard, *op. cit.*, p. 715n.

[3] Cf. Danzel und Guhrauer, *Lessing*, neue Ausgabe, II[11], Beilage, p. 7; and *Wilhelm von Humboldts Tagebücher*, I, 132n.

[4] Cf. Danzel und Guhrauer, *Lessing*, neue Ausgabe, II[11], Beilage, p. 7.

[5] Cited by Béclard, *op. cit.*, p. 716.

[6] LXXX, 111.

and fill them with tears and sweet sentiment. Both respect the unities, both proceed with a certain realism. However, while the German author is content to portray the lower nobility and the upper bourgeoisie, Mercier brings the middle class and even the proletariat on the stage. Likewise, Lessing attacks social abuses in a guarded fashion, while the French author crusades openly against social inequality. Finally, Mercier goes beyond Lessing's realism, and stressing the details of domestic life and the importance of money and material things, approaches an almost modern naturalism.[7]

To sum up, there is no appreciable influence of Lessing and Mercier on each other. The critic who wrote the *Dramaturgie*, *Miss Sara*, and *Emilia* belonged to an earlier generation than the author of the *Nouvel essai*, *l'Indigent*, and *la Brouette du vinaigrier* in both time and thought. Similar in their desire to be the reformers of their respective theaters, similar in their condemnation of French classicism, the German was conservative in his opinions and analytical in his methods. Mercier, on the other hand, was more radical in his views, and was possessed of more enthusiasm than love of order and system.

With the position of Lessing and Mercier clarified, we can now turn to the German middle-class drama. Mercier maintained in the *Nouvel essai* that "nature had impelled the Germans to fall into the useful and picturesque genre that is called (in France) the 'drame.' "[8] A study of some of the countless plays of Sprickmann, Schröder, Iffland, Grossmann, Gemmingen, Soden, and Kotzebue will confirm this contention and will indicate the similarity of the thought and technique of these two men to Mercier's theories and practice. With the exception of Sprickmann, they were all closely connected with the theater, and hence must certainly have come in contact with the Frenchman's plays which, it will be remembered, were seen so often on the German stage in the 1770's and 1780's.

[7] There is no evidence that Mercier was influenced by Lessing's plays. However, in 1780, he knew and appreciated *Emilia*, cf. Danzel und Guhrauer, *Lessing*, neue Ausgabe, II[11], Beilage, pp. 6f.

[8] *Nouvel essai*, p. 108n.

The few plays of the Westphalian Anton Matthias Sprickmann (1749-1833) that have been preserved are quite in the spirit of Lessing and are not particularly reminiscent of Mercier. Some of them, however, belong to the genre of the "drame," and it will be of interest to discuss them here briefly. *Die natürliche Tochter* (1773), a "rührendes Lustspiel," stands half way between Diderot and Lessing, and the *Sturm und Drang*.[9] While the willingness of the noble hero to marry a middle-class girl despite the difference in rank is a democratic touch that recalls Mercier, the whole characterization points to *Minna von Barnhelm*. We shall pass over *Eulalie* (1777), a kind of *Sturm und Drang* version of *Emilia*,[10] and *Das Mißverständnis* (1778), an insignificant comedy with English characters, and deal with *Der Schmuck* (1779) in greater detail. While the influence of Lessing is still unmistakable, the play none the less approaches the Familiengemälde of Mercier, Schröder, Iffland, and Grossmann in its bourgeois realism and its republicanism. Major Wegfort is the rough but kind father of the virtuous and tearful daughter, both of whom we meet so frequently in works of this kind. He has democratic inclinations and would see his child wed a peasant rather than a count. Karl, another of the chief characters, is serious, virtuous, and glories in the "bliss of furthering the general welfare of humanity." There is, then, no reason to assume that Mercier had any direct influence on the Westphalian poet. Similarity of idea, we must always remember, does not prove influence. At most, Sprickmann's democratic and humanitarian tendencies may have been stimulated and strengthened by contact with Mercier's polemics and dramas.

Since most of the plays of Friedrich Ludwig Schröder (1744-1816) are imitations of foreign models other than dramas by Mercier, it is only in his few original productions that we may look for traces of the Frenchman's influence.[11] *Der Fähndrich*

---

[9] *Die natürliche Tochter* was not available to me. It is discussed by J. Venhofen, *Sprickmanns Jugendjahre und dichterische Frühzeit* (Münster, 1909), pp. 22ff.

[10] Cf. Erich Schmidt in the *Allgemeine deutsche Biographie*, xxxv, 305ff.

[11] According to Tieck, "Die geschichtliche Entwicklung der neueren Bühne," p. 371, Schröder's *Testament*, an adaptation of the *London Prodigal*, is written in the spirit of "Mercier, Sedaine, and others after Diderot." It would scarcely be

(1782), a comedy, shows a number of similarities in plot with various of Mercier's "drames." Its hero belongs to the tradition of the brave officer, who like Durimel in *le Déserteur* meets with difficulties in his career because of his unwillingness to debase himself before an insolent superior. Like the magistrate of *le Juge*, Schröder's hero is finally revealed as the illegitimate son of a noble. Similarly, his beloved, like Charlotte in *l'Indigent*, turns out not to be his sister, after all, as was feared. In addition, secret donations to the poor, emphasis on parental authority, and the attitude that love and devotion are found only in the underprivileged, all to be sure common to the bourgeois, humanitarian theater in England, France, and Germany, are to be found in *Der Fähndrich* and in various of Mercier's plays.

Der Vetter in Lissabon (1784) also shows a number of points of likeness with the Frenchman's dramas. It has the subtitle "Familiengemälde," and is free from the comic elements found in Schröder's other original works. Again, it has only three acts, a form favored by the Frenchman. If we believe the report of Schröder's editor, Bülow, that the German actor had sketched the plot of *Der Vetter* in 1781,[12] then its similarity to Mercier's *Habitant de la Guadeloupe* (1782) must, of course, be pure coincidence.[13] Still it is valuable to note such a striking parallelism of interest. In the French play a rich merchant returns home from a lengthy stay abroad, first, however, circulating a report of his poverty. His wealthy cousins spurn him, but a poor relative, a widow, welcomes him warmly. He eventually reveals that he is rich and then marries her. The affluent cousin from Portugal pursues a similar course. Concealing his identity, he gains the friendship of the good husband and his daughter Sophie but the enmity of the arrogant wife and stepchildren. He finally saves the family from financial ruin, reveals himself, and weds the daughter. Various traits in Schröder's play seem to have been taken from others of Mercier's "drames" and modified to suit the German

---

profitable, I think, to investigate all the adaptations Schröder made. Such a study would doubtless only show a relationship similar to that noted below.

[12] *Schröders dramatische Werke*, III, iv.

[13] According to Gaiffe, *op. cit.*, p. 58, Mercier's play is adapted from *Miss Sidney Bidluph* (1761-1767), a novel by Mrs. Frances Sheridan.

author's immediate purpose. Sophie's dead husband is the French officer of the *Déserteur-Soldaten* tradition who becomes involved with the daughter of a German bourgeois family. The forlorn and hungry child of the opening scenes recalls the misery shown in *l'Indigent,* and the reconciliation of the husband and wife through the offices of Sophie's suitor, the cousin, has a none too exact parallel in the restoration of normal marital relations in *le Faux ami,* which is also brought about by a virtuous young man in quest of a relative's hand. Moreover, Schröder's play breathes the atmosphere of money and debts that had become so popular in European drama as a result of such plays as the *London Merchant* and *la Brouette du vinaigrier.* It allows, too, for a good bit of moralizing, especially by the cousin, whose hatred of evil is as great as Mercier's, and it ends in one of those touching and tearful scenes of remorse and reconciliation in which the Frenchman excels.

A similar scene of forgiveness and happiness terminates *Das Portrait der Mutter* (1786). The opening of the play is laid in a "small, wretched room" and shows us the hero, hungry, in debt, and pursued by creditors, a background familiar from *l'Indigent.* Aside from its beginning and end, however, the tone of Schröder's piece recalls the *comédie gaie* of say Beaumarchais rather than Mercier's "drame." The hero speaks of himself as a "true comedian," and the dialogue, as typical of the German author, is much more rapid and clever than that of the moralizing Mercier.

Another comedy, *Ehrgeiz und Liebe* (1788), is unique among the original plays of Schröder in that it treats the problem of class distinction. Like Mercier, Schröder is on the side of the bourgeoisie, but he is content to idealize middle-class virtue and does not introduce class collision into his play. In fact, the rich merchant recognizes the necessity of a class society. He instructs his son to dress according to his social rank, and tells him that if he wishes to be really noble, he must be kind to his inferiors and modest toward the aristocracy. The son, who at first does not wish to lower himself to a marriage with a farmer's daughter, finally consents to a union, which as in *la Brouette du vinaigrier,* joins the upper and lower strata of the nonnoble class. Finally, the desire of the merchant to better humanity is typical of Mercier and the age, and his donations of money to free an honest man from prison reproduces the charitable action of Mercier's Montesquieu.

A summary of the relation of Schröder to Mercier yields the following results. We have seen above that the German playwright adapted *Jenneval* and *le Juge* for the German stage. Further, *Olinde et Sophronie* and *la Brouette du vinaigrier* were presented at Hamburg during his directorship.[14] As a practical playwright, then, Schröder took his material wherever he could find it, and thus occasionally borrowed from Mercier. We have also noted the great similarity of interest of the two men. Both wrote in the moralizing, lachrymose, humanitarian, middle-class tradition. Schröder's dramas, however, are in general freer from the preaching that so mars the French author's work, and contain more dramatic action, better dialogue, and often very real comedy. On the other hand, they lack the serious social conviction that gives Mercier's "drames" whatever worth they may possess.

Iffland is the most characteristic author of the Eighteenth Century German middle-class drama and hence by hypothesis has much in common with Mercier. He was, also, we remember, a personal friend of the French author, acted in his plays, and wrote a sequel to one of them.[15] It would be an endless task to peruse all of his eighty dramas in order to prove an influence by Mercier. However, a study of some of his more important earlier works will indicate the similarity of thought and technique of the two men.

Iffland's first play shows a definite trace of his knowledge of Mercier. The tragedy *Albert von Thurneisen* (1781) is in the tradition of *le Déserteur* and its German imitations. Thurneisen, a captain, has incurred the enmity of his major because he has saved the life of a young soldier, who when treated inhumanly, rebels against his superior. Thurneisen later deserts the field of battle and is sentenced to be executed, not, to be sure, like the French soldier by his own parent, but still by one very close to him, the father of the girl he loves. *Albert von Thurneisen* belongs to the tearful and sentimental genre of the "drame," and incidents of its

---

[14] Cf. above, "Mercier in German Translation," "Mercier on the German Stage."
[15] *Ibid.*, cf. also p. 68.

plot seem to be taken from *le Déserteur*. However, it contains more action and is much more stirring than the French play.

The next important piece of our author, *Verbrechen aus Ehrsucht* (1784), the first member of a trilogy concerned with the fall and redemption (in bourgeois society, of course) of one Eduard Ruhberg, has the subtitle "Familiengemälde." Except for the fact that as in *Jenneval* a young man steals money from his father, there are no close parallels in plot with any of Mercier's plays. The whole atmosphere, however, reminds us of *la Brouette du vinaigrier*. In both dramas money is the deciding factor, in both, men of finance are faced with ruin. The moral tirade and the "language of the heart" are greatly in evidence in both works. There is also a tendency in the German play to glorify the bourgeoisie at the expense of the nobility, but Iffland, like Schröder, is more conservative than the revolutionary Mercier,[16] and does not attack the validity of class distinction.

Like Mercier and young Schiller, Iffland is convinced of the "influence of the drama upon the morals" of the spectators and expresses the hope that his play *Bewußtsein* will cause the playgoers to shed tears and to be more tolerant of the misfortunes of others in the future.[17] This piece (1786) and *Reue versöhnt* (1788), both devoted to the fortunes of Ruhberg, give a picture of family life in accord with Mercier's definition of the "drame." While there is no direct influence of the Frenchman visible in either, both resemble his plays in that they are lachrymose, show the merchant and the ordinary citizen in a more favorable light than the nobility and the court circle, and end in touching scenes of forgiveness.

Other plays of Iffland, *Die Jäger* (1785), *Frauenstand* (1790), *Die Hagestolzen* (1791), *Die Advokaten* (1795), and *Der Spieler* (1796), are pervaded by the same bourgeois, family atmosphere. In most cases there is a middle-class father who conceals the kindest of hearts beneath a crude exterior. He is contrasted favor-

---

[16] In the *Nouvel essai* (pp. 221n., ixf.) Mercier attacks the "horrible inequalities of wealth" that put "inhuman distances between citizens," and implies that an exclusively bourgeois society would be desirable. In his plays, however, he is not so radical as in theory.

[17] *Vorrede, Theatralische Werke* (Leipzig, 1827-1828), III, 5, 8.

ably with members of the nobility and like the vinegar merchant, eulogizes and typifies bourgeois virtue. He follows Mercier's Montesquieu in practicing secret charity. The atmosphere in which he moves is one of moralizing, exaggerated feeling, tears, humanitarianism, and money. His petty misfortunes end in a touching tableau of forgiveness and domestic felicity. He is deeply conscious of the fact that he is a German, and in this, to be sure, differs from Mercier's more cosmopolitan figure. Several of these plays deal with subjects suggested or already treated by the French author. *Die Hagestolzen*, for instance, is concerned in part with the simple life of the farmer,[18] *Die Advokaten* with the idealized magistrate, *Der Spieler* once again with the motif of military insubordination.

Direct borrowings are rare, but it is evident that Iffland and Mercier are working in the same realm of thought and that they treat similar subjects and characters in a similar manner. This relationship becomes even clearer from a statement of the German playwright after a performance of *Verbrechen aus Ehrsucht* in 1784. It is exciting, he thinks, to see the members of a large audience give way to their emotions and break into tears, for that shows that noble feelings have been aroused in them. Then having left the gathering, they transfer this emotion to the members of their family. Moreover, the emotion does not die completely and may be revived easily in the future.[19] It will be remembered that the emotional appeal of the theater and its effect on the daily life of the spectator are cardinal points of the *Nouvel essai*. Both Mercier and Iffland were preachers who wished to move the masses to virtue by appealing to their tender feelings.

Nicht mehr als sechs Schüsseln (1780) by Gustav Friedrich Wilhelm Grossmann (1746-1796), incorporates perhaps even more

---

[18] Cf. the *Nouvel essai*, p. 112: "A-t-on sensément peint . . . le cultivateur honnête, ayant pour domicile les champs que fécondent ses mains, élevant ses enfants au travail et dans cette pureté de mœurs que nous ne soupçonnons pas."

[19] In the *Theatralische Laufbahn*, p. 55. As noted above, p. 121n., there is an interesting parallel to this in a statement of Wilhelm in Book iv of the *Sendung*, written in 1783: "Daß jeder einzeln zu Hause mit den Seinigen und in den Seinigen die guten edeln Taten und lebendigen Eindrücke des Stückes nachempfinden würde." Iffland: "Die meisten Menschen verlassen mit innigem Wohlwollen die Versammlung, bringen es mit sich in ihren häuslichen Zirkel, und verbreiten es auf ihre Angehörigen. Lange noch tönt die Stimmung nach. . . ."

than Schröder's and Iffland's plays, Mercier's idea of the "drame." Grossmann was well acquainted with French language and literature, having made German adaptations of *Pygmalion* and *le Barbier de Séville*. As a member of Seyler's company in Gotha, and later as director of the Prince Elector's Court Theater in Bonn, he must have known Mercier's plays, since they were performed in both cities.[20] In addition, as we have noted above, he made use of an incident of *le Déserteur* for his drama *Henriette* (1777).[21]

Sechs Schüsseln is called a "Familiengemälde" and deserves the appellation, portraying the "fine moment of human life that reveals the interior of a family" which we have seen the French author thinks is essential for the "drame." The setting and action are realistic to the point of naturalism. The Hofrat is a capable, good-hearted, honorable servant of the state who is outwardly harsh, rough, and at times even boorish. He receives his wife's noble relatives in a dressing gown and consequently is dubbed "roturier" by them. His relationship to his sweet, virtuous, fainting daughter is one of tyranny and tenderness. He has the same unfortunate proclivity to preach that characterizes Mercier's personages, and plays, as Goethe remarks with more perspicacity than sympathy, "Haushofmeister zu Trost und Erbauung" of all his guests.[22] Despite his apparent severity, he pities the unfortunate and is happy if he can alleviate their distress. Indeed *Nicht mehr als sechs Schüsseln* seems to have been written in illustration of Mercier's contention that in the home of the honest bourgeois, manners and morals are good, decent, frank and varied.[23]

Grossmann's drama also contains an attack on the nobility as severe as Mercier himself ever made or even advocated. The nobles portrayed are vicious caricatures and must finally acknowledge defeat at the hands of the virtuous and highly idealized citizens. The Hofrat hates the corrupt courtier as much as the Frenchman, for whom he is the scourge of humanity.[24] Like Mercier's magistrate, too, the Hofrat is the soul of integrity and refuses to

[20] Cf. above, "Mercier on the German Stage."
[21] Cf. above, p. ooo.
[22] *Dichtung und Wahrheit, Werke,* xxviii, 196.
[23] *Nouvel essai,* p. 84.
[24] *Ibid.,* pp. 138f.

decide a suit against a poor widow in favor of persons in more favored circumstances.

In character, sentiment, and plot, then, *Nicht mehr als sechs Schüsseln* is an excellent example of Mercier's theories put into practice. Only in the Hofrat's *Sturm und Drang* son, in the genuine humor of the slightly inebriated guests, and in the German patriotism expressed, does Grossmann deviate from the Mercier tradition. His piece, as well as any of the French author's own "drames," shows that more than realism, moral tirades, and democratic propaganda is necessary for an artistic play.

The dramaturgical writings and the bourgeois plays of Otto Heinrich von Gemmingen (1755-1836) doubtless owe more to Diderot and Lessing than to the author of the *Nouvel essai*.[25] In the fragmentary *Mannheimer Dramaturgie für das Jahr 1779*,[26] which contains reviews of some thirty-five plays presented by Seyler, Gemmingen follows his more famous Hamburg predecessor in preferring Shakespeare and the English tradition to French classicism. He condemns Greek subjects for modern plays and finds the French tragedy nothing more than a "metropolitan convention." Further, he expresses disapproval of unities that destroy dramatic illusion, stresses the moral usefulness of the theater, desires truth and naturalism, prefers prose to poetry in the drama, demands proper costuming, and insists on a national theater for Germany. We recognize these views as also being held by Mercier. Most of them, however, can be found as well in either the *Dramaturgie* or in Diderot's theoretic writings on the drama.[27]

Gemmingen's affinity with Diderot is further indicated by the title of the one play of his that is still remembered, *Der deutsche Hausvater* (1780),[28] an adaptation of *le Père de famille*. The pater-

---

[25] Cf. *Das Drama der klassischen Periode*, hrsg. von Adolf Hauffen (DNL), II¹, 3.

[26] The *Mannheimer Dramaturgie* was not available to me. It is discussed at length in Flaischlen, *Gemmingen*, pp. 68-78.

[27] Elsewhere Gemmingen emphasizes the high rank of the poet; cf. *Von dem Einflusse, den eine Akademie auf den Geist der Nation haben sollte* (1779), in Flaischlen, *op. cit.*, pp. 56f.: "Dünke dich bei jedem neuen Unternehmen, du seiest Gottes Prophet, Triebrad des Weltpols, seiest berufen, die Welt zu belehren, zu unterstützen die Natur in ihrem Vorhaben, mit ihr zu wirken auf die Menschheit."

[28] Gemmingen also translated Rousseau's *Pygmalion* and Shakespeare's *Richard III*. His bourgeois play, *Die Erbschaft* (1779), was not available to me. The one-act comedy bearing the same name and appearing in Vol. VII of the *Deutsche*

familias who watches over the welfare of his grown children and instructs them by means of lengthy sermons, and the son who loves below his rank are taken from Diderot, while the painter and the countess, as Hauffen points out,[29] are added from *Emilia*. Gemmingen follows Diderot in portraying an unequal marriage, but he goes beyond his more conventional predecessor and in the republican spirit implied in the *Nouvel essai* avoids having his bourgeois heroine turn out at the last moment to be of the nobility. Still the father recognizes in general the necessity of class distinction and regrets in particular his son's *mésalliance* which he fears might disturb the established order. The defense of the peasants and their rights against the nobility is the only other hint of sympathy in *Der deutsche Hausvater* with the more advanced theories of Mercier. By and large, there is really little definite indication of any specific influence of the younger Frenchman on Gemmingen.

While Count Julius von Soden (1754-1831) is best known for his *Ignez de Castro* (1784), a play in the vein of young Schiller, Klinger, and Törring, his bourgeois dramas, the products of the next decade, are of more interest to us here. While Soden may have known Mercier's works, his own plays, written at a time when the Frenchman's popularity had been supplanted by that of Iffland and Kotzebue, do not show any striking points of likeness.[30] However, it is interesting to note that *Die deutsche Hausmutter* (1797), *Der Blinde* (1798), and *Versöhnung und Ruhe, oder Menschenhaß und Reue, zweiter Teil* (1801) are Familiengemälde in the Mercier tradition. In them as in Mercier's plays, the rôle of secret charity, of sweet sentiment and tears, of reconciliation and forgiveness, of moralizing, is very great. In addition, *Der Blinde*

Schaubühne (Augsburg, 1789), and in Vienna in 1796, is attributed to him by the catalogues of the Harvard University and the New York City Public Libraries, but according to Flaischlen, *op. cit.*, pp. 145ff., is by another author.

[29] *Op. cit.*, p. 4.

[30] O. Hachtmann, *Graf Julius Heinrich von Soden als Dramatiker* (Göttingen, 1902), p. 14, relates that Soden was an occasional visitor at the Ansbach court while Lady Craven was there. At that time Mercier's brother, Charles-André, was in residence as secretary of the "Literary Society of Ansbach" (cf. Baldensperger, "Notes sur le frère de Sébastien Mercier," *Revue d'Histoire littéraire de la France*, XIX (1912), 411ff.), and may have called Soden's attention to Louis-Sébastien's dramas.

attacks the corrupt upper classes. Its hero believes that virtue and righteousness, not lions and leopards form the true coat of arms of nobility, and that *"edel"* and *"Adel"* are synonymous. In general an air of humanitarianism, sentimentality, and of sympathy for the middle class, characterizes these plays of Soden and those of Iffland and Mercier. There is, however, as in the case of Iffland, a sense of nationalism in them that is quite foreign to the plays of the French author.

To investigate the numerous sentimental dramas of one of Germany's greatest and most prolific playwrights, August von Kotzebue (1761-1819) in order to document Mercier's influence would be a thankless and scarcely profitable task, and would also lead us beyond our period. The author of *Menschenhaß und Reue* was by no means averse to taking material from German or foreign contemporaries and predecessors. While Holzmann's comprehensive study does not indicate that Kotzebue had any knowledge of the Frenchman,[31] L. F. Thompson suggests that he knew the *Nouvel essai* and that his early plays follow Mercier's theories. Thompson also draws the distinction that the French author's dramas were so moral that they occasionally failed to be dramatic, whereas Kotzebue's works were so dramatic that they often in the estimation of his contemporaries failed to be moral.[32]

The work of this group of authors of the middle-class drama belongs to the genre of the "drame" that Mercier had advocated so vigorously and illustrated so abundantly. In general, the same sentimental, humanitarian, democratic spirit pervades their literary productions and those of the Frenchman. While Sprickmann is still under the influence of the conservative Lessing and Gemmingen is an avowed disciple of Diderot, Schröder, Iffland, and Grossmann are indebted in theory to the *Nouvel essai,* and in practice to such plays as *le Déserteur, l'Indigent, la Brouette du*

---

[31] *Family Relationships in the Dramas of August von Kotzebue* (Princeton, 1935).

[32] *Kotzebue.* "Bibliothèque de la Revue de littérature comparée," Nr. 51 (Paris, 1928), pp. 110f. Ch. Rabany, *Kotzebue* (Paris et Nancy, 1893), pp. 240ff., discusses Kotzebue's *Hugo Grotius* (1803), a play in the tradition of the Soldatenstück. The struggle of the young hero, Moritz Helderbusch, between his military duty and his loyalty to his adopted father, Grotius, is vaguely reminiscent of *le Déserteur,* but other points of likeness do not exist.

vinaigrier, and *le Juge.* Soden and Kotzebue, on the other hand, were active in a period when Mercier's popularity and appeal in Germany were already almost extinct and hence were less affected. Within certain limits, then, the French author left his imprint on these minor playwrights and satellites as well as on the more independent "geniuses" of the *Sturm und Drang.*

X

SUMMARY AND CONCLUSION

WITH THE WANING of the rationalistic period and the rise of the romantic movement the significance of Mercier in Germany comes to an end. Before bringing this investigation to a conclusion, however, it may be of assistance to the reader to retrace the steps by which we have sought to establish the relationship of the French writer to German literature. The introductory chapter was intended to differentiate the theories of Mercier from those of his French contemporaries, Rousseau, Beaumarchais, and especially Diderot. The rest of our study fell into two parts. Chapters ii, iii, iv attempted to determine the extent and general nature of the Frenchman's German popularity, and also to furnish the necessary background for the ensuing investigation of his specific relationship to certain German men of letters. Chapters v, vi, vii, viii, ix then dealt with Mercier and Wieland, Goethe, Schiller, the *Sturm und Drang,* and the middle-class drama. While the chapters devoted to Mercier in German translation (ii), Mercier and Wieland (v), Mercier and Schiller (vii), and Mercier and the *Sturm und Drang* (viii), offer a new examination of material already traversed in part by other scholars, those chapters concerned with Mercier on the German stage (iii), the reception of Mercier by German critics (iv), Mercier and Goethe (vi), and Mercier and the bourgeois drama (ix), offer completely new material.

The conclusions may be summarized as follows. Mercier's German popularity was very extensive. At least seventy-five editions of his various works appeared in German in the last thirty years of the Eighteenth Century. Among these *Jenneval, le Déserteur, la Brouette du vinaigrier, l'An 2440, Jezennemours,* and the *Tableau de Paris* were the most frequently translated and imitated. Three or four German works that Mercier had adapted were even translated back into the original language. His plays were performed frequently on the German stage for over twenty years, and were acted by almost every important contemporary German player. One, *la Brouette du vinaigrier*, was given in translation down past the middle of the Nineteenth Century. The outstanding literary journals of the period, in particular the *Göttingische Anzeigen* and the *Allgemeine Literaturzeitung*, devoted many pages to the discussion of the merit of his works, and almost all German men of letters were familiar with one or more of them. Wieland knew *l'An 2440* and used it extensively for his own utopian *Goldene Spiegel*. The debt of Goethe to the *Nouvel essai* for the discussion of the drama in the early books of the *Theatralische Sendung*, although not recognized by previous Goethe scholars, is unmistakable. While Schiller's early treatises on the theater do not owe as much to Mercier's discourse as the *Sendung* does, influence is nevertheless very probable. Further traces of the German dramatist's knowledge of the Frenchman can also be found in *Don Carlos* and the fragment, *Die Polizei*. At least three members of the *Sturm und Drang* group, Wagner, Lenz, and Klinger were influenced by Mercier's writings on the drama, while the *Nouvel essai* and several of the plays not only helped to determine the direction of the German literary revolt of the 1770's, but were in translation a part of it. Finally, the actor playwrights, Schröder, Iffland, Grossmann, and others, made use of Mercier's technique and produced "drames" in accord with his precepts.

The profile of Mercier's German appeal has already been outlined in the conclusion of Chapter IV, "The Reception of Mercier by German Critics." During the eighth decade of the century the Germans were attracted especially by Mercier's plays, but after 1780 their chief interest passed to his social and political works. The year 1785, approximately, marks the high point of his German vogue. The nature of his appeal, however, does not change greatly throughout the entire time he was before the German reading public. He was appreciated as an exponent of humanitarian and democratic ideas, as a lover of virtue and tender sentiment, and as the champion of a newer, more realistic form.

The reasons for Mercier's great popularity in Germany have been indicated briefly here and there in our work and may be summed up as follows. In the first place, Germans were still very

receptive to French culture. Despite Lessing and contrary to the
dictum of the average German *Literaturgeschichte,* they still suf-
fered from an inferiority complex, and turned, to be sure a bit
resentfully, to the West for patterns, stimulation, and confirmation
of their own ideas. In the second place, Mercier offered a convenient summary of the democratic, progressive French thought of
Diderot, Rousseau, and Voltaire. Again, there was no emphasis
on merely formal aspects to raise a barrier between the Frenchman and his German followers, both he and they considering content of much greater significance than mode of expression. Finally,
Mercier was one of the few Frenchmen of his time who was willing
to admit that German literature existed at all, and this liberal and
cosmopolitan point of view was flattering to his German contemporaries. In this vein he wrote in the *Satires contre Racine et
Boileau* in 1808:[1]

> Nous vîmes de nos jours la vaste Germanie
> S'amimer tout à coup aux rayons de génie.
> Là sont les esprits sains et les cœurs vertueux:
> Ils ont chéri mon nom, et j'en rends grâce aux cieux.
> Les étourneaux français n'ont point telle sagesse.

In the course of our discussion of the influence of Mercier on
Wieland, Goethe, Schiller, the *Stürmer und Dränger,* and the
authors of the middle-class drama, we continually have called attention to similarity of thought, even when no influence could be
documented, as significant of the universality of certain ideas in
Europe at the time. Tolerance, humanitarianism, democracy, the
rights of emotion were in the air, and hence it was often difficult
to distinguish between an influence of Diderot, Rousseau, Lessing,
or Mercier on the writer under consideration. On the other hand,
we have noted several points of disagreement between Mercier and
his German followers. These are important as indicative of certain
basic dissimilarities of the French and German mind. Mercier
was cosmopolitan in his outlook, the Germans more conscious of
their German nationality. The French critic subordinated everything in his plays and theories to a moral purpose, while the Germans, never leaving the didactic element entirely out of consider-

[1] P. 17.

ation, also maintained that a work of art was an expression of the personal feelings of its creator; in other words, he was interested primarily in society, they in the individual. Finally, the Germans were more deeply religious than Mercier, and were consequently unwilling to reduce religion to reason.

In addition, then, to having given an account of Mercier in Germany: the extent, duration, and the nature of his appeal, and his influence on certain German poets and playwrights, I hope to have shed some light on German thought and culture in the three decades from the *Hamburgische Dramaturgie* to the rise of Napoleon. Further, it is also hoped that my investigation may perhaps have contributed something toward the understanding of the progress and the assimilation of ideas at an extremely interesting and critical time in Western civilization.

APPENDIX I

(TO CHAPTER II)

GERMAN TRANSLATIONS OF MERCIER'S WORKS

Heinsius	Heinsius, Allgemeines Bücher-Lexikon (Leipzig, 1812-1894)
Jördens	K. H. Jördens, Lexikon deutscher Dichter und Prosaisten (Leipzig, 1806-1811)
Kayser	Kayser, Vollständiges Bücher-Lexikon (Leipzig, 1834-1912)
Kontz	A. Kontz, les Drames de la jeunesse de Schiller (Paris, 1899)
Mentzel	E. Mentzel, Geschichte der Schauspielkunst in Frankfurt am Main (Frankfurt, 1882)
Meusel	J. G. Meusel, Das gelehrte Deutschland, 5. Ausgabe (Lemgo, 1796-1834)
Meusel-Lexikon	Meusel, Lexikon der von 1750 bis 1800 verstorbenen deutschen Schriftsteller (Leipzig, 1802-1816)
Nationalbibliothek in Wien	Kataloge der Theatersammlung der Nationalbibliothek in Wien, hrsg. von der Generaldirektion der Nationalbibliothek (Wien, 1928-1934)
NBSW	Neue Bibliothek der schönen Wissenschaften (1765-1806)
NDBibl	Neue (allgemeine) deutsche Bibliothek (1793-1806)
RTK	Reichard, Theater-Kalender (1775-1800)
Schiller-Goedeke	Schillers sämtliche Schriften, hrsg. von Goedeke (Stuttgart, 1867-1876)
Schlösser	R. Schlösser, Vom Hamburger Nationaltheater zur Gothaer Hofbühne. "Theatergeschichtliche Forschungen," Nr. 13 (Hamburg und Leipzig, 1895)
Schlösser-Gotter	Schlösser, Gotter. "Theatergeschichtliche Forschungen," Nr. 10 (Hamburg und Leipzig, 1894)
Schmid	Chr. H. Schmids Chronologie des deutschen Theaters, hrsg. von Legband. "Schriften der Gesellschaft für Theatergeschichte," Nr. 1 (Berlin, 1902)
Schmidt-Wagner[1]	E. Schmidt, Heinrich Leopold Wagner (Jena, 1875)

Schmidt-Wagner[11]	——, 2 Auflage (Jena, 1879)
Schreyvogel	Joseph Schreyvogels Tagebücher, hrsg. von Karl Glossy. "Schriften der Gesellschaft für Theatergeschichte," Nrs. 2, 3 (Berlin, 1903)
Schubart	Deutsche Chronik (1774-1778)
Stettenheim	L. Stettenheim, Schillers Fragment: "Die Polizei" (Berlin, 1893)
Stockmayer	K. H. von Stockmayer, Das deutsche Soldatenstück des 18. Jahrhunderts. "Literarhistorische Forschungen," hrsg. von J. Schick und M. von Waldberg, Nr. 10 (Weimar, 1898)
Sulzer	Sulzer, Allgemeine Theorie der schönen Künste, neue vermehrte zweite Auflage (Leipzig, 1792-1799)
Walter-Archiv	F. Walter, Archiv und Bibliothek des großh. Hof- und Nationaltheaters in Mannheim (Leipzig, 1899)
Weiße	Christian Felix Weißens Selbstbiographie, hrsg. von Chr. E. Weiße und S. G. Frisch (Leipzig, 1806)
Weisstein	F. von Zobeltitz, Bibliothek Weisstein (Leipzig, 1913)
Wolter-Großmann	Jos. Wolter, Großmann (Köln, 1901)
Wurzbach	Wurzbach, Biographisches Lexikon des Kaisertums Österreich (Wien, 1856-1891)
Zollinger-Beziehungen	Zollinger, "Merciers Beziehungen zur deutschen Literatur," *Zeitschrift für französische Sprache und Literatur,* xxv (1902), 87ff.
Zollinger-Mercier	Zollinger, Louis-Sébastien Mercier als Dramatiker und Dramaturg (Straßburg, 1899)

LIST OF TRANSLATIONS

A. PLAYS

1 Jenneval, ou le Barnevelt français, drame en 5 actes et en prose, par M. Mercier, Paris, 1769.

1a *Jenneval, oder der französische Barnevelt, ein Schauspiel aus dem Französischen des Mercier, Frankfurt am Main: Varrentrapp, 1770.
Cf. ADM, 1771, 152; Fernbach, I, 143.
Meusel-Lexikon, III, 256, and Goedeke, V, 250, attribute the translation to J. H. Faber. RTK, 1776, 205, attributes it to Johann André. Meusel, I, 72, does not list it among André's works.

1aa *Jenneval, Basel: Schweighäuser, 1770.
Cf. Kayser, VI¹¹, 64.

1b *Die Gefahren der Verführung, ein Schauspiel in 4 Aufzügen, nach dem französischen Drama Jenneval frei bearbeitet von Schröder, Hamburg: Herold, 1781.
Cf. AV, 1781, 761.

1ba *Die Gefahren der Verführung, oder Jugend hat selten Tugend, Schauspiel in 4 Aufzügen nach dem Jenneval des Mercier von Schröder, Mannheim, 1780.
This is in manuscript form. Cf. Walter-Archiv, II, 24.

1bb *Die Gefahren der Verführung, "Hamburgisches Theater," Hamburg: Herold, 1778-1782, Vol. IV.
Cf. Fernbach, I, 305-306.

1bc *Die Gefahren der Verführung, Schauspiel in 4 Aufzügen, "Im kaiserl. königl. Nationaltheater aufgeführte Schauspiele," Wien: Gräffer, 1783.
Cf. Walter-Archiv, II, 103-104.

1bd Die Gefahren der Verführung, ein Schauspiel in 4 Aufzügen nach dem französischen Drama: Jenneval, frei bearbeitet von Schröder, "Deutsche Schaubühne," III, Augsburg, 1791.
Harvard University Library.

1be *Die Gefahren der Verführung, Schauspiel nach dem Französischen von Schröder, Hamburg, 1796.
Cf. Fernbach, I, 108.

1bf Die Gefahren der Verführung, "Schröders dramatische Werke," hrsg. von Bülow, Berlin, 1831. Vol. I.
Columbia University Library.

2 Le Déserteur, drame en 5 actes et en prose, par M. Mercier, Paris, 1770.

2a *Der Deserteur, ein Drama in 5 Akten, freie Übersetzung aus dem Französischen des Herrn Mercier, Mannheim: Schwan, 1771.
According to ADM, 1772, 16of., this has the new happy ending.
Schmid, 202, and Meusel, VII, 403f., attribute this to C. F. Schwan.

2aa *Der Deserteur, Schauspiel in 5 Aufzügen aus dem Französischen des Mercier in einer freien Übersetzung, zweite Auflage, Mannheim: Schwan, 1771.
Cf. Walter-Archiv, II, 14.

2ab *Der Deserteur, Drama in 5 Aufzügen nach Mercier, Mannheim, 1782.
This is in manuscript form. Cf. Walter-Archiv, II, 14.

2ac *Der Deserteur, ein Schauspiel, Mannheim: Schwan, 1791.
Cf. Zollinger-Mercier, 78, who refers to Ersch, "Literatur der schönen Künste," neue Ausgabe, Leipzig, 1840, 570.

2ad *Der Deserteur, oder die teutschen Truppen in Frankreich, Schauspiel in 4 Akten nach Mercier von Stegmayer.
Played in Vienna in May, 1814. Cf. Schreyvogel, II, 403.

2b Der Deserteur, ein Drama in 5 Handlungen von Herrn Mercier, übersetzt von C. A. von Beulwitz, Berlin: Lange, 1771.
Jena Universitätsbibliothek.

2ba *Der Deserteur, ein Drama in 5 Handlungen von Herrn Mercier, übersetzt von einem Offizier, zweite Auflage, welche mit einer zweiten fünften Handlung, nach welcher das Stück einen glücklichen Ausgang nimmt, vermehrt ist, Berlin: Lange, 1774.
Cf. ADM, 1775, 90; Fernbach, I, 60; Meusel-Lexikon, I, 379; Goedeke, V, 252.

2bb *Der Deserteur, for the Kochische Gesellschaft, by C. H. Schmid.
Cf. Stockmayer, 92f.

2c *Der Deserteur, aus dem Französischen, Hamburg, 1771.
Cf. ADM, 1772, 16of.
RTK, 1776, 198, attributes this to Madam Zink.
Schmid, 202, refers to a translation by Wittenberg, which may be this one. Meusel, VIII, 572ff., does not list it among Wittenberg's works.

2d *Durimel, oder die Einquartierung der Franzosen, ein rührendes Lustspiel nach dem Französischen, Prag: Höchenberger, 1771.
According to ADM, 1772, 16of., this has the new happy ending.
FGA, 1781, 135; Wurzbach, XX, 435; Meusel, V, 465, attribute this to J. J. Nunn.

2e *Der Deserteur, ein Drama aus dem Französischen des Herrn Mercier, Berlin, 1774.
Meusel-Lexikon, xv, 49, and Kayser, vi[11], 64, attribute this to F. F. Westarp.

2f *Das Kriegsrecht, eine Tragödie, Lüneburg, 1781.
According to Stockmayer, 93, this is "weiter nichts als der Deserteur von Mercier."

Imitations

2g *Der österreichische Deserteur, militärisches Lustspiel in 5 Aufzügen, "Marinellische Schaubühne," Wien, 1790-1791, Vol. iv.
Wurzbach, viii, 315, and Goedeke, v, 327, attribute this to K. F. Hensler. Stockmayer, 94, has not seen this, but believes it to be an imitation of Sedaine's operetta.

2h *Der ungarische Deserteur, oder der Kopf von Bronze, Schauspiel in 3 Aufzügen, Erfurt, 1814.
Kayser, vi[11], 83, attributes this to C. W. Schall.

2i *Der Deserteur, "Rührende Erzählungen aus Dichtern übersetzt," Leipzig und Frankfurt: Krieger, 1778.
Cf. AV, 1778, 762.
Published at Giessen according to FGA, Jan. 19, 1779.

2j *Die Kriegsgefangenen, oder große Begebenheiten aus kleinen Ursachen, Lustspiel in 5 Akten von Stephanie dem jüngeren, Wien, 1771. Cf. Stockmayer, 31f.; Schlösser, 41.

2k Der Freiherr von Bardenfels, ein bürgerliches Trauerspiel in 3 Aufzügen von H. C. H. von Trautzschen, "Deutsches Theater," ii, Leipzig: Jacobäer, 1773.
Harvard University Library.
The similarity is slight.

2l Der Graf von Walltron, oder die Subordination, ein Originaltrauerspiel in 5 Aufzügen, von H. F. Möller, Frankfurt am Main: Eichenbergische Erben, 1776.
ADM, 1778, 67, lists this and three other editions in 1776-1777.
Cf. Schlösser, 52, and Zollinger-Mercier, 28.
This was available to me only in a French translation: le Compte de Waltron, ou la Subordination, pièce en 3 actes, arrangée par Dalainval, Paris, 1789.
Columbia University Library.

2m *Der Deserteur aus Kindesliebe, ein Schauspiel, Wien, 1773.
Meusel, vii, 653, and Wurzbach, xxxviii, 224, attribute this to Stephanie der jüngere.

According to Schlösser, 41, and Devrient, ii, 288, this owes something to Mercier's play. According to Stockmayer, 25, it is dependent on Sedaine's operetta. According to ADM, 1774, 55, its source is a "bekannte Zeitungsgeschichte."

2n *Der Deserteur aus Kindesliebe, von Gotter nach Mercier.
Cf. Mentzel, 520.
Schlösser-Gotter, 188ff., and Meusel-Lexikon, iv, 292ff., do not list this among Gotter's works.

No connection with Mercier's work

Der Deserteur, eine Posse in einem Akt, Wien, 1808.
This was available to me in "Theater von Kotzebue," Leipzig und Wien, 1840-1841, xxi, 295ff.; Columbia University Library.

3 Olinde et Sophronie, drame héroïque en 5 actes et en prose, par M. Mercier, Paris, 1771.

3a *Olint und Sophronia, ein heroisches Drama in ungebundener Rede und 5 Aufzügen aus dem Französischen des Herrn Mercier übersetzt, Frankfurt am Main: Varrentrapp, 1771.
Cf. ADM, 1772, 154ff.; RTK, 1776, 209; Fernbach, i, 217; Walter-Archiv, ii, 44; Kayser, vi^{ii}, 64.

3b Olinth und Sophronie, ein heroisches Schauspiel in 5 Aufzügen nach dem Französischen des Mercier in reimfreien Iamben von B. C. d'Arien, Wien: Jahn, 1788.
New York City Public Library.

4 L'Indigent, drame en 4 actes, en prose, par M. Mercier, Paris, 1772.

4a Der Dürftige, ein Schauspiel in 4 Aufzügen aus dem Französischen des Hn. Mercier, Mannheim: Schwan, 1772.
Bibliothèque nationale.
Meusel, vii, 403; Goedeke, v, 252; and Kayser, vi^{ii}, 64, attribute this to Schwan.

4b *Der Dürftige, ein Drama in 4 Aufzügen aus dem Französischen des Herrn Mercier, Breslau und Leipzig: Gutsch, 1772.
Meusel-Lexikon, ix, 173; Kayser, vi^{ii}, 64; and RTK, 1779, 149, attribute this to J. Milack.

4ba *Der Dürftige, "Dramatische Werke des Herrn Mercier," i, Breslau: Gutsch, 1778.
Cf. AV, 1779, 107.
This volume also contains a translation of le Faux ami. Cf. *5aa*. ..

4c *Die dürftige Familie, ein Schauspiel in 4 Aufzügen von Mercier, Hamburg: Bode, 1773.

Cf. ADM, 1774, 104, and FGA, Dec. 24, 1773.
RTK, 1779, 149, attributes this to H. Heinrichs.

4d *Die dürftige Familie, Schauspiel in 3 Aufzügen nach Mercier, Wien, 1781.
Cf. Walter-Archiv, II, 16.

4da *Der dürftige Familie, Schauspiel in 3 Aufzügen nach Mercier, "Im kaiserl. königl. Nationaltheater aufgeführte Schauspiele," Wien: Gräffer, 1783.
Cf. Walter-Archiv, II, 104.

Imitation

4e Armut und Tugend, ein kleines Schauspiel in einem Aufzuge, zum Besten der Armen, Leipzig: Dyk, 1772.
Cf. ADM, 1773, 123, and Zollinger-Mercier, 53f.
This was available to me in "Lustspiele von Weiße," Karlsruhe, 1778, Vol. II; Columbia University Library.

5 Le Faux ami, drame en 3 actes, en prose, par M. Mercier, Paris, 1772.

5a *Der falsche Freund, ein Drama in 3 Aufzügen aus dem Französischen des Herrn Mercier übersetzt, Breslau: Gutsch, 1772.
Cf. ADM, 1775, 91.
Meusel-Lexikon, x, 173, and Kayser, vi[ii], 64, attribute this to J. Milack.

5aa *Der falsche Freund, "Dramatische Werke des Herrn Mercier," I, Breslau: Gutsch, 1778.
Cf. AV, 1779, 107.
This volume also contains a translation of l'Indigent. Cf. *4ba*.

5ab *Der falsche Freund, Drama von Mercier, Breslau: Gutsch, 1805.
Cf. Fernbach, I, 99.
Kayser, vi[ii], 64, lists an edition at Leipzig: Nauck, 1805, which is doubtless this one.

5b *Der falsche Freund, ein Drama in 3 Aufzügen aus dem Französischen des Herrn Mercier, Breslau, 1774.
Meusel-Lexikon, xv, 50; Ersch, II, 373; and Zollinger-Mercier, 81, attribute this to F. F. Westarp.

6 Jean Hennuyer, évêque de Lisieux, drame en 3 actes, Londres, 1772.

6a *Johann Hennüyer, Bischof von Lisieux, Drama in 3 Aufzügen, Leipzig: Schwickert, 1773.
Cf. ADM, 1774, 102f.

RTK, 1779, 160; Ersch-Supplément, v, 325; Kayser, vi^{ii}, 41; and Weiße, 239, attribute this to C. F. Weisse.

6b *Johann Hennüyer, Bischof von Lisieux, ein Drama in 3 Aufzügen aus dem Französischen des Herrn von Voltaire, Hamburg und Güstrow: Buchenröder und Ritter, 1774.
Cf. ADM, 1774, 103, and RTK, 1779, 160.
Ersch-Supplément, i, 325, attributes this to J. G. P. Thiele.

7 Le Juge, drame en 3 actes, en prose, par M. Mercier, Paris, 1774.

7a *Der Richter, ein Schauspiel in 3 Aufzügen, aus dem Französischen des Mercier, "Theaterstücke von A. von Knigge," i, Hanau und Offenbach: Schulz, 1779.
Cf. ADM, 1780, 55; FGA, April 13-16, 1779; Meusel-Lexikon, vii, 123.

7aa *Der Richter, "Sammlung ausländischer Schauspiele für die deutsche Bühne umgearbeitet" von A. von K., i, Heidelberg: Geb. Pfähler, 1784.
Cf. ALZ, May 19, 1785; Fernbach, i, 245.

7b Der Richter, ein Schauspiel nach Mercier in 2 Aufzügen, aufgeführt auf dem kaiserl. königl. Nat. Hoftheater, Wien, 1781.
New York City Public Library.
This is an adaptation of Knigge's version by Schröder. Cf. ALZ, May 19, 1785.

8 Natalie, drame en 4 actes, par M. Mercier, Paris, 1775.

8a *Natalie, ein Drama in 4 Akten nach dem Französischen des Mercier, Gotha: Ettinger, 1778.
Cf. AV, 1779, 127; ADBibl, xli (1780), 452.
Meusel, iii, 193f., and Kayser, vi^{ii}, 64, attribute this to C. G. von Helmolt.

8aa Natalie, ein Drama in 4 Akten nach dem Französischen des Mercier, "Theater der Ausländer, Verdeutschungen," i, Gotha: Ettinger, 1778, 285ff.
Bibliothèque nationale.
ADM, 1780, 115f., attributes this to von Helmolt.

8b *Natalie, ein Drama in 4 Handlungen von Herrn Mercier, aus dem Französischen übersetzt von C. A. von B., Berlin: Lange, 1778.
Cf. AV, 1778, 465f.
Attributed by Meusel, i, 276f., and Kayser, vi^{ii}, 68, to von Beulwitz, and listed as published at Gotha.

9 La Brouette du vinaigrier, drame en 3 actes, par M. Mercier, Paris, 1775.

9a Der Schubkarn des Essighändlers, ein Lustspiel in 3 Aufzügen, aus dem Französischen des Herrn Mercier, Frankfurt am Main: Eichenbergische Erben, 1775.
Hamburg Universitätsbibliothek.
ADM, 1777, 134f.; Kontz, 191; and Weisstein, 1, 666, attribute this to H. L. Wagner.

9aa *Der Schubkarn des Essighändlers, 2d ed., 1776.
Cf. Kontz, 191.

9ab *Der Schubkarn des Essighändlers, ein Lustspiel in 3 Aufzügen, "Neue Schauspiele für das Chf. Theater in München," IV, Augsburg: Stage, 1776.
Cf. ADM, 1778, 69, and Schubart, 1776, III, Schluß.

9ac *Der Schubkarn des Essighändlers, "Gesammelte Schauspiele," Frankfurt, 1780.
Cf. Schmidt-Wagner[ii], 130.

9ad Der Schubkarn des Essighändlers, ein Lustspiel in 3 Aufzügen, aus dem Französischen des Herrn Mercier, 1804.
New York City Public Library.
This is Wagner's translation. Wrongly attributed to von Brahm by the New York City Public Library catalogue.

9ae Der Schubkarn des Essighändlers, "H. L. Wagners gesammelte Werke," hrsg. von L. Hirschberg, 1, Potsdam, 1923, 185ff.
Columbia University Library.

9b Der Essigmann mit seinem Schubkarrn, ein Drama von 3 Akten aus dem Französischen des Herrn Mercier, für das Herzoglich-Gothaische Hoftheater übersetzt von H. von H., Gotha: Ettinger, 1776.
Bibliothèque nationale.
FGA, March 30 and April 2, 1779, and Meusel, III, 193f., attribute this to von Helmolt.

9ba *Der Essigmann mit seinem Schubkarrn, ein Drama in 3 Akten von Mercier, übersetzt von H. von H., Gotha: Ettinger, 1803.
Cf. Fernbach, 1, 84.

9c *Der Schubkarn des Essighändlers, ein Lustspiel in 3 Aufzügen, "Neues Wiener Theater," II, Wien: Kurzböck, 1776.
Cf. ADM, 1777, 72f.
According to Meusel, 1, 399, this was also available by itself. Goedeke, V, 313, and RTK, 1776, 269, attribute this M. von Brahm.

9d *Der Schubkarn des Essigkrämers, "Neues französisches Theater," 1, Leipzig: Müller, 1776.

Cf. ADM, 1777, 133, and RTK, 1776, 220.

Schmidt-Wagner[1], 21, attributes this to Becker.

9e *Der Essigmann mit seinem Schubkarrn, Drama von Mercier, ins Deutsche übersetzt von M. (1775-1777).
According to Mentzel, 519, this was written by Marchand for the Kurpf. Hofschauspieler in Frankfort.

9f *Der Essigmann mit seinem Schubkarren, Drama in 3 Aufzügen nach Mercier.
Played at Weimar in 1798; attributed to Schröder. Cf. Burkhardt, 28

9g *Der Essighändler, Schauspiel von Mercier, übersetzt und neu bearbeitet, 2 Akten, Berlin: Hayns Erben, 1846.
Cf. Grethlein, 171.

9h *Der Essighändler, Schauspiel für die deutsche Bühnen-Darstellung neu bearbeitet und in einem Akt zusammengezogen von Karl Grunert, "Classische Theaterbibliothek aller Nationen," xxxix, Stuttgart, 1868.
Cf. British Museum General Catalogue of Books, under "Mercier," and ADB, x, 51.

Sequel

9i Das Erbteil des Vaters, ein Schauspiel in 4 Aufzügen, Fortsetzung des Schauspiels: der Essighändler von Mercier, "Dramatische Werke," Leipzig, 1798-1807, Vol. xvi.
Cf. Fernbach, i, 349f.
This was available to me in "Ifflands theatralische Werke," Leipzig, 1827-1828, Vol. ix.

10 La Destruction de la Ligue, ou la Réduction de Paris, pièce nationale en 4 actes. Amsterdam, 1782.

10a *Die Zerstörung des heiligen Bundes, oder die Übergabe von Paris, ein Nationalschauspiel aus dem Französischen des Mercier, Leipzig, 1782.
Meusel, viii, 488, and Kayser, vi[11], 64, attribute this to C. A. Wichmann.

10b *Die Zerstörung der Ligue, Genf, 1782.
Cf. Zollinger-Beziehungen, 114n.

11 Portrait de Philippe ii, roi d'Espagne, par M. Mercier, auteur du Tableau de Paris (précédé d'un précis historique), Amsterdam, 1785.

11a Philipp der Zweite, König von Spanien, von Mercier, "Thalia," i[11], 1787.
This is a translation of the Précis by Schiller.

11b *Philipp der Zweite, König von Spanien, ein dramatisches Gemälde von Mercier, aus dem Französischen, Liegnitz und Leipzig: Siegert, 1788.
Cf. ADBibl. xcv (1790), 233; Heinsius, ii, 1001; Schiller-Goedeke, iv, 88n.

12 Le Ci-devant noble, comédie en 3 actes, en prose, par M. Mercier, Paris, 1792.

12a *Der Adliche, wie er weiland war, Lustspiel in 3 Akten, aus dem Französischen des Mercier, Hamburg: Matthießen, 1792.
Cf. Fernbach, i, 3; Ersch-Supplément, i, 325; Kayser, vi^{ii}, 64.

Miscellaneous

13 *Schauspiele vom Verfasser des Jahres 2440, Heidelberg, 1784.
Cf. Sulzer, i, 560a, and RTK, 1785, 165.
The contents of this collection is unknown to me.

14 Montesquieu à Marseille, pièce en 3 actes, par M. Mercier, Lausanne, 1784.

14a Montesquieu, oder die unbekannte Wohltat, ein Schauspiel in 3 Handlungen für die Mannheimer Nationalschaubühne, Mannheim: Schwan und Götz, 1787.
This was available to me in "Deutsche Schaubühne," viii, Augsburg, 1789; Harvard University Library.
Attributed by Ersch-Supplément, i, 325, to Dalberg.
The similarity to Mercier's work is slight. This is rather an imitation of J. Pilhes, le Bienfait anonyme, comédie en 3 actes et en prose, Paris, 1785.

15 *Der ungegründete Verdacht, Lustspiel in einem Akt, nach Mercier von von Brahm.
Cf. Wolter-Großmann, vii; Meusel, i, 399; RTK, 1776, 220.
I was unable to discover the original of this.

B. OTHER WORKS

16 L'Homme sauvage, histoire traduite de . . . par M. Mercier, Paris, 1767.

16a *Der Naturmensch, von Mercier, aus dem Französischen übersetzt von C. A. J. Brückmann, Hamburg und Leipzig: Matthießen, 1787.
Cf. ALZ, Oct. 25, 1786, Dec. 5, 1787; Meusel, i, 452; Kayser, iv, 85.

17 Songes philosophiques, par M. Mercier, Londres et Paris, 1768.
Augmented version: Songes et visions philosophiques, "Voyages

imaginaires, songes, visions et romans cabalistiques," XXXII, Amsterdam et Paris, 1788.

17a *Erscheinungen und Träume, von Mercier und einigen deutschen Gelehrten, übersetzt und herausgegeben von G. Schatz, Leipzig: Dyk, 1791. 2 vols.
Cf. Meusel-Lexikon, XII, 92.
ALZ, Sept. 24, 1792, and NBSW, XLV (1792), 141ff., list Maass, Manso, Dyk, and Schatz as the authors of the German dreams.

17b *Merciers philosophische Träume und Visionen, nach der neusten Pariser Ausgabe verdeutscht, Dresden und Leipzig: Richter, 1791. 2 vols.
Cf. ALZ, Dec. 23, 1793.

17ba *Philosophische Träume und Visionen, aus dem Französischen, Dresden: Richter, 1807.
Cf. Kayser, IV, 85; Heinsius, II, 1001.

17c *Die Stimme der Natur, oder die schöne Lüge, ein Lustspiel in einem Akt aus dem Französischen des Herrn Armand, "Neues Wienerisches Theater," Wien, 1775.
Cf. ADM, 1776, 40; GGA, April 24, 1777; Nationalbibliothek in Wien, I, 51.
Goedeke, V, 313, attributes this to M. von Brahm.
According to a note in Merciers Nachtmütze, I, 144 (*24a*), the dream, "de l'Amour," was dramatized by Armand as "le Cri de la nature."

18 L'An 2440, rêve s'il en fût jamais, Amsterdam, 1770.

18a Das Jahr 2440, ein Traum aller Träume, London (Leipzig), 1772.
Columbia University Library.
Kayser, III, 235, and Weiße, 239, attributed this to C. F. Weisse.

18aa *Das Jahr 2440, ein Traum aller Träume, aus dem Französischen des Mercier, neue Auflage, Leipzig: Schwickert, 1782.
Cf. Kayser, III, 235, and Heinsius, II, 478.

18b *A new translation of l'An 2440 is announced by the Intelligenzblatt of ALZ, Feb. 25, 1795, to be made by Posselt, and to be published in Tübingen by Cotta.
Meusel, VI, 152, does not mention this among the works of E. L. Posselt, who was writing on the French Revolution at this period.

Imitations

18c *Das Jahr 1850, oder Gedanken über die Armenanstalten, den öffentlichen Gottesdienst, den Huldigungseid eines schweizerischen Kantons, Frankfurt und Leipzig, 1777.
Cf. Zollinger-Beziehungen, 93.

18d *Das Jahr 2440, zum zweitenmale geträumt, ein Traum, deren es wohl träumerischere gegeben hat, Leipzig: Weygand, 1783.
Attributed by Meusel, VIII, 280, and Kayser, III, 235, to K. H. Wachsmuth.
ADBibl, LVIII (1784), 126, attributes this to Witzel.

18e *Das Jahr 2500, oder der Traum Alradis, aus einer arabischen Handschrift des 16. Jahrhunderts, Berlin: Maurer, 1794-1795. 2 vols.
Meusel, V, 119, and Kayser, III, 235, attribute this to D. G. G. Mehring.

19 Du Théâtre, ou Nouvel essai sur l'art dramatique, Amsterdam, 1773.

19a *Neuer Versuch über die Schauspielkunst, aus dem Französischen, mit einem Anhang aus Goethes Brieftasche, Leipzig: Schwickert, 1776.
By H. L. Wagner. Cf. Schmidt-Wagner[ii], 132n.

20 Éloges et discours philosophiques, qui ont concouru pour les prix de l'Académie française et de plusieurs autres académies, par l'auteur de l'ouvrage intitulé "l'An 2440," Amsterdam, 1776.

20a Philosophische Abhandlungen und Lobreden über Preisaufgaben der französischen und verschiedener andrer Akademien, von dem Verfasser des Werks, das Jahr 2440, aus dem Französischen übersetzt, Leipzig: Kummer, 1777-1778. 2 vols.
Jena Universitätsbibliothek.
Ersch, II, 372, and Meusel, I, 529, attribute this to K. A. Caesar.

20b *Philosophische Abhandlungen über verschiedene wichtige Gegenstände, von Mercier, dem Verfasser des Werks: das Jahr 2440, aus dem Französischen übersetzt, Salzburg: Mayer, 1788.
Cf. ALZ, Feb. 18, 1791; Heinsius, II, 1000; Kayser, IV, 85.

21 Jezennemours, roman dramatique, Amsterdam, 1776.
Reprinted with the title: Histoire d'une jeune luthérienne, par M. Mercier, Neuchâtel, 1785.

21a *Jezennemours, ein dramatischer Roman aus dem Französischen, Leipzig: Schneider, 1778.
Cf. AV, 1778, 461; Ersch, II, 373.

21b *Geschichte eines jungen lutherischen Frauenzimmers, von dem Verfasser des Jahrs 2440, Leipzig: Schneider, 1787.
Cf. ADBibl, LXXVII (1787), 120; ALZ, Feb. 5, 1795.

21c *Belcour und Antonie, ein Sittengemälde nach Mercier, von Leopold Baron von Lehndorf, Neustadt an der Aisch: Riedel, 1791. 2 vols.

Cf. ALZ, Feb. 5, 1795; Meusel, IV, 392.

21d *Geschichte einer jungen Protestantin, aus dem Französischen, Frankfurt am Main: Eichenberg, 1793.
Cf. Kayser, VI[111], 94.

22 Tableau de Paris, Hambourg et Neuchâtel, 1781. 2 vols.
Tableau de Paris, nouvelle édition, corrigée et augmentée, Amsterdam, 1782-1788. 12 vols.

22a Schilderung von Paris, aus dem Französischen auszugsweise übersetzt, Breslau: Löwe, 1783. 4 vols.
Jena Universitätsbibliothek.
Attributed by Meusel, I, 491, and Jördens, I, 244, to S. ꞏG. Bürde.

22b Paris, ein Gemälde von Mercier, verdeutscht von B. G. Walch, Leipzig: Schwickert, 1783-1784. 4 vols.
Jena Universitätsbibliothek.

22c Merciers neustes Gemälde von Paris, für Reisende und Nichtreisende, Leipzig: Jacobäer, 1789. 2 vols.
Jena Universitätsbibliothek.
Meusel, VI, 259; Kayser, IV, 85; and Béclard, 627n., attribute this to Reichard.

22d *Historisch-kritische Enzyclopädie über verschiedene Gegenstände, Begebenheiten und Charaktere berühmter Menschen, hrsg. von H. G. Hoff, Preßburg: Mahler, 1787.
Contains translations of passages about d'Argenson and the Paris police, taken from the Tableau de Paris. Cf. Stettenheim, 34f.

Imitation

22e Neustes Gemälde von Berlin, auf das Jahr 1798, nach Mercier, Kölln: Hammer, 1798.
Bibliothèque nationale.

23 Portraits des rois de France, par M. Mercier, Neuchâtel, 1783. 4 vols.

23a *Gemälde der Könige von Frankreich, von Mercier nach der zweiten Originalausgabe zum erstenmal übersetzt, Meißen: Erbstein, 1792-1794. 3 vols.
Cf. ALZ, July 10, 1794.
NDBibl, VI (1793), 334; Meusel, V, 369; and Kayser, IV, 85, attribute this to F. S. Mursinna.

24 Mon Bonnet de nuit, par M. Mercier, Neuchâtel, 1784. 4 vols.

24a Merciers Nachtmütze, Berlin: Unger, 1784-1786. 4 vols.
Columbia University Library.

By Reichard and others: Friederika Unger, J. K. Müchler. Cf.
Nachtmütze, I, iv; Kayser, IV, 85; Ersch, II, 374.

No connection with Mercier's work

*Die frikassierte Nachtmütze, eine komische Geschichte in 4 Büchern, Leipzig, 1776.
Cf. ADBibl, XXXII (1777), 122.

25 La Solitude considérée, relativement à l'esprit et au cœur, ouvrage
traduit de l'allemand par Mercier, Paris, 1788.

25a *Mercier über die Einsamkeit und ihren Einfluß auf Geist und
Herz, nach Zimmermann, ein Buch für die reifere Jugend beiderlei
Geschlechts, übersetzt und mit psychologischen Reflexionen begleitet von Professor Heydenreich, Leipzig: Weygand, 1797.
Cf. Kayser, VI, 85; Heinsius, II, 1000; Meusel, XI, 352.

26 Fictions morales, par M. Mercier, Paris, 1792. 3 vols.

26a *Moralische Dichtungen, aus dem Französischen, I, Hamburg:
Campe, 1792.
Cf. Kayser, IV, 85, and Heinsius, II, 1000.

26b *La Sympathie, "traduite en Allemand . . . en Suédois," Stockholm,
1797.
Cf. Ersch-Supplément, I, 325.
This story is contained in the Fictions morales.

No connection with Mercier's work

*Moralische Erzählungen, Leipzig: Brockhaus, 1771.
According to Ersch, II, 372f., this is a translation of Contes
moraux, ou les hommes comme il y en a peu, Paris, 1768.

27 Le Nouveau Paris, par le cit. Mercier, Paris (1797-1800). 6 vols.

27a *Das neue Paris, vom Bürger Mercier, übersetzt vom Bürger K. F.
Cramer, Braunschweig: Vieweg, 1800. 2 vols.
Cf. NDBibl, LXV (1801), 140; Kayser, IV, 85; Jördens, VI, 602.

28 Ansichten der Hauptstadt des französischen Kaiserreichs vom Jahr
1806 an, von Pinkerton, Mercier und K. F. Cramer, Amsterdam,
1807-1808.
Bibliothèque nationale.

Miscellaneous

29 *Moralische Erzählungen zur Ergänzung der Frankfurter Landbibliothek, 1771ff.
According to Fürst, 32, this contains translations of stories by
Mercier.

30 *Vathek, conte arabe, 1787.
This is generally attributed to William Beckford. Cf. Catalogue of
the Bibliothèque nationale under "Beckford."

30a *"Traduit en Allemand . . . Mannheim, 1788."
Cf. Ersch, II, 374f.

31 *Das Schicksal nach Mercier, "Amalthea," I, 1789.
Meusel, III, 298, attributes this to K. H. Heydenreich.
I was unable to discover the original of this.

No connection with Mercier

*Gerhard von Velsen, ein historischer Roman von Mercier, aus
dem Französischen übersetzt, Berlin: Langenhoff, 1796.
Cf. NDBibl, xxxix (1798), 76.
The original is by Mercier de Compiègne. Cf. ALZ, Jan. 18, 1796.

APPENDIX II

ADDITIONAL BIBLIOGRAPHY

Only those works are cited which have been of direct aid in the investigation.

A. EDITIONS

Diderot, Denis. Œuvres complètes. Éd. J. Assézat. Paris, 1875-1877.

Gemmingen, Heinrich von. Das Drama der klassischen Periode. Hrsg. von Adolf Hauffen. Vol. 2¹. "DNL." Stuttgart.

Gerstenberg, Heinrich Wilhelm von. Rezensionen. Hrsg. von O. Fischer. "Deutsche Literaturdenkmale des 18. und 19. Jahrhunderts," Nr. 128. Berlin, 1904.

Gerstenberg, Heinrich Wilhelm von. Vermischte Schriften. Altona, 1815-1816.

Goethe, Johann Wolfgang von. Der junge Goethe. Neue Ausgabe. Hrsg. von Max Morris. Leipzig, 1909-1912.

Goethe, Johann Wolfgang von. Goethes Werke. Hrsg. im Auftrage der Großherzogin Sophie von Sachsen. Weimar, 1887-1919.

Goethe, Johann Wolfgang von. Wilhelm Meisters theatralische Sendung. Hrsg. von Harry Maync. Stuttgart und Berlin, 1911.

Hamann, Johann Georg. Hamanns Leben und Schriften. Zweite Ausgabe. Hrsg. von C. H. Gildemeister. Gotha, 1875.

Heinse, Wilhelm. Sämtliche Werke. Hrsg. von Carl Schüddenkopf. Leipzig, 1903-1925.

Herder, Johann Gottfried. Herders sämtliche Werke. Hrsg. von Bernhard Suphan. Berlin, 1877-1913.

Humboldt, Wilhelm von. Wilhelm von Humboldts Tagebücher. Hrsg. von Albert Leitzmann. Berlin, 1916-1918.

Iffland, A. W. Ifflands Briefe an seine Schwester Louise und andere Verwandte. Hrsg. von Ludwig Geiger. "Schriften der Gesellschaft für Theatergeschichte," Nr. 5. Berlin, 1904.

Iffland, A. W. Ifflands Briefe, meist an seine Schwester nebst andern Aktenstücken. Hrsg. von Ludwig Geiger. "Schriften der Gesellschaft für Theatergeschichte," Nr. 6. Berlin, 1905.

Iffland, A. W. Theatralische Werke, Leipzig, 1827-1828.

Iffland, A. W. Über meine theatralische Laufbahn. "Deutsche Literaturdenkmale des 18. und 19. Jahrhunderts," Nr. 24. Stuttgart, 1886.

Klinger, F. M. Betrachtungen und Gedanken. Köln, 1803-1805.

Klinger, F. M. Sturm und Drang. Hrsg. von Karl Freye. Bong & Co. Dritter Teil.

Lenz, J. M. R. Briefe von und an Lenz. Hrsg. von Karl Freye und Wolfgang Stammler. Leipzig, 1918.

Lenz, J. M. R. Gesammelte Schriften. Hrsg. von Franz Blei. München und Leipzig, 1900-1913.

Lessing, Gotthold Ephraim. Lessings Hamburgische Dramaturgie. Hrsg. von Julius Petersen. Bong & Co.

Lessing, Gotthold Ephraim. Lessings sämtliche Schriften. Hrsg. von Karl Lachmann und Franz Muncker. Göschen, 1886-1924.

Rousseau, Jean-Jacques. Petits chefs-d'œuvre de J.-J. Rousseau. Paris, 1870.

Schiller, Friedrich von. Schillers Briefe. Hrsg. von Fritz Jonas. Stuttgart, Leipzig, Berlin, Wien, Einleitung: 1892.

Schiller, Friedrich von. Schillers Briefwechsel mit Körner. 2d ed. Hrsg. von Karl Goedeke. Leipzig, 1878.

Schiller, Friedrich von. Schillers dramatische Entwürfe und Fragmente. Hrsg. von Gustav Kettner. Stuttgart, 1899.

Schiller, Friedrich von. Schillers sämtliche Schriften. Hrsg. von Karl Goedeke. Stuttgart, 1867-1876.

Schiller, Friedrich von. Schillers Werke. Hrsg. von Ludwig Bellermann. Leipzig und Wien.

Schiller, Friedrich von. Schillers Werke. Hrsg. von Robert Boxberger. "DNL." Berlin und Stuttgart.

Schröder, Friedrich Ludwig. Schröders dramatische Werke. Hrsg. von Eduard von Bülow. Berlin, 1831.

Wagner, Heinrich Leopold. Die Kindermörderin. Hrsg. von Erich Schmidt. "Deutsche Literaturdenkmale des 18. und 19. Jahrhunderts," Nr. 13. Heilbronn, 1883.

Wagner, Heinrich Leopold. Sturm und Drang. Hrsg. von Karl Freye. Bong & Co. Zweiter Teil.

Wagner, Heinrich Leopold. Voltaire am Abend seiner Apotheose. Hrsg. von Bernhard Seuffert. "Deutsche Literaturdenkmale des 18. und 19. Jahrhunderts." Nr. 2. Stuttgart, 1881.

Wieland, Christoph Martin. Ausgewählte Briefe von Wieland. Zürich, 1815-1816.

Wieland, Christoph Martin. Wielands Briefe an Sophie von Laroche. Hrsg. von Franz Horn. Berlin, 1820.

Wieland, Christoph Martin. Wielands gesammelte Schriften. Hrsg. von der deutschen Kommission der Königlich Preußischen Akademie der Wissenschaften. Berlin, 1909ff.

B. To Chapter III: "Mercier on the German Stage"

Altenburg, Otto. "Aus der Geschichte des Theaters in Pommern." *Baltische Studien*, N. F., xxxiii[1] (1931), 199ff,

Brachvogel, A. E. Geschichte des Königlichen Theaters zu Berlin. Berlin, 1877-1878.

Brandes, Johann Christian. Meine Lebensgeschichte. Hrsg. von Willibald Franke. München, 1923.

Burkhardt, C. A. H. Das Repertoire des Weimarischen Theaters unter Goethes Leitung. "Theatergeschichtliche Forschungen," Nr. 1. Hamburg und Leipzig, 1891.

Costenoble, Carl Ludwig. Tagebücher. Hrsg. von Alexander von Weilen. "Schriften der Gesellschaft für Theatergeschichte," Nr. 18. Berlin, 1912.

Deneke, Otto. Göttinger Theater im 18. Jahrhundert. "Göttingische Nebenstunden," Nr. 8. Göttingen, 1930.

Fuchs, D. Chronologisches Tagebuch des Großherzoglich Hessischen Hoftheaters. Darmstadt, 1832.

Fühler, Armas Sten. Das Schauspielrepertoire des Mannheimer Hof- und Nationaltheaters im Geschmackswandel des 18. und 19. Jahrhunderts. Heidelberg, 1935.

Groß, Edgar. J. F. F. Fleck. "Schriften der Gesellschaft für Theatergeschichte," Nr. 22. Berlin, 1914.

Hagen, E. A. Geschichte des Theaters in Preußen. Königsberg, 1854.

Hampe, Theodor. Die Entwicklung des Theaterwesens in Nürnberg. Nürnberg, 1900.

Härle, H. Ifflands Schauspielkunst. "Schriften der Gesellschaft für Theatergeschichte," Nr. 34. Berlin, 1925.

Heine, Carl. "Die ausländischen Dramen im Spielplane des Weimarischen Theaters unter Goethes Leitung." *Zeitschrift für vergleichende Literaturgeschichte*, N. F., iv (1891), 313ff.

Hodermann, Richard. Geschichte des Gothaischen Hoftheaters 1775-1779. "Theatergeschichtliche Forschungen," Nr. 9. Hamburg und Leipzig, 1894.

Kasten, Otto. Das Theater in Köln während der Franzosenzeit. "Die Schaubühne," Nr. 2. Bonn, 1928.

Knudsen, Hans. "Mannheimer Schauspieler-Briefe." *Mannheimer Geschichtsblätter*. Hrsg. vom Mannheimer Altertumsverein, xxxviii (1937), 90ff.

Koffka, Wilhelm. Iffland und Dalberg. Leipzig, 1865.

Krauß, Rudolf. Das Stuttgarter Hoftheater. Stuttgart, 1908.

Küstner, Karl Th. Rückblick auf das Leipziger Stadttheater. Leipzig, 1830.

Legband, Paul. Münchener Bühne und Literatur im 18. Jahrhundert.

"Oberbayerisches Archiv für vaterländische Geschichte," Nr. 51. München, 1904.

Litzmann, Berthold. Friedrich Ludwig Schröder. Hamburg und Leipzig, 1890-1894.

Maas, Hermann. Das Mainzer Theater vom Beginn der zweiten Franzosenherrschaft bis zur Einweihung des Neuen Schauspielhauses. Gießen, 1928.

Mentzel, E. Geschichte der Schauspielkunst in Frankfurt am Main. Frankfurt, 1882.

Olivier, Jean-Jacques. Les Comédiens français dans les cours d'Allemagne au XVIIIe siècle. Paris, 1901-1905.

Peth, Jakob. Geschichte des Theaters und der Musik zu Mainz. Mainz, 1879.

Prölss, Robert. Geschichte des Hoftheaters zu Dresden. Dresden, 1878.

Pukánszky-Kádár, Iolantha. Geschichte des deutschen Theaters in Ungarn. "Schriften der deutschen Akademie in München," Nr. 14. München, 1933.

Reichard, H. A. O. Selbstbiographie. Hrsg. von Hermann Uhde. Stuttgart, 1877.

Reichard, H. A. O. Theater-Journal für Deutschland. 1777-1784.

Rötscher, Heinrich Th. Seydelmanns Leben und Wirken. Berlin, 1845.

Rupp, Fritz. Reichard. Marburg, 1908.

Schink, Johann Friedrich. Zusätze und Berichtigungen zu der Gallerie von deutschen Schauspielern und Schauspielerinnen. Hrsg. von Richard Maria Werner. "Schriften der Gesellschaft für Theatergeschichte." Nr. 13. Berlin, 1910.

Schlösser, Rudolf. Vom Hamburger Nationaltheater zur Gothaer Hofbühne. "Theatergeschichtliche Forschungen," Nr. 13. Hamburg und Leipzig, 1895.

Schmid, Christian Heinrich. Chronologie des deutschen Theaters. Hrsg. von Paul Legband. "Schriften der Gesellschaft für Theatergeschichte," Nr. 1. Berlin, 1902.

Schreyvogel, Joseph. Tagebücher. Hrsg. von Karl Glossy. "Schriften der Gesellschaft für Theatergeschichte," Nrs. 2, 3. Berlin, 1903.

Vasterling, Heinz. Das Theater in der freien Reichsstadt Kaufbeuren. Braunschweig, 1934.

Vogl, Frank. Das Bergische Nationaltheater. Düsseldorf, 1930.

Wahle, Julius. Das Weimarer Hoftheater unter Goethes Leitung. "Schriften der Goethe-Gesellschaft," Nr. 6. Weimar, 1892.

Walter, Friedrich. Archiv und Bibliothek des großh. Hof- und Nationaltheaters in Mannheim. Leipzig, 1899.

Weil, Rudolf. Das Berliner Theaterpublikum unter A. W. Ifflands

Direktion. "Schriften der Gesellschaft für Theatergeschichte," Nr. 44. Berlin, 1932.

Wenzel Dennerlein, I. G. Geschichte des Würzburger Theaters. Würzburg, 1853.

Witzig, Erich. Johann David Beil. "Germanische Studien," Nr. 47. Berlin, 1927.

Wlassack, Eduard. Chronik des kaiserl. königl. Hof-Burgtheaters. Wien, 1876.

Wollrabe, Ludwig. Chronologie sämtlicher Hamburger Bühnen. Hamburg, 1847.

Wolter, Joseph. G. F. W. Großmann. Köln, 1901.

C. GENERAL

Arnold, Robert Franz. Allgemeine Bücherkunde. 3d ed. Berlin und Leipzig, 1931.

Aubertin, Charles. L'Esprit public au xviiie siècle. 2d ed. Paris, 1873.

d'Avalon Cousin. Merciériana. Paris, 1834.

Bachaumont, Louis Petit de. Mémoires secrets. London, 1784-1789.

Baldensperger, Fernand. "Notes sur le frère de Sébastien Mercier." *Revue d'Histoire littéraire de la France,* XIX (1912), 411ff.

Bengesco, Georges. Voltaire, Bibliographie de ses œuvres. Paris, 1882-1890.

Berendt, Hans. Goethes "Wilhelm Meister." Dortmund, 1911.

Berger, Karl. Schiller. Sein Leben und seine Werke. 7 ed. München, 1912.

Bitterling, Richard. Joh. Fr. Schink. "Theatergeschichtliche Forschungen." Nr. 23. Leipzig und Hamburg, 1911.

Brecht, Walter. Heinse und der ästhetische Immoralismus. Berlin, 1911.

Brunetière, F. Les Époques du théâtre français. Nouv. éd. Paris, 1896.

Bürger, Gottfried August. Briefe von und an Bürger. Hrsg. von Adolf Strodtmann. Berlin, 1874.

Danzel, T. W. und Guhrauer, G. E. Lessing. Neue Ausgabe. Leipzig, prefaces: 1849-1853.

Danzel, T. W. und Guhrauer, G. E. Lessing. 2d ed. Hrsg. von W. von Maltzahn und R. Boxberger. Berlin, 1880-1881.

Deutsche Bibliothek der schönen Wissenschaften. Hrsg. von Ch. A. Klotz. 1767-1772.

Der Deutsche Merkur. Hrsg. von Wieland. 1773-1810.

Diezmann, August. Goethe und die lustige Zeit in Weimar. Leipzig, 1857.

Eggert, C. A. "Goethe und Diderot." *Euphorion,* IV (1897), 301ff.

Eggli, Edmond. "Diderot et Schiller." *Revue de littérature comparée,* I (1921), 68ff.

Eggli, Edmond. Schiller et le romantisme français. Paris, 1927.

Eschenburg, Johann Joachim. Beispielsammlung zur Theorie und Literatur der schönen Wissenschaften. Berlin und Stettin, 1788-1795.

Faguet, Émile. Dix-huitième siècle. Paris, preface: 1890.

Flaischlen, Cäsar. Otto Heinrich von Gemmingen. Stuttgart, 1890.

Flögel, Karl Friedrich. Geschichte der komischen Literatur. Liegnitz und Leipzig, 1784-1787.

Friedrich, Theodor. Die "Anmerkungen übers Theater." "Probefahrten." Hrsg. von Albert Köster. Nr. 13. Leipzig, 1908.

Fuchs, Albert. Les Apports français dans l'œuvre de Wieland. Paris, 1934.

Gaiffe, Félix. Le Drame en France au xviiie siècle. Paris, 1910.

Geiger, Ludwig. Charlotte von Schiller und ihre Freunde. Berlin, preface: 1908.

Geiger, Ludwig. "Einundzwanzig Briefe von Marianne von Eybenberg." Goethe-Jahrbuch, xiv (1893), 27ff.

Geiger, Ludwig. "Schiller und Diderot." Marbacher Schillerbuch, i (1905), 81ff.

Gensel, Walter. Cronegk. Sein Leben und seine Schriften. Berlin, 1894.

Gervinus, G. G. Geschichte der deutschen Dichtung. 5 ed. Leipzig, 1871-1874.

Grimm, F. Melchior. Correspondance littéraire. Éd. Maurice Tourneux. Paris, 1877-1882.

Hachtmann, Otto. Graf Julius Heinrich von Soden als Dramatiker. Göttingen, 1902.

Hettner, Hermann. Geschichte der deutschen Litteratur im 18. Jahrhundert. Hrsg. von Georg Witkowski. Leipzig, 1929.

Heymach, Ferdinand. "Ramond de Carbonnières." Jahresbericht des Fürstlich Waldeckschen Gymnasiums zu Corbach. Mengeringhausen. 1887.

Hill, Wilhelm. Die deutschen Theaterzeitschriften des 18. Jahrhunderts. "Forschungen." Hrsg. von Franz Muncker. Nr. 49. Weimar, 1915.

Holzmann, Albert William. Family Relationships in the Dramas of August von Kotzebue. Princeton, 1935.

Humboldt, Wilhelm von. Neue Briefe Wilhelm von Humboldts an Schiller. Hrsg. von Friedrich Clemens Ebrard. Berlin, 1911.

Iacuzzi, Alfred. The European Vogue of Favart. New York, 1932.

Isambert, Gustave. La Vie à Paris pendant une année de la Révolution. Paris, 1896.

Jacobi, Friedrich Heinrich. Jacobis auserlesener Briefwechsel. Hrsg. von Friedrich Roth. Leipzig, 1825-1827.

Jahn, Kurt. "Wilhelm Meisters theatralische Sendung und der humoristische Roman der Engländer." *Germanisch-Romanische Monatsschrift,* v (1913), 225ff.

Keudel, Elise von. Goethe als Benutzer der Weimarer Bibliothek. Weimar, 1931.

Korff, Hermann. Voltaire im literarischen Deutschland des 18. Jahrhunderts. "Beiträge zur neueren Literaturgeschichte," N. F., Nrs. 10, 11. Heidelberg, 1917-1918.

Köster, Albert. "Die allgemeinen Tendenzen der Geniebewegung im 18. Jahrhundert." *Die deutsche Literatur der Aufklärungszeit.* Heidelberg, 1925.

Köster, Albert. "Wilhelm Meisters theatralische Sendung." *Zeitschrift für den deutschen Unterricht,* xxvi (1912), 209ff.

Krogmann, W. "Die Anfänge des Wilhelm Meister." *Zeitschrift für deutsche Philologie,* lvii (1932), 56ff.

La Harpe, Jean François de. Œuvres diverses. Paris, 1826.

Lappenberg, J. M. Briefe von und an Klopstock, Braunschweig, 1867.

Lemaître, Jules. Théories et impressions. "Nouvelle bibliothèque littéraire." Paris, no date.

Lespinasse, Julie de. Lettres de Mlle de Lespinasse. Éd. Eugène Asse. Paris, notice: 1876.

Leyser, J. A. Joachim Heinrich Campe. Braunschweig, 1877.

Lichtenberger, André. Le Socialisme au xviiie siècle. Paris, 1895.

Lieder, Frederick W. C. Don Carlos. "Oxford German Series." New York and London, 1912.

Louvet, L. "Mercier." *Nouvelle biographie générale.* Éd. Hoefer. xxxv (1865), 19ff.

Matenko, Percy. Tieck and Solger. New York and Berlin, 1933.

Melchinger, Siegfried. Dramaturgie des Sturms und Drangs. Gotha, 1929.

Merz, Elsbeth. Tell im Drama vor und nach Schiller. "Sprache und Dichtung," Nr. 31. Bern, 1925.

Michiels, Alfred. Histoire des idées littéraires en France au xixe siècle. Paris, 1842.

Minor, Jacob. Weiße und seine Beziehungen zur deutschen Literatur. Innsbruck, 1880.

Mis, Léon. "Sébastien Mercier, Schiller und Otto Ludwig." *Euphorion,* xxix (1928), 190ff.

Monroy, Else von. Goethes Briefwechsel mit Georg und Caroline Sartorius. Weimar, 1931.

Monselet, Charles. Les Oubliés et les dédaignés. Alençon, 1857.

Morris, Max. Goethes und Herders Anteil an dem Jahrgang 1772 der Frankfurter gelehrten Anzeigen. Stuttgart und Berlin, 1909.

Morsch, H. "Goethes Festspiel: Des Epimenides Erwachen." *Goethe-Jahrbuch*, xiv (1893), 212ff.

Neuse, Werner. Wege zur deutschen Kultur. Chicago and Philadelphia, 1937.

Nicolai, Friedrich. Leben Justus Mösers. Berlin und Stettin, 1797.

Nolte, F. O. The Early Middle Class Drama. Lancaster, Pa., 1935.

Oppermann, Heinrich Albert. Die Göttinger gelehrten Anzeigen. Hannover, 1844.

Petsch, Robert. Deutsche Dramaturgie. 2d ed. Hamburg, 1921.

Quérard, J. M. La France littéraire. Paris, 1827-1864.

Rabany, Ch. Kotzebue. Paris et Nancy, 1893.

Reynaud, Louis. Histoire générale de l'influence française en Allemagne. 2d ed. Paris, 1915.

Rieger, M. Klinger. Darmstadt, 1880-1896.

Rosanow, M. N. Lenz. German translation by C. von Gütschow. Leipzig, 1909.

Rovillain, Eugène. "L'Abbé Prévost et *l'Homme sauvage* de Sébastien Mercier." *PMLA,* xlv (1930), 822ff.

San-Giorgiu, Jon. Sébastien Merciers dramaturgische Ideen im "Sturm und Drang." Basel, 1921.

Schlösser, Rudolf. Rameaus Neffe. "Forschungen zur neueren Literaturgeschichte," Nr. 15, Berlin, 1900.

Schmidt, Erich. Lenz und Klinger. Berlin, 1878.

Seuffert, Bernhard. Goethes Theater-Roman. Graz, Wien, Leipzig, 1924.

Seuffert, Bernhard. "Wielands Berufung nach Weimar." *Vierteljahrschrift für Literaturgeschichte,* i (188), 342ff.

Staël, Mme de. De l'Allemagne. 2d ed. Paris, 1814.

Stockmeyer, Clara. Soziale Probleme im Drama des Sturmes und Dranges. "Deutsche Forschungen," Nr. 5. Frankfurt am Main, 1922.

Thompson, L. F. Kotzebue. A Survey of his Progress in France and England. "Bibliothèque de la Revue de littérature comparée," Nr. 51. Paris, 1928.

Tieck, Ludwig. "Die geschichtliche Entwicklung der neueren Bühne." *Kritische Schriften.* Leipzig, 1848-1852. ii, 315ff.

Ulmann, Hans. Das deutsche Bürgertum in deutschen Tragödien des 18. und 19. Jahrhunderts. Elberfeld, 1923.

Valentin, Caroline. Theater und Musik am Fürstlich Leiningischen Hofe. "Neujahrsblätter." Hrsg. von der Gesellschaft für fränkische Geschichte, Nr. 15. Würzburg, 1921.

Van Tieghem, Paul. La Littérature comparée. Paris, 1931.

Venhofen, Johannes. Sprickmanns Jugendjahre und dichterische Frühzeit. Münster, 1909.

Vogt, Oskar. Der goldene Spiegel "Forschungen zur neueren Literaturgeschichte," Nr. 26. Berlin, 1904.

Walzel, Oskar. "Das bürgerliche Drama." *Vom Geistesleben alter und neuer Zeit.* Leipzig, 1922.

Werner, Oscar Helmuth. The Unmarried Mother in German Literature. New York, 1917.

Werner, Richard Maria. Ludwig Philipp Hahn. "Quellen und Forschungen," Nr. 22. Straßburg, 1877.

Wittmer, Louis. Charles de Villers. Genève, 1908.

Zollinger, Oskar. "Eine Utopie des 18. Jahrhunderts vor der spanischen Inquisition." *Zeitschrift für französische Sprache und Literatur,* XIX (1897), 305ff.

INDEX

INDEX

239